JOSEPH BEUYS

MANRESA

A Spiritual Geography

1966

In the middle of the 1960s, Joseph Beuys found in the Fluxus movement a way to broaden the older concept of art based on artistic disciplines, making it possible for art to encompass any human activity, and enabling it to be an instrument in the transformation of the world.

Various Beuys actions from the period dramatised initiation journeys, incantations and invocations, using ritual forms to centre on the activation of special points of energy. These rituals have been compared to the ecstasy techniques of shamans, and could be seen as inquiries into cultural energy points that 'a shaman might have "visited" thanks to a special aptitude for magical flight'[1]: 'Auf zu dir fliege ich, Manresa' (I am flying to you too, Manresa), wrote Beuys in the script of the action MANRESA (Galerie Schmela, Düsseldorf, 15/12/1966). Manresa, a site of transformational, reparative energy.

Beuys's action-demonstration MANRESA draws its spiritual substrate from Ignatius of Loyola, who the artist read and reread during his spiritual crisis of the 1950s. Loyola had abandoned his weapons after being wounded in battled, and converted himself into a pilgrim. Creating a transformational army of souls, Loyola activated individual self-determination and laid out a theoretical and practical groundwork with his *Spiritual Exercises*, which he wrote in Manresa during his stay there in 1522–23, after a period of illumination at Montserrat. Beuys found in Loyola a biographical similitude: the crash of his military plane near Crimea in 1943, along with his mission as an artist dedicated to social transformation, called to follow the principle of freedom and self-determination, leading thereby to his social art.

In the action-demonstration MANRESA, the site that is invoked becomes a concept, a hot spot in the south of the Eurasian continent, a 'brown space' where the transformation of man is possible, a *Braunraum*. It finds its counterpoint at the Thorvaldsen Museum in Copenhagen, associated with Henning Christiansen and Bjørn Nørgaard, Beuys's two collaborators.

Friedhelm Mennekes analyses the symbology of the action MANRESA, the similitudes between Beuys and Loyola and how they overcame their respective personal crises; he further explores the 'Christic' ritual in the action, and what it means as an activation of the Christ impulse and the point of inflection for the advent of the highest idea in Beuysian thought: 'social sculpture'. Harald Szeemann reviews the action MANRESA as an homage to Alfred and Monika Schmela, extracting the political and social dictates to be drawn from it, while Klaus D. Pohl addresses the freedom Fluxus affords Beuys when it comes to creating an expanded art through a multidisciplinary, collaborative action, which sets his 'artistic theory' into motion. My contribution delves into the values of a spiritual and mystical geography, centred on Manresa, which becomes a concept and universal symbol after Ignatius of Loyola's own stage there, finding continuity with Joseph Beuys's reworking and updating of 20th century art. The fundamental testimony of Henning Christiansen and Bjørn Nørgaard, who narrate their experience, rounds off this new monograph, entitled *Joseph Beuys – MANRESA: A Spiritual Geography*. The volume further includes the script and photographs of the action, preparatory drawings and photographs of the objects displayed in it, all of which are now at the Hessisches Landesmuseum Darmstadt.

Following the example of Loyola, the action MANRESA opens the door for Beuys to evolve his work towards social sculpture. The mystery of this action lies in the question 'Where is Element 3?', which is repeated insistently in the script. Beuys gives us the answer in the catalogue for his exhibition at the Guggenheim Museum: 'On the 22nd of June, 1967, Beuys founded the German Student Party in Room 13 of the Staatlische Kunstakademie in Düsseldorf'.[2]

This would be Beuys's first disembarkation in the political arena, when he decides to undertake a crusade through art for social, political and economic change.

Pilar Parcerisas
Editor

1
Alois Martin Müller, 'Chamanes', *Beuysnobiscum. Joseph Beuys*, Madrid: Museo Nacional Centro de Arte Reina Sofía, 1994, p. 225 [exh. cat.].

2
Caroline Tisdall, *Joseph Beuys*, New York: Guggenheim Museum, 1979, p. 113 [exh. cat.].

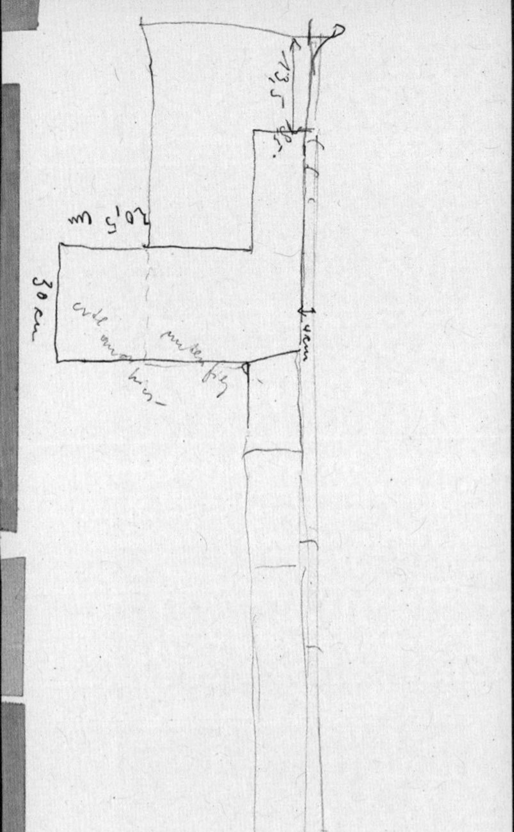

Konstruktionszeichnung (Construction Drawing), 1966. 39.9 × 17.2 cm.

6

13.5 cm
8.5 cm

30.5 cm
30 cm

under felt
here too perhaps

20 cm

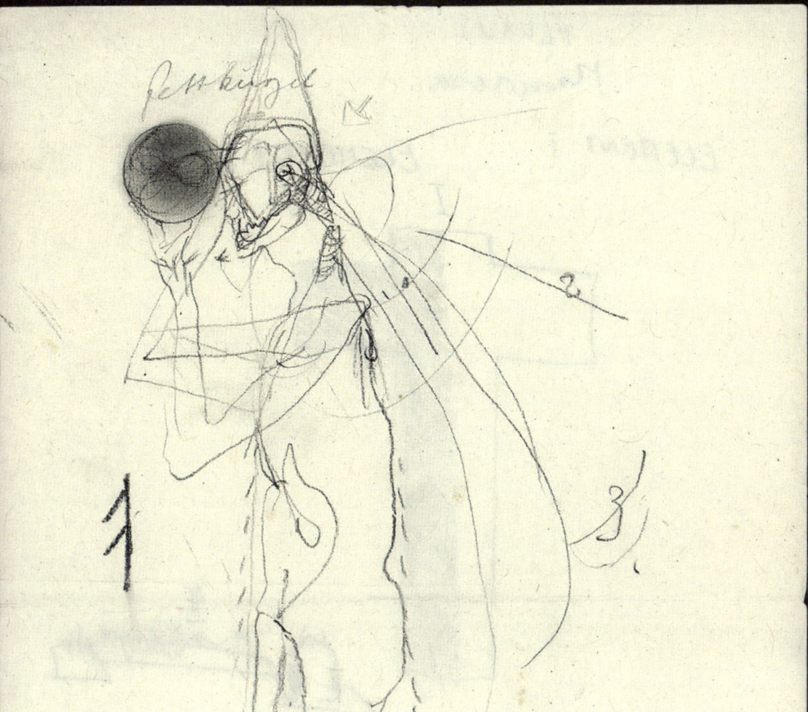

Untitled, from *The Secret Block for a Secret Person in Ireland*, 1965. 29.7 × 21cm.

7

Ball of fat

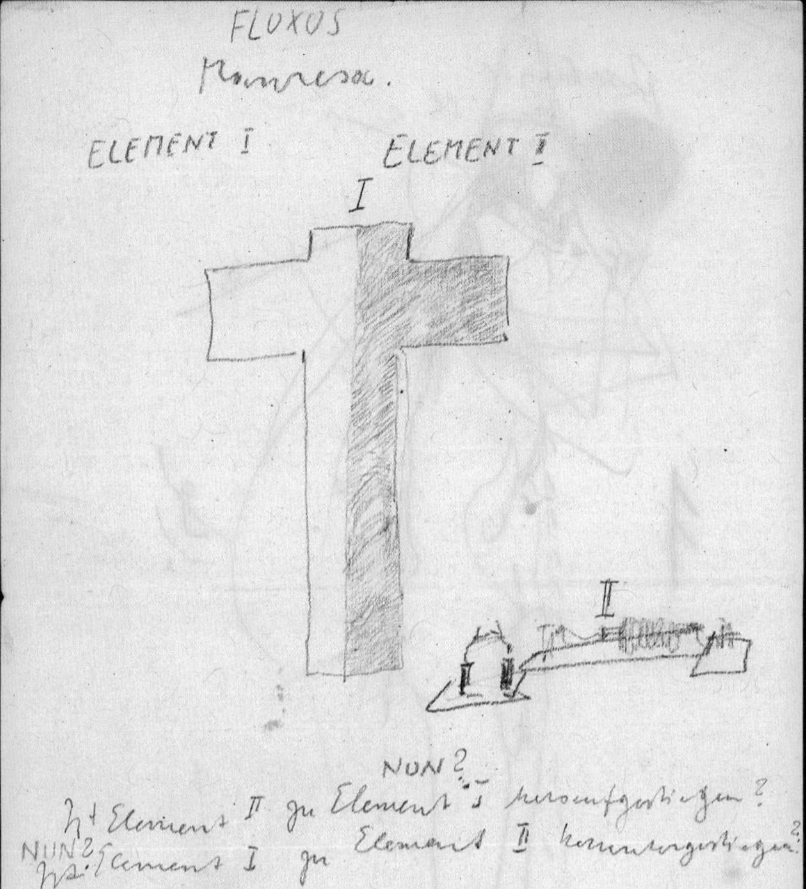

Partitur zu MANRESA (MANRESA Score), 1966. 29.7 × 21 cm.

FLUXUS
Manresa.
ELEMENT I ELEMENT II

NOW?
Has Element II gone up to Element I?
NOW?
Has Element I gone down to Element II?
Tape recording
Bjørn Nørgaard with recording tape same clothes

I carry Bjørn N on my shoulders

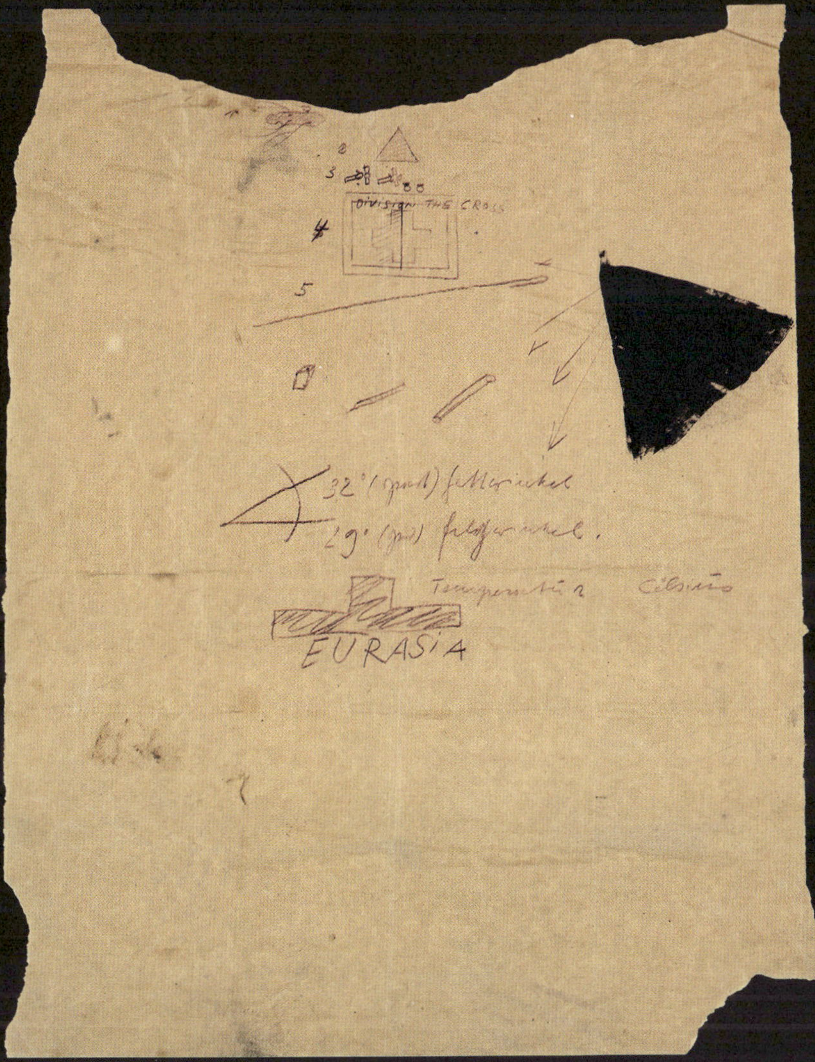

Partitur zu Eurasia (Eurasia Score), 1966. 55 × 44.5 cm.

1 2
3
DIVISION OF THE CROSS
4
5

32° (degrees) fat angle
29° (degrees) felt angle

Temperature centigrade
EURASIA

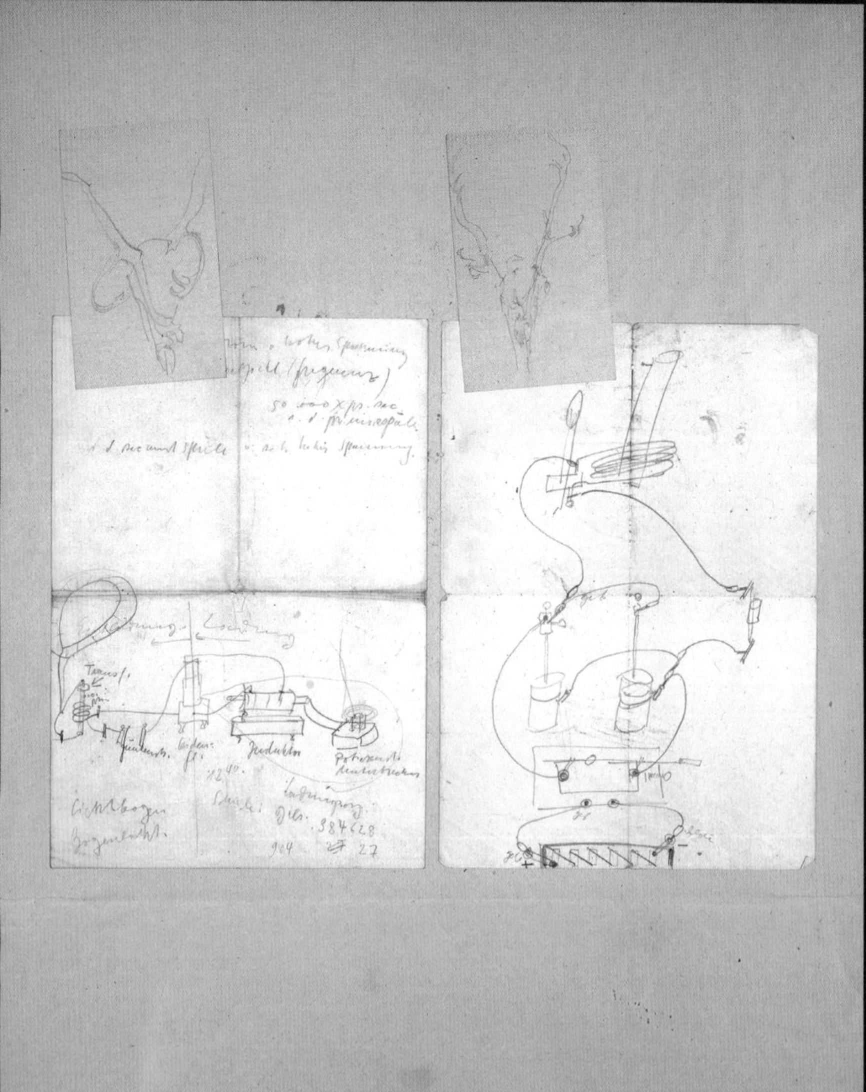

Untitled, from *The Secret Block for a Secret Person in Ireland*, 1965, 64.5 × 48.2 cm.

current, high tension (frequency)
50,000 x per sec.
in the primary coil
in the secondary coil very high tension

Discharge - Charge
Transformer

Spark streaming	Leyden jar	Inductor	Rotary circuit breaker
Voltaic Arc	1240	[illegible] charge	
Arc lamp	Institute: Gels. 384628		
	904	27	

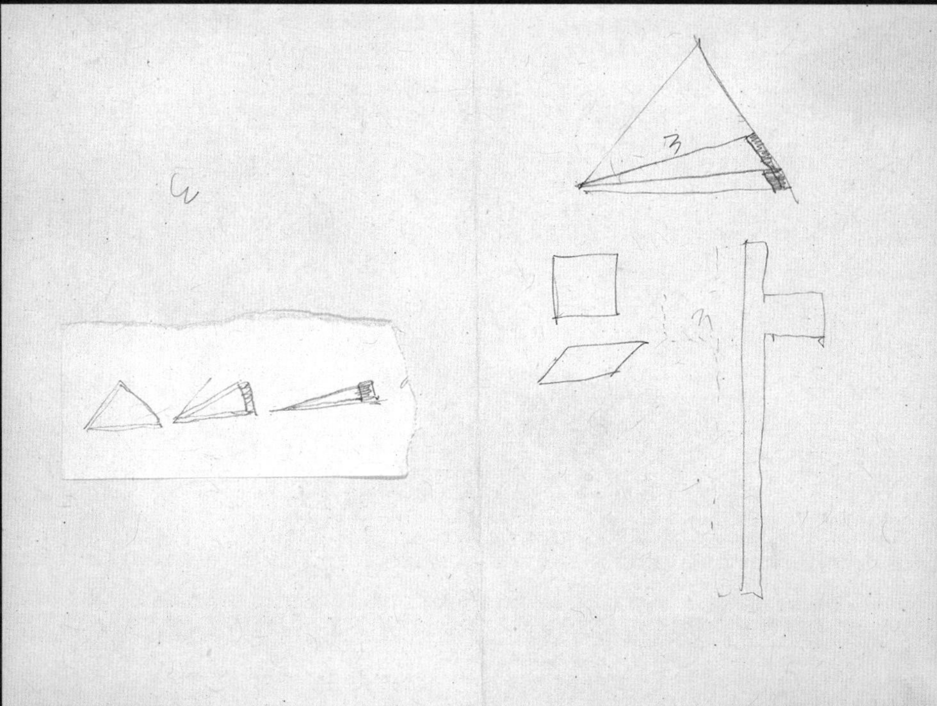

Score for MANRESA, 1966. 20.8 × 29.6 cm.

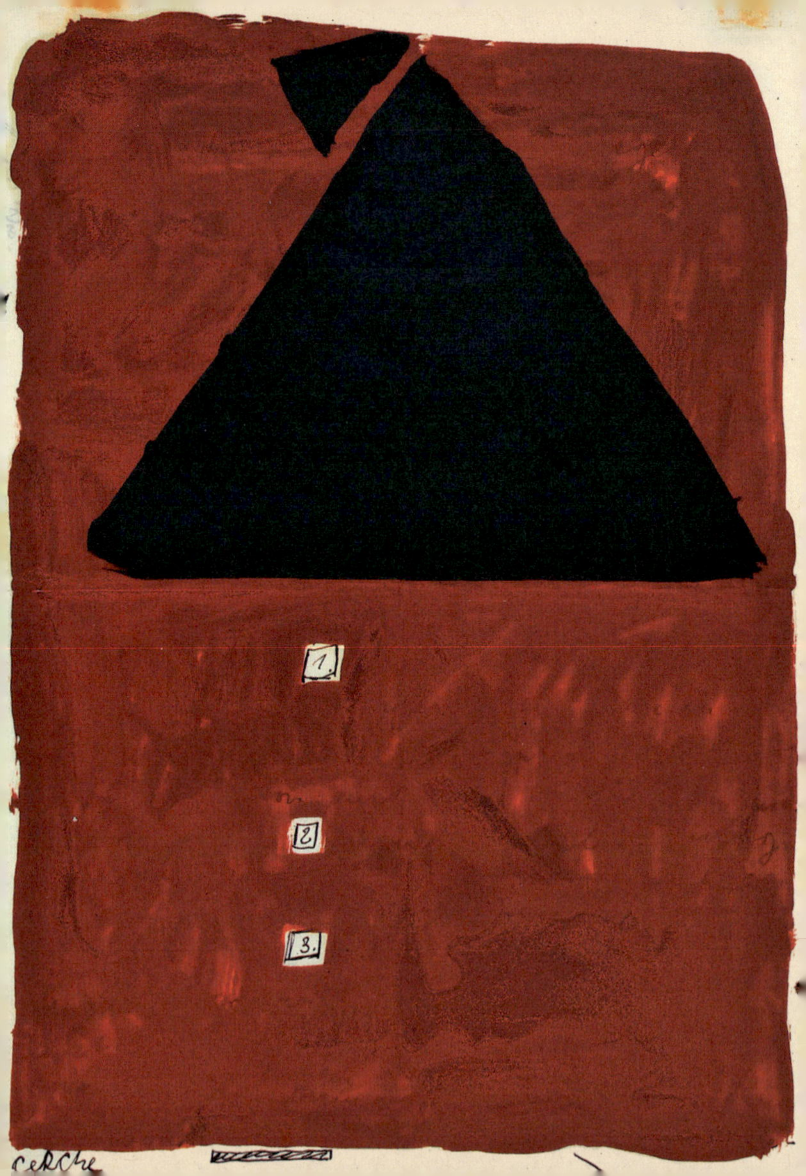
1.
2.
3.
ceRche

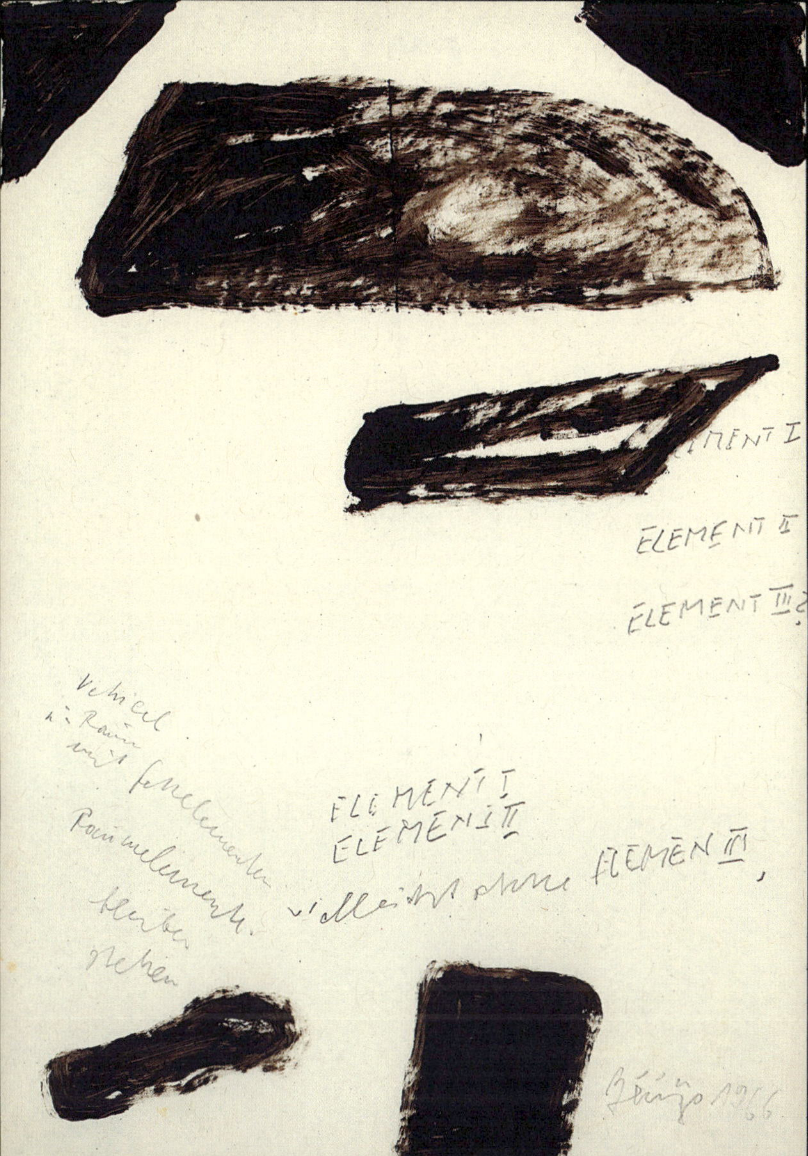

Partitur zu MANRESA (Score for MANRESA), 1966. 29.7 × 21 cm.

ELEMENT I
ELEMENT II
ELEMENT III?

ELEMENT I
ELEMENT II
perhaps without ELEMENT III

Vehicle
in space
with fat elements

elements of space
are kept
as they are

Beuys 1966

Hier spricht FLUXUS
FLUXUS

Nun?
Ist Element 2 zu Element 1 heraufgestiegen?

Nun?
Ist Element 1 zu Element 2 heruntergestiegen?

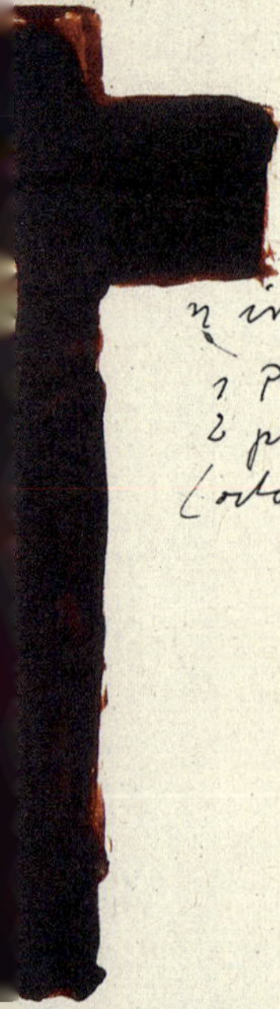

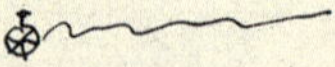

η ist der Schnittpunkt dreier Strichlinien

1 Plastik
2 potentielle Arithmetik
(oder [illegible] 1 u. 2 integriert)

und Element 3

Fettecke
Fettecke
Filterfettecke
Filzecke
Braunräume

„Guten Tag wo gehen Sie hin"?

„Thorwaldsen Museum

auch zu dir fliege ich MANRESA

Hier spricht FLUXUS [FLUXUS Speaking], 1966. 29.5 × 21 cm.

This is FLUXUS speaking
FLUXUS

Now?
Has Element 2 climbed up to Element 1?
Now?
Has Element 1 climbed down to Element 2?

n is the intersection of three transmitting lines
1 sculpture
2 potential arithmetic
(or also 1 and 2 integrated)
and Element 3

fat corner
fat corner
filter fat corner
felt corner
brown spaces
"Good morning where are you going?"
: "Thorvaldsen Museum"
I am flying to you too, MANRESA

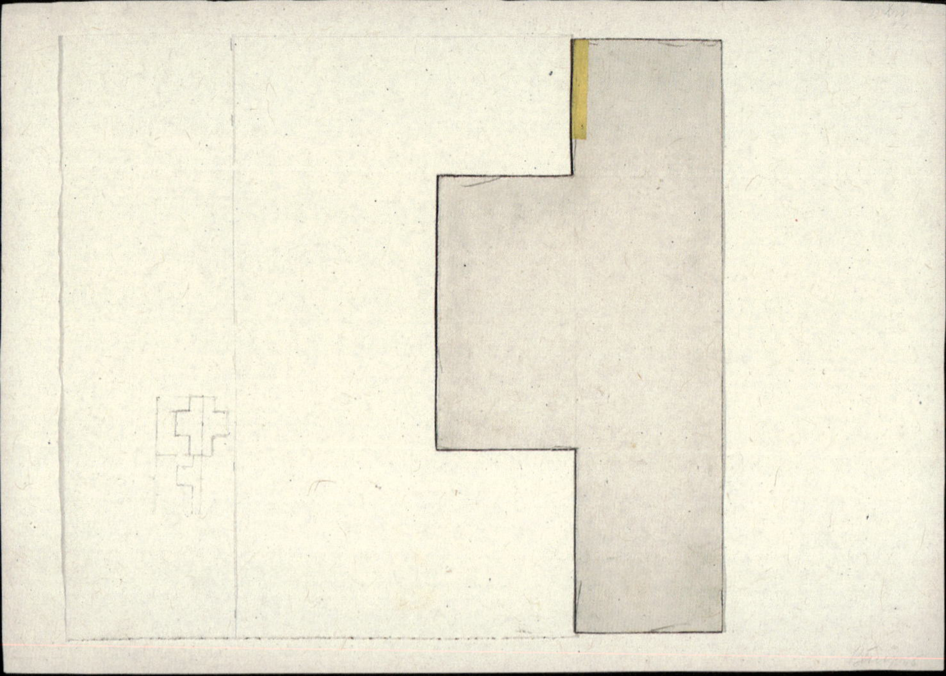

Study for Felt Cross, 1966. 52.8 × 79 cm.

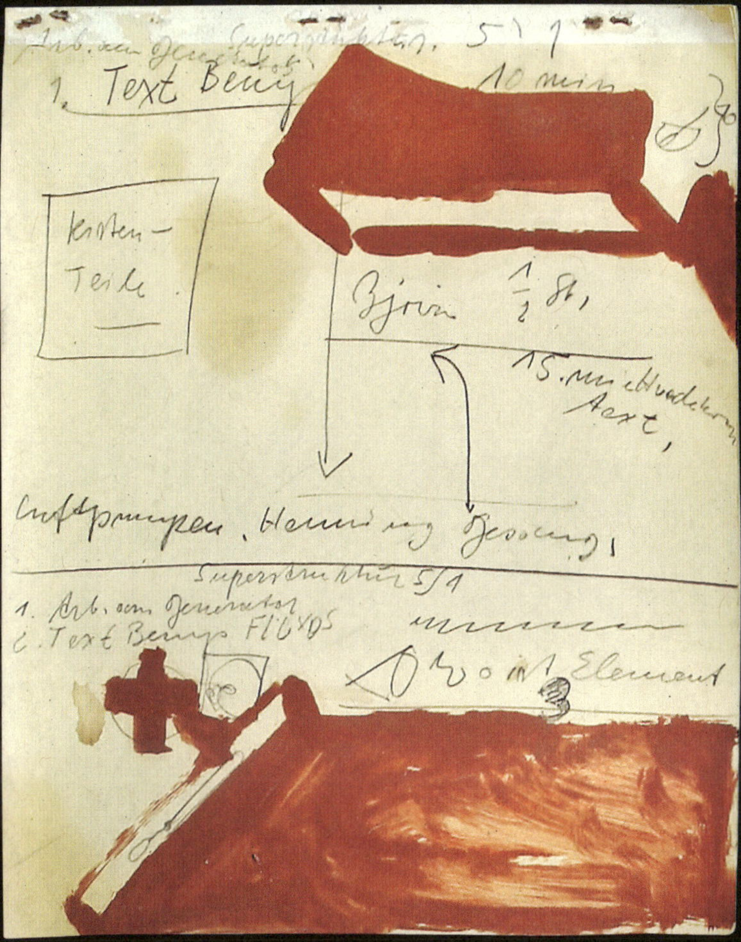

Partitur für MANRESA (Score for MANRESA), 1966. 26 × 21 × 1.5 cm.

Superstructure 5
Pieces with the generator
1. Text Beuys 10 min.

Pieces of
the box Bjørn ½ hour

15 min. text *Hvedekorn*

Bicycle pumps, Henning sings,

Superstructure 5/1
1. Pieces with the generator
2. Text Beuys FLUXUS
Where is Element
3

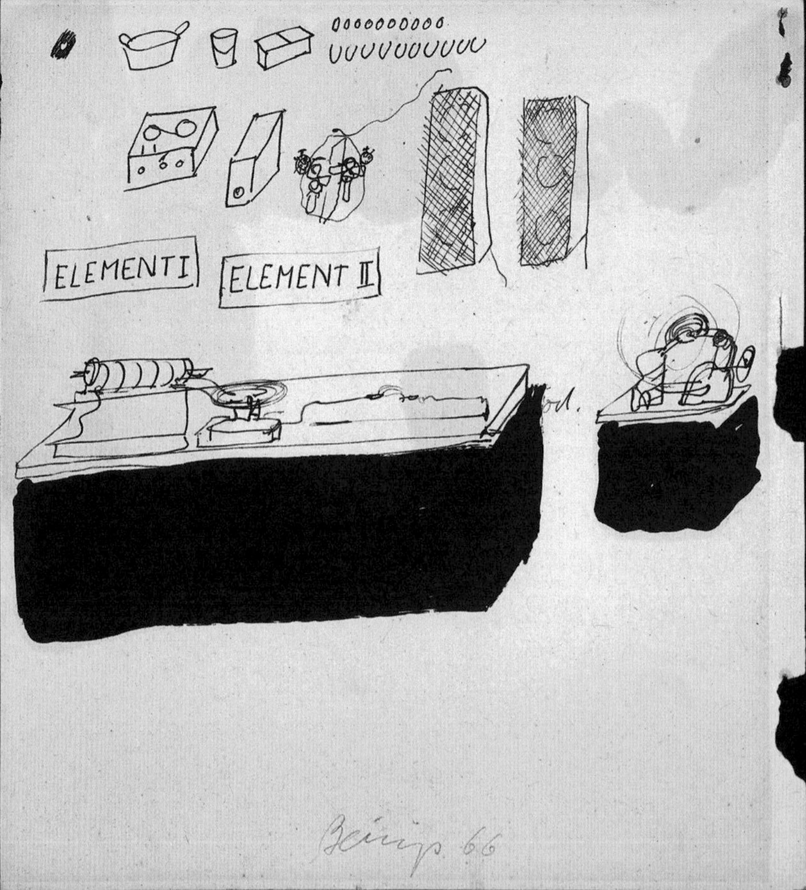

Element I, Element II, 1966. 21 × 19.7 cm.

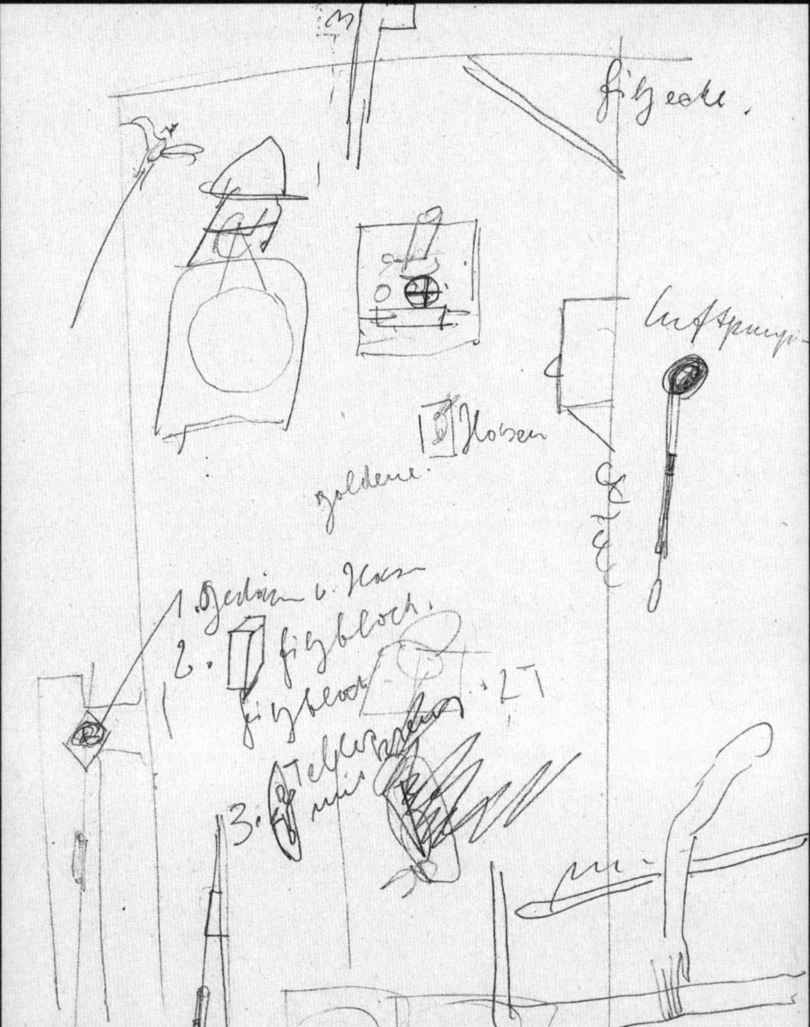

Gedärm von Hasen (Hare Innards), 1966. 38.7 × 30.2 cm.

felt corner

bicycle pump

golden hares

1. Hare innards
2. felt block
   felt block
3. Plate
   with crucifix

Wo ist Element 3
Hier spricht FLUXUS
Nun:
Ist Element 1 zu Element 2 heruntergestiegen?
Nun?
Ist Element 2 zu Element 1 heruntergestiegen?
Guten Tag wo gehen Sie hin?
Thorwaldsen Museum
n ist der Schnittpunkt zweier Strahllinien
Plastik 1 potentielle Arithmetik 2
u. Element 3
Fettecke.
Fettecke.

Wo ist Element 3? (Where is Element 3?), 1966. 29.5 × 21 cm.

50,000 V per sec. in the primary coiling

n

vocal: Where is Element 3
This is FLUXUS speaking
FLUXUS

Now?
Has Element 1 climbed down to Element 2?
Now?
Has Element 2 climbed down to Element 1?

21

Good morning, where are you going?
: "Thorvaldsen Museum"
To the beautiful valley of Manresa

n is the intersection of three transmitting lines
sculptural expression 1 potential arithmetic 2
(with pencil: or a sculptural expression and potential arithmetic "n" integrated
Marcel Duchamp)
And Element 3

fat corner
fat corner

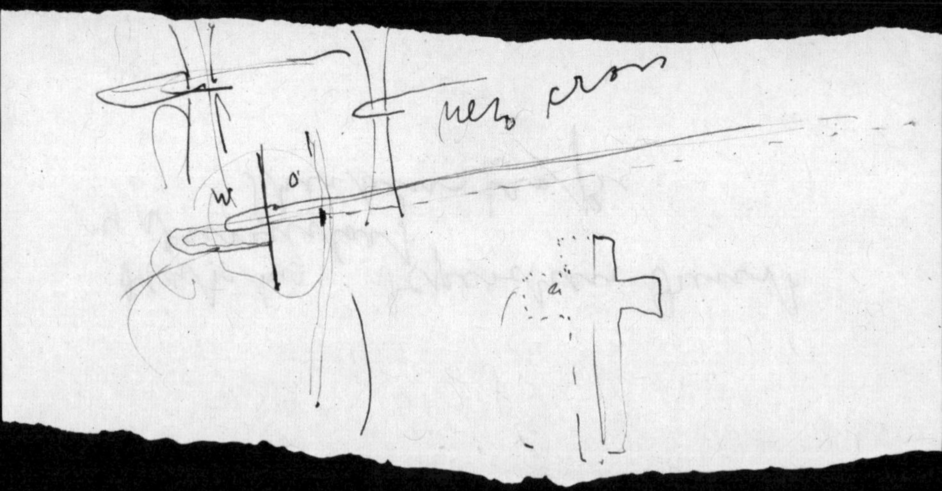

Zu MANRESA (On MANRESA), 1966. 9.7 × 20.9 cm.

New Cross

W E

n

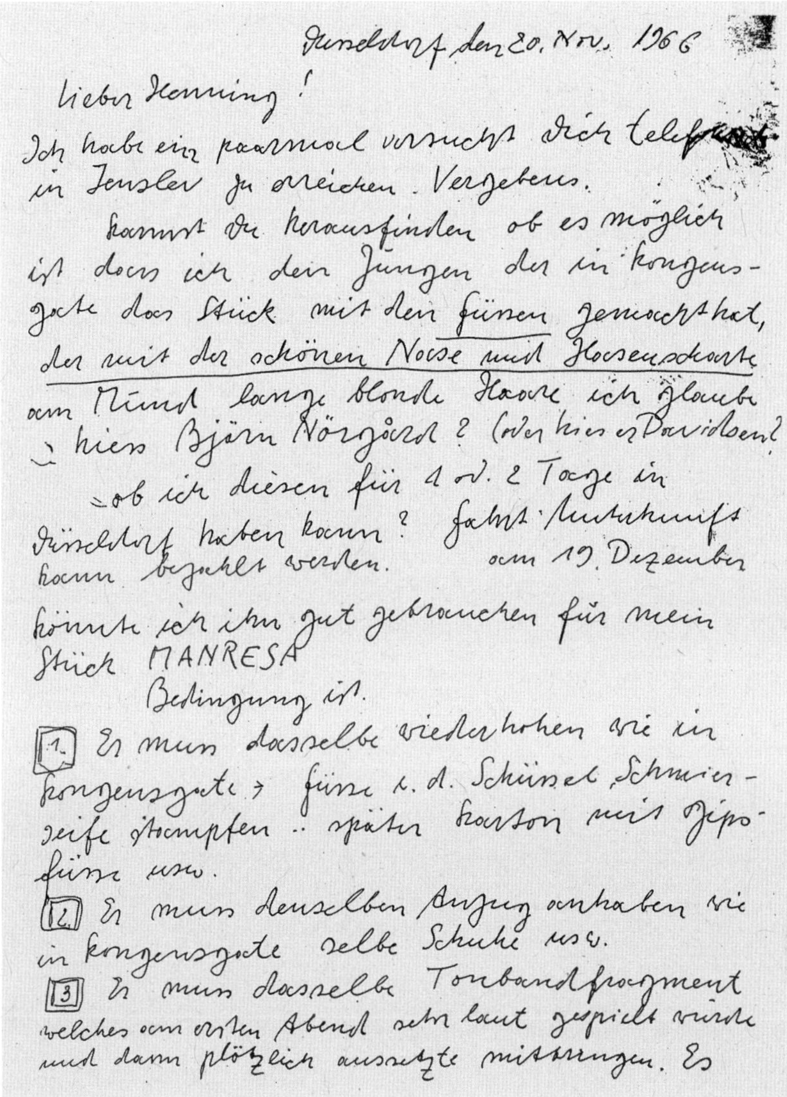

Düsseldorf, den 20. Nov. 1966

Lieber Henning!

Ich habe ein paarmal versucht dich telef… in Jensler zu erreichen. Vergebens.

Kannst Du herausfinden ob es möglich ist dass ich den Jungen der in Kongensgate das Stück mit den Füssen gemacht hat, der mit der schönen Nase und Hasenscharte am Mund lange blonde Haare ich glaube hiess Björn Nörgård? (oder hiess er Davidsen?)

ob ich diesen für 1 od. 2 Tage in Düsseldorf haben kann? Fahrt Unterkunft kann bezahlt werden. am 19. Dezember könnte ich ihn gut gebrauchen für mein Stück MANRESA

Bedingung ist.

1. Er muss dasselbe wiederholen wie in Kongensgate → Füsse i. d. Schüssel Schmierseife stampfen .. später Karton mit Gipsfüsse usw.
2. Er muss denselben Anzug anhaben wie in Kongensgate selbe Schuhe usw.
3. Er muss dasselbe Tonbandfragment welches am ersten Abend sehr laut gespielt wurde und dann plötzlich aussetzte mitbringen. Es

Düsseldorf, 20 November 1966

Dear Henning:

I have tried to call you various times at Jensler. No luck.

Could you find out if it is possible for me to have the young man who did the piece with the feet at Kongensgate, the one with the beautiful nose and the harelip, long blond hair, I think he was called Bjørn Nørgaard? (or was his name Davidsen?)

If I could have him for 1 or 2 days in Düsseldorf? Journey and lodgings can be paid for. On 19 December I could find a good use for him in my piece MANRESA.

Conditions:

1. He must repeat the same thing as in Kongensgate — stamp feet in a bowl of brown soap... later on cardboard box with plaster feet, etc.
2. He must wear the same suit as in Kongensgate, same shoes, etc.
3. He must bring the same piece of tape that was played very loudly on the first night and then suddenly stopped. On it the word

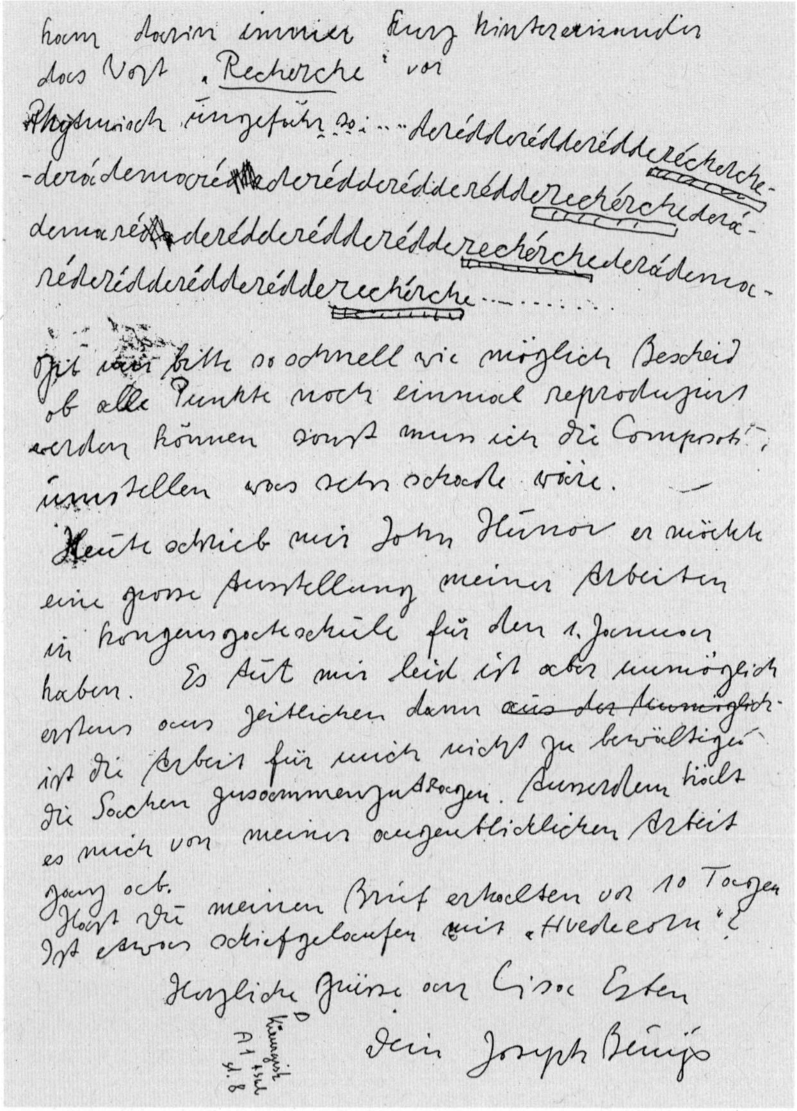
kam darin immer kurz hintereinander
das Wort „Recherche" vor
Rhythmisch ungefähr so:....derédderédderéddeŕécherche-
derádemaréd derédderédderéddeŕecherchederá-
demaréd derédderédderéddeŕecherchederádema-
réderédderédderéddeŕecherche........
Gib mir bitte so schnell wie möglich Bescheid
ob alle Punkte noch einmal reproduziert
werden können sonst muss ich die Composition
umstellen was sehr schade wäre.
Heute schrieb mir John Hunov er möchte
eine grosse Ausstellung meiner Arbeiten
in Kongensgadeschule für den 1. Januar
haben. Es tut mir leid ist aber unmöglich
erstens aus zeitlichen dann ~~aus der Unmöglich-~~
ist die Arbeit für mich nicht zu bewältigen
die Sachen zusammenzutragen. Ausserdem hält
es mich von meiner augenblicklichen Arbeit
ganz ab.
Hast du meinen Brief erhalten vor 10 Tagen
Ist etwas schiefgelaufen mit „Hvedecorn"?
Herzliche Grüsse an Lisa Esten
Dein Joseph Beuys

Joseph Beuys, letter to Henning Christiansen to plan the action MANRESA, 1966.

'recherche' was repeated at short intervals. Rhythmically it was more or less like this: .... derédderédderéddeŕécherche-

deráddemarédderédderédderéddeŕechérchederá-

demaréderédderédderéddeŕechérchederádema-

réderédderédderéddeŕechérche ....

Please, let me know as soon as you can if all these points can be done again if not, I will have to retouch the composition which would be a shame for it.

Today John Hunor wrote me he wants to have a large exhibition of my work at the school in Kongensgate for 1 January. I am sorry but it is not possible first for reasons of time and later ~~for the impossib~~ because I cannot do all this work — recompiling things. Also, it takes away from me doing my current work.

Did you receive my letter of 10 days ago?

Perhaps there are problems with «Hvedecorn»?

Best regards to Lisa Esten

Yours Joseph Beuys

HOMMAGE AN SCHMELA

7 VERANSTALTUNGEN

in der Galerie Schmela
Düsseldorf, Hunsrücken-
straße 16, zu denen Sie
herzlich eingeladen sind

89

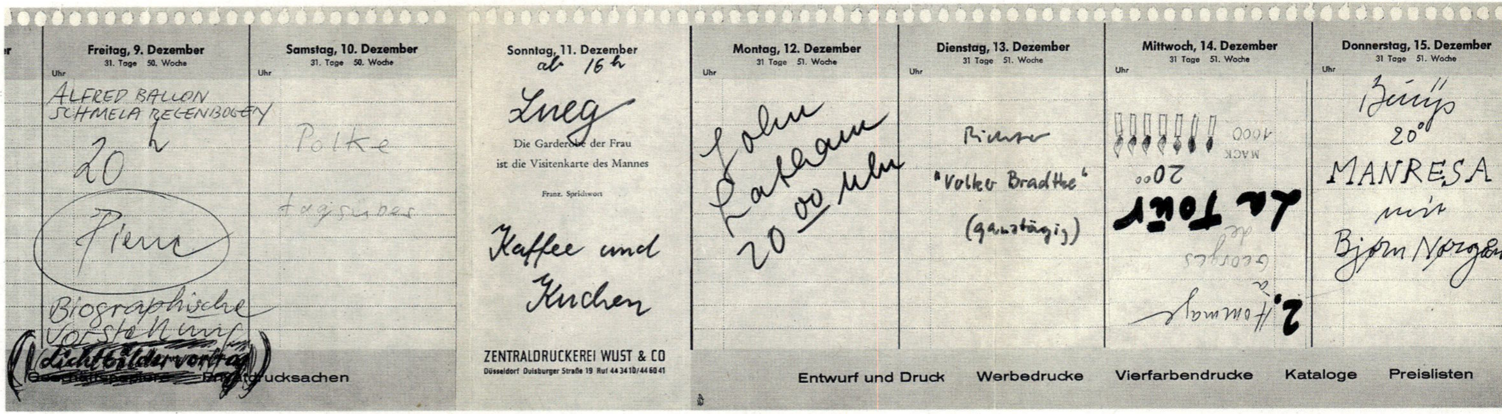

Programme for the activities carried out from 9 to 15 December 1966, in homage to Galerie Schmela, 16 Hunsrücken, Düsseldorf, before it moved.

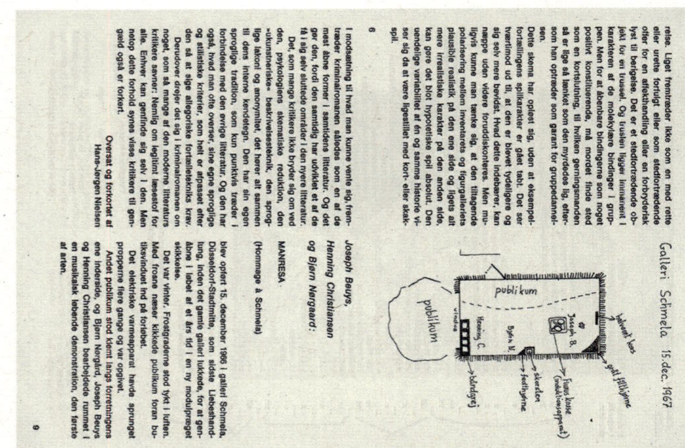

reise. Liget fremtræder ikke som en med rette eller urette forfulgt eller som stedfortrædende offer for en affekthandling eller en forbryderisk lyst til berigelse. Det er et stedfortrædende objekt for en trussel. Og truslen ligger immanent i karakteren af de molekylære bindinger i gruppen. Men for at åbenbare bindingerne som noget positivt konstituerende, må mordet finde sted som en kortslutning, til hvilken gerningsmanden så er lige så lænket som den myrdedes lig, eftersom han optræder som garant for gruppedannelsen.

Dette skema har opløst sig, uden at eksempelfortællingens spilkarakter er gået tabt. Det ser tværtimod ud til, at den er blevet tydeligere og sig selv mere bevidst. Hvad dette indebærer, kan næppe uden videre foruddiskonteres. Men muligvis kunne man tænke sig, at den tiltagende polarisering mellem inventarets og figurgalleriets plausible realistik på den ene side og ligets alt mere irrealistiske karakter på den anden side, kan gøre det blot hypotetiske spil absolut. Den uendelige variabilitet af én og samme historie viser sig da at være ligestillet med kort- eller skakspil.

6

I modsætning til hvad man kunne vente sig, fremtræder kriminalromanen således som en af de mest åbne former i samtidens litteratur. Og det gør den, fordi den samtidig har udviklet et af de få i sig selv sluttede områder i den nyere litteratur.

Det, som mange kritikere ikke bryder sig om ved den, psykologiens skematiske reduktion, den »ukunstneriske« beskrivelsesteknik, den sproglige lakoni og anonymitet, det hører alt sammen til dens interne kendetegn. Den har sin egen sproglige tradition, som kun punktvis træder i forbindelse med den øvrige litteratur. Og den har også, hvad man ofte overser, sine egne sproglige og stilistiske kriterier, som helt er afpasset efter den så at sige allegoriske fortælleteknisk krav.

Derudover drejer det sig i kriminalromanen om noget, som så mange af den moderne litteraturs kritikere savner: Nemlig om legitimt læsestof for alle. Enhver kan genfinde sig selv i den. Men netop dette forhold synes visse kritikere til gengæld også er forkert.

Oversat og forkortet af
Hans-Jørgen Nielsen

Joseph Beuys,
Henning Christiansen
og Bjørn Nørgaard:

MANRESA

(Hommage à Schmela)

blev opført 15. december 1966 i galleri Schmela, Düsseldorf-Stadtmitte, som sidste Liebeshandlung, inden det gamle galleri lukkede, for at genåbne i løbet af et års tid i en ny modulpræget skikkelse.

Det var vinter. Frostgraderne stod tykt i luften. Med frosne næser kikkede publikum foran butiksvinduet ind på forløbet.

Det elektriske varmeapparat havde sprunget propperne flere gange og var opgivet.

Andet publikum stod klemt langs forretningens ene inderside, og Bjørn Nørgård, Joseph Beuys og Henning Christiansen bearbejdede rummet i en musikalsk løbende demonstration, den første af arten.

9

Script for the action MANRESA, published in the magazine *ta'* 4 in August–September 1967, in Copenhagen. The script was prepared by Henning Christiansen and appeared signed by Beuys, Christiansen and Nørgaard. The first page was hand modified by Joseph Beuys.

Klokken var 20.00, da båndstemmen forkyndte:
(J. B.):

5 elementer i organisk delt form.

Hier spricht Fluxus / / Fluxus
Hier spricht Fluxus / / Fluxus

NUN?
NUN? ist Element 2 zu Element 1 heraufgestiegen
NUN? ist Element 1 zu Element 2 heruntergestiegen
NUN? ist Element 2 zu Element 1 heraufgestiegen
NUN? ist Element 1 zu Element 2 heruntergestiegen

—

NUN? ist Element 2 zu Element 1 heraufgestiegen
NUN? ist Element 1 zu Element 2 heruntergestiegen
NUN? ist Element 2 zu Element 1 heraufgestiegen
NUN? ist Element 1 zu Element 2 heruntergestiegen

—

n ist der Schnittpunkt dreier Strahllinien
eins Plastik
zwei potentielle Arithmetik
oder auch eins und zwei integriert
und Element 3

n ist der Schnittpunkt dreier Strahllinien
eins Plastik
zwei potentielle Arithmetik
oder auch eins und zwei integriert
und Element 3

—

Fettecke / Fettecke
Filterfettecke
Filzecke

—

BRAUNRÄUME

Guten Tag, wo gehen Sie hin?
Thorvaldsen-Museum

Guten Tag, wo gehen Sie hin?
Thorvaldsen-Museum

NUN? ist Element 2 zu Element 1 heraufgestiegen
NUN? ist Element 1 zu Element 2 heruntergestiegen

In = Hier spricht u.s.w.
a = Nun ist u.s.w.
a/l = halveret a
x = n ist u.s.w.
v = fettecke u.s.w.
vu = Guten Tag u.s.w.
y = auf zu Dir u.s.w.

n ist der Schnittpunkt dreier Strahllinien
eins Plastik
zwei potentielle Arithmetik
oder auch eins und zwei integriert
und Element 3

Fettecke / Fettecke
Filterfettecke
Filzecke

—

BRAUNRÄUME

Guten Tag, wo gehen Sie hin?
Thorvaldsen-Museum

—

Guten Tag, wo gehen Sie hin?
Thorvaldsen-Museum

Hier spricht Fluxus / / Fluxus

NUN? ist Element 2 zu Element 1 heraufgestiegen
NUN? ist Element 1 zu Element 2 heruntergestiegen

—

NUN? ist Element 2 zu Element 1 heraufgestiegen
NUN? ist Element 1 zu Element 2 heruntergestiegen

n ist der Schnittpunkt dreier Strahllinien
eins Plastik
zwei potentielle Arithmetik
oder auch eins und zwei integriert
und Element 3

—

Fettecke / Fettecke
Filterfettecke
Filzecke

—

BRAUNRÄUME

Guten Tag, wo gehen Sie hin?
Thorvaldsen-Museum

NUN? ist Element 2 zu Element 1 heraufgestiegen
NUN? ist Element 1 zu Element 2 heruntergestiegen

n ist der Schnittpunkt dreier Strahllinien
eins Plastik
zwei potentielle Arithmetik
oder auch eins und zwei integriert
und Element 3

Guten Tag, wo gehen Sie hin?
Thorvaldsen-Museum

Hier spricht Fluxus / / Fluxus

Guten Tag, wo gehen Sie hin?
Thorvaldsen-Museum

Auf zu Dir fliege ich MANRESA

10

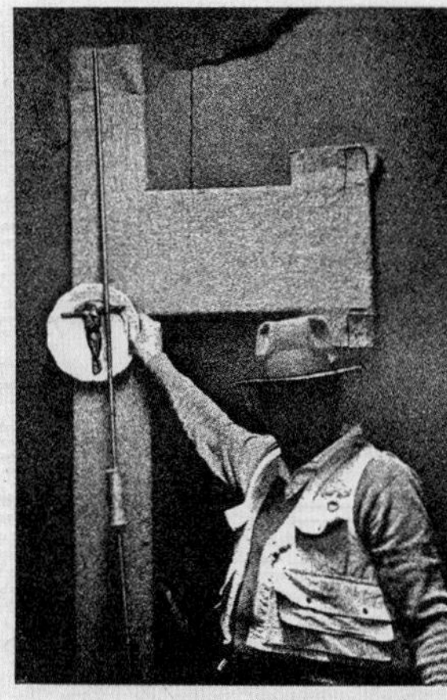

(n er 3 stråleliniers snitpunkt, skal ikke opfattes som uendelighed, men som mulighed.
1 er plastik (skulptur) – 2 potentiel (potens) aritmetisk, eller begge. Nødvendigt for at alt »stemmer« er, at element 3 er til stede.

Forvandlingen fra fedthjørne til filthjørne sker over felterfedthjørne / / Filthjørne fører direkte til **brunrummene.** Et muligt brunrum er Thorvaldsens musæum og herfra: M A N R E S A.)

(H.C.):
Ikke kann
Ikke Ikke kann
Ikke Ikke Ikke kann
Ikke Ikke Ikke Ikke kann
Ikke Ikke Ikke Ikke Ikke
Ikke Ikke Ikke Ikke Ikke Ikke
kann kann kann kann kann kann
kann kann kann kann kann
kann kann kann kann Ikke
kann kann kann Ikke
kann kann Ikke
kann Ikke

11

Rummet er helt sortmalet
I baggrunden det halverede filtkors (gråt)
Hvert femte minut slukkes lyset et minut

(J.B.):
Spydet anbragt foran korset.
Tallerken med terracotta-korsfæstet mand føres til punktet.
På ryggen filtsol på papgrund.
26 luftpumper med fedt klemt om indsugningen, suges ud og slynges mod væggen – bliver hængende – – glider langsomt mod gulvet.
Fugl på stang vifter flyvende med vingerne.
Filtblok føres mod korspunktet. (Stadig gentagelse.)
Wo ist Element drei?
Lyd af gnister }
Lys af gnister } fra induktionsapparat.
Hareører

(B.N.):
Et vilkårligt antal vilkårligt valgt materiale behandles og sættes i forhold til egne ben.

En 15 cm høj træramme fyldes med elektriske pærer. Rammen dækkes med et blåt klæde, pærerne knuses med fødderne.

En kubusformet lerklods (30×30×30 cm) betrukket med blåt klæde. Den stampes roligt ud til en pudeformet masse.

(H.C.):
herfra ⟶ og ⟶ dertil
derfra ⟶ og ⟶ hertil
kaffe ⟶ kop
klang ⟵ (hånd / hånd) ⟵ teske

(J.B.):
Den forgyldte hare elektrificeres – lyser i mørket.
Se harens indvolde.
Geislerrør gnides – snart lang snart kort.
Wo ist Element drei?
Lillebitteambulancemilitær
flytterkorsetmodjordebesvær
Wo ist Element drei?

(H.C.):
ikke ikke ikke ikke ikke ikke ikkeikkeikke ikke
ikke ikke ikke ikke ikke ikke
ikke ikke ikkeikkeikke ikke ikke

(B.N.):
På samme træramme udspændes et ståltrådsnet. Med gyngende og hoppende bevægelser ødelægges nettet.

På en hård masonitplade udtrykkes en stor klump brun sæbe. Med glidende bevægelser smøres hele pladen ind i sæben med fødderne.

Står i en papkasse. Fylder den langsomt med mel. Bevæger ustandseligt fødderne og resten af benene.

(J.B.):
En patentflaske med mælk
En patentflaske af bly.

(H.C.):
kann kann kann kann kann kann kann kann
kann kann kann

kann kannkann kann kann kann kann kann
kann kann

(B.N.):
I en beholder med vand opløses en stor mængde brun sæbe, ved at plaske i vandet med benene.

Hver fod indstøbes i hver sin gipsklods.

ET BÅND GENTAGER EN SOLDATERHILSEN OPTAGET FRA DANMARKS RADIO af typen: 789 Jensen sender hilsen til Karen på Samsø o.s.v.

(H.C.):
.... og hans energiplan ....joseph beuys .... joseph beuys er professor ved Düssel .... citatet er centralt ...... GEGENRAUM ....varmekagen er anbragt midt på scenen og løser sit indhold .... beuys forsøgt at indkredse ...... viste beuys .... en almindelig spadserestok ...... forlængede med ...... beuys ligeledes med den gule ...... beuys går klædt i .... at beuys er mystiker .... antinatur .... skiller er kropsvarmen .... beuys med sine fødder .... professor beuys's lærestol .... berlinmuren 5 cm ...... kaputhauen

Opsummeret for tysk hørelse

(J.B.):
To jernklodser forbundet med gaze.
Wo ist Element drei?

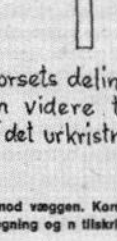

Korsets deling, muliggør
en videre transport
af det urkristne budskab.

Korset står mod væggen. Korsets anden halvdel antydes med kridtstregning og n tilskrives.

12

(H.C.):
Climb up skrives med kridt på væggen.

kann ikke
kann kann ikke
kann kann kann ikke
kann kann kann kann ikke
kann kann kann kann kann
kann kann kann kann kann kann
ikke ikke ikke ikke ikke ikke
ikke ikke ikke ikke ikke
ikke ikke ikke ikke kann
ikke ikke ikke kann
ikke ikke kann
ikke kann

(J.B.):
Induktionsapparat trækkes for gnister. Hænderne hvæser og drukner i

(H.C.):
kraftige søjleklange fra højttalerne ....
ON THE LINE (perceptive constructions)

Poul Nielsen:

FIGURATIV MUSIK

En re-interpretation af Strawinskys neoklassicisme

> Incidentally, I still consider Dostoievsky to be the greatest Russian after Pushkin. Now, when one is supposed to reveal so much of oneself by one's choice of Freud or Jung, Strawinsky or Schönberg, Dostoievsky or Tolstoj, I am a Dostoievskyan.
>
> Igor Strawinsky

1. Frontstillingen dodekafoni/neoklassicisme

Det er vist i almindelighed accepteret, at de to bærende strømninger i dette århundredes europæiske musikudvikling: neoklassicismen og serialismen (dodekafonien) i deres udspring havde fælles funktion: at opfylde et behov for sikkerhed. Deres opståen skyldtes ikke bare, at de ledende komponister i musikkens eksplosive nybrud omkring verdenskrig I, Strawinsky og Schönberg, pludselig blev bløde i knæene, da perspektiverne i det, de havde gjort, stod klart for dem, men også den specielle, indremusikalske problematik, som frigørelsen fra tonalitetens hegemoni havde afsløret. »Musikkens fulde frihed måtte forekomme ham at være en trussel, straks den var vundet«, skriver musikkritikeren Adorno om Strawinsky: »Med lynklar skarphed stod al musiks rådvildhed siden da klart for ham: hvordan det, der er emanciperet fra de forudgivne referencerammer, kan opnå forbindtlighed kun i kraft af sig selv«.

Det har siden ca. 1950 (herhjemme siden ca. 1960) været lige så almindeligt accepteret at forkaste den ene af disse løsninger, neoklassicismen, til fordel for den anden, serialismen. Denne frontstilling var faktisk en drivende kraft bag efterkrigstidens musik-avantgardisme. Kritikeren André Hodeir kaldte neoklassicismen for vort århundredes særlige kræftskade. Stockhausen udslyngede parolen »Kein neo –!«, og Boulez motiverede sin afvisning af neoklassicismen ved at påpege, at den er baseret »sur une esthétique de réconstitution«, mens dodekafonien adlyder »une dialectique de l'évolution«. Det, der lå bag efterkrigs-generationens forkastelse af neoklassicismen, var æstetisk allergi støttet af a) antagonisme mellem komponisten og det historiserende musikliv og b) komponisternes håb om etableringen af en forpligtende musikalsk sprogtilstand, der kunne påberåbe sig samme legitimation og autenticitet, som tonaliteten havde kunnet.

Og hvordan er så situationen i dag? Renlivet traditionalisme er nu som altid suspekt. Dette smitter af på vurderingen af neoklassicismen. Spørgsmålet er imidlertid, om dette er rimeligt. I det hele taget er det tvivlsomt, om neoklassicismen er så éntydigt et fænomen, at det er forsvarligt fortsat at opretholde den simple sammenkobling af neoklassicisme og traditionalisme.

13

JOSEPH BEUYS, HENNING CHRISTIANSEN AND BJØRN NØRGAARD

MANRESA (HOMAGE TO SCHMELA)

Performed on 15 December 1966 in the Galerie Schmela in the centre of Düsseldorf, as a last 'act of love' before the old gallery closed. It would open its doors again a year later, with a new modular interior.

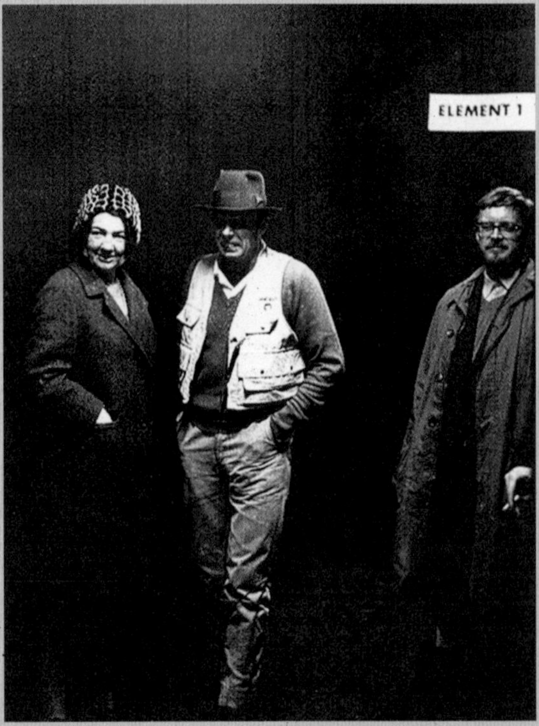

A

It was winter. Frosty temperatures stiffened the air. With frozen noses, part of the audience looked through the window at the goings-on.

The electric heater had blown the fuses several times and had been abandoned.

The other part of the audience stood inside, huddled along one side of the gallery, where Bjørn Nørgaard, Joseph Beuys and Henning Christiansen carried out a musical demonstration that was the first of its kind.

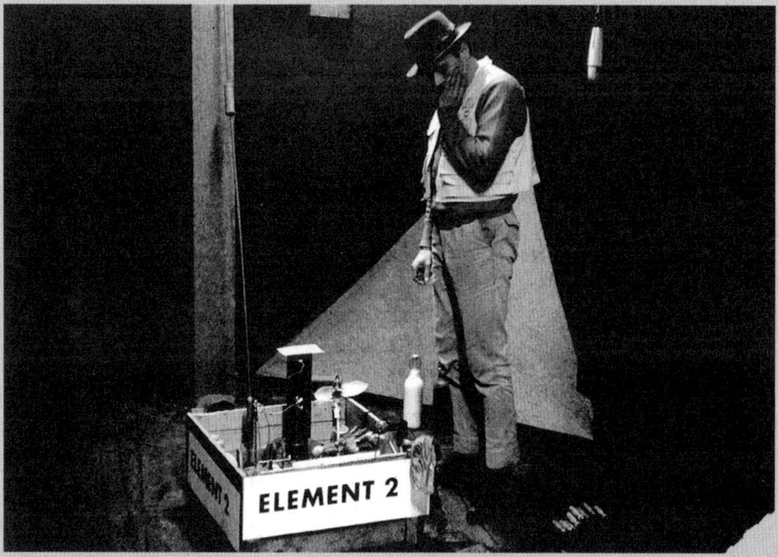

B

It was 8p.m. when the taped voice announced:

J.B.

This is Fluxus speaking/ /Fluxus
This is Fluxus speaking/ /Fluxus

Now? Has Element 2 climbed up to Element 1?
Now? Has Element 1 climbed down to Element 2?
Now? Has Element 2 climbed up to Element 1?
Now? Has Element 1 climbed down to Element 2?
–
Now? Has Element 2 climbed up to Element 1?
Now? Has Element 1 climbed down to Element 2?
Now? Has Element 2 climbed up to Element 1?
Now? Has Element 1 climbed down to Element 2?
–
n is the intersection of three transmitting lines[1]
one sculpture
two potential arithmetic
or one and two integrated
and Element 3

n is the intersection of three transmitting lines
one sculpture
two potential arithmetic
or one and two integrated
and Element 3

5	–
elements	Fat corner / Fat corner
in	Filter fat corner
divided	Felt corner
organic	–
form:	BROWN SPACES
in	Good morning, where are you going?
in	Thorvaldsen Museum
–	
a	Good morning, where are you going?
a	Thorvaldsen Museum
–	
x	Now? Has Element 2 climbed up to Element 1?
x	Now? Has Element 1 climbed down to Element 2?
–	
v	n is the intersection of three transmitting lines
–	one sculpture
vu	two potential arithmetic
vu	or one and two integrated
–	and Element 3
a/l	
–	Fat corner / Fat corner
x	Filter fat corner
–	Felt corner
v	–
–	BROWN SPACES
vu	
vu	Good morning, where are you going?
–	Thorvaldsen Museum
in	–
–	Good morning, where are you going?
a	Thorvaldsen Museum
–	
x	This is Fluxus speaking/ /Fluxus
–	
v	Now? Has Element 2 climbed up to Element 1?
–	Now? Has Element 1 climbed down to Element 2?
vu	–
–	Now? Has Element 2 climbed up to Element 1?
a/l	Now? Has Element 1 climbed down to Element 2?
–	
x	
–	
vu	
–	
in	
vu	
y	

in = This is Fluxus, etc.
a = Now?, etc.
a/l = half of 'a'
x = n is, etc.
v = Fat corner, etc.
vu = Good morning, etc.
y = I am flying, etc.

n is the intersection of three lines
one is sculpture
two potential arithmetic
or one and two integrated
and Element 3
–
Fat corner / Fat corner
Filter fat corner
Felt corner
–
BROWN SPACES

Good morning, where are you going?
Thorvaldsen Museum

Now? Has Element 2 climbed up to Element 1?
Now? Has Element 1 climbed down to Element 2?

n is the intersection of three lines
one is sculpture
two potential arithmetic
or one and two integrated
and Element 3

Good morning, where are you going?
Thorvaldsen Museum

This is Fluxus speaking/ /Fluxus

Good morning, where are you going?
Thorvaldsen Museum

I am flying to you too, Manresa

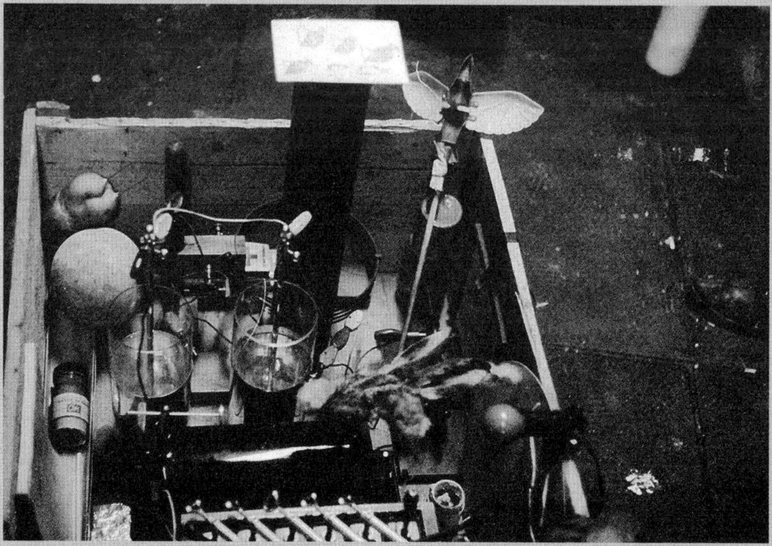

C

(n is the intersection of three lines of radiation, and should not be understood as infinity, but as a possibility.

1 is plastic expression (sculpture) - 2 potential arithmetic (potency) or both of them at once. For everything to "agree", Element 3 needs to be present.

The transformation from fat corner to felt corner takes place via the filter fat corner//the felt corner leads directly to the brown spaces. A possible brown space is the Thorvaldsen Museum and from here: MANRESA.)

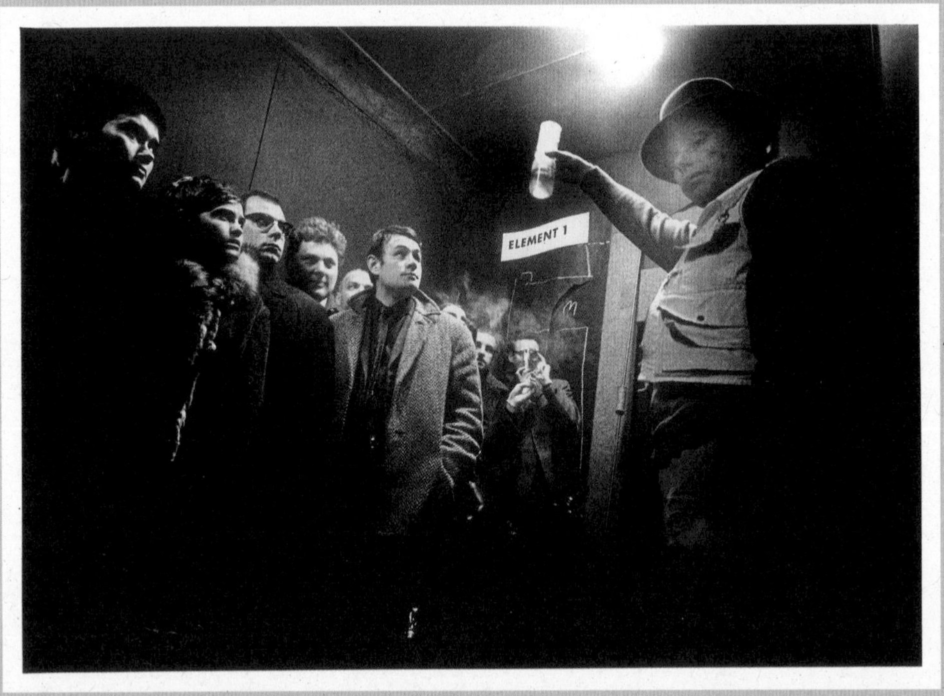

D

H.C.

ikke kann[2]
ikke ikke kann
ikke ikke ikke kann
ikke ikke ikke ikke kann
ikke ikke ikke ikke ikke
ikke ikke ikke ikke ikke ikke
kann kann kann kann kann kann
kann kann kann kann kann
kann kann kann kann ikke
kann kann kann ikke
kann kann ikke
kann ikke

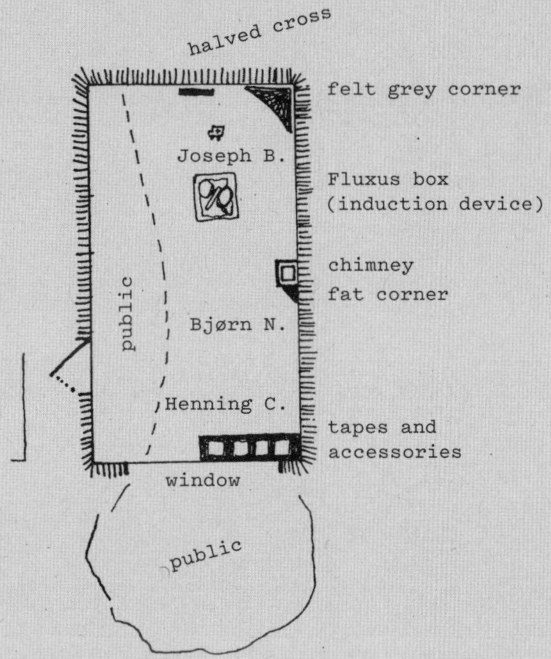

The room is painted black
In the background, the halved felt cross (grey)
Every five minutes the light goes off for a minute

J.B.

The spear is placed in front of the cross.
Terracotta man crucified on a plate, is led to the point.
On the back, a felt sun on a cardboard support.
26 bicycle pumps with fat squeezed into their air valves, which is sucked up and flung against the wall - sticks - slowly slides to the ground.
Bird on the pole fans its wings.
Felt block is guided against the intersection. (Continuous repetition)

Where is Element three?

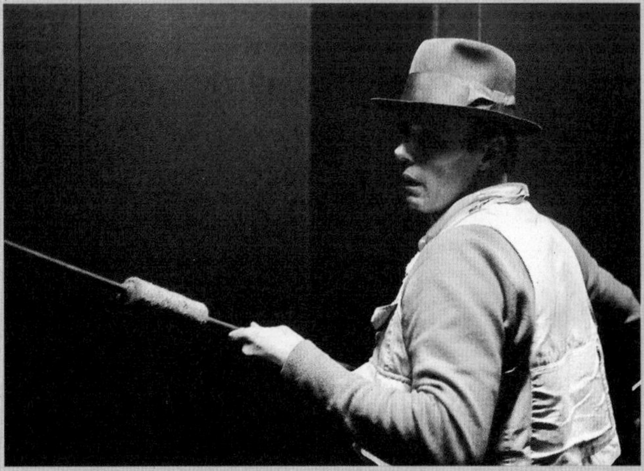

E

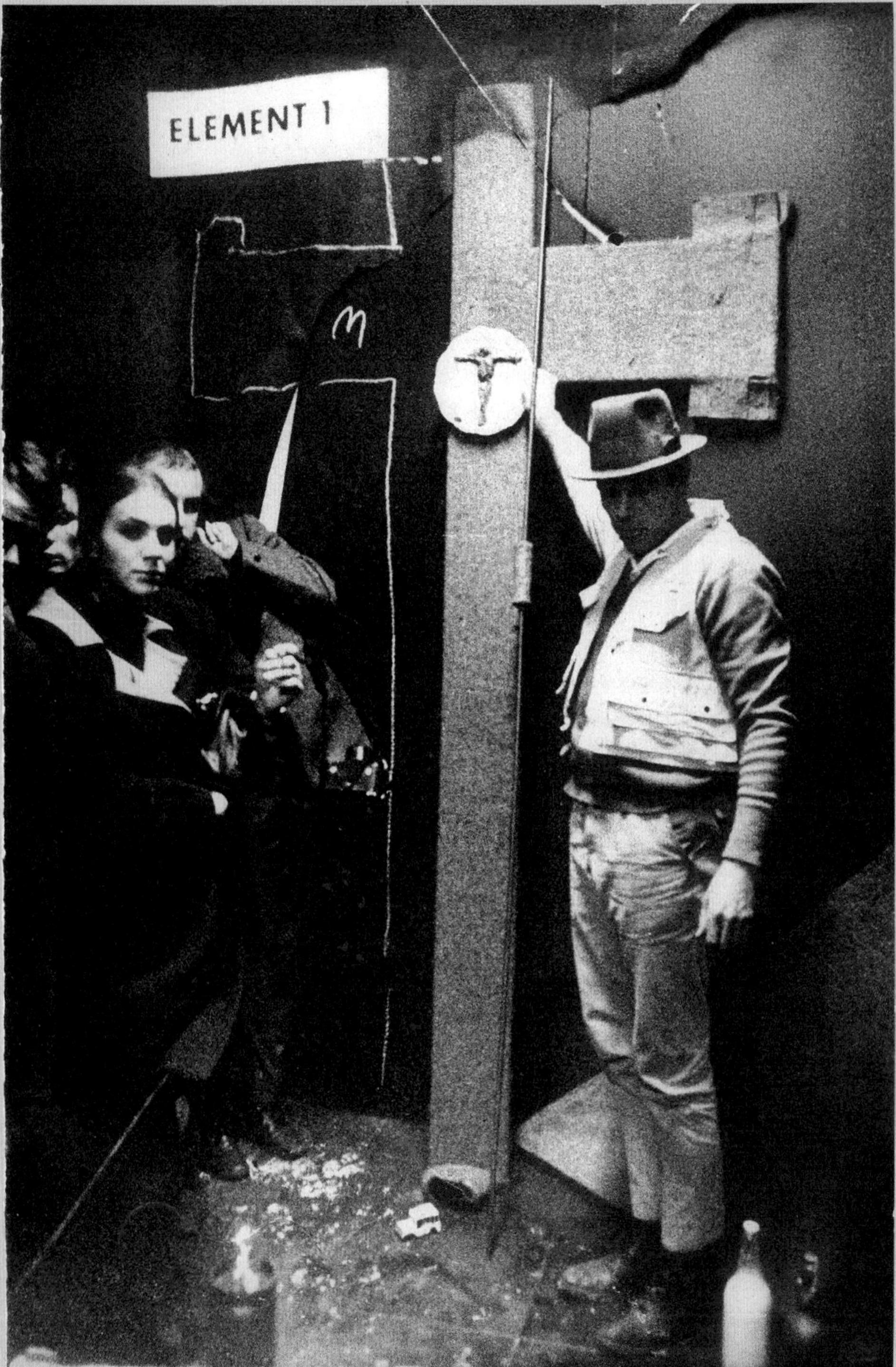

F

G

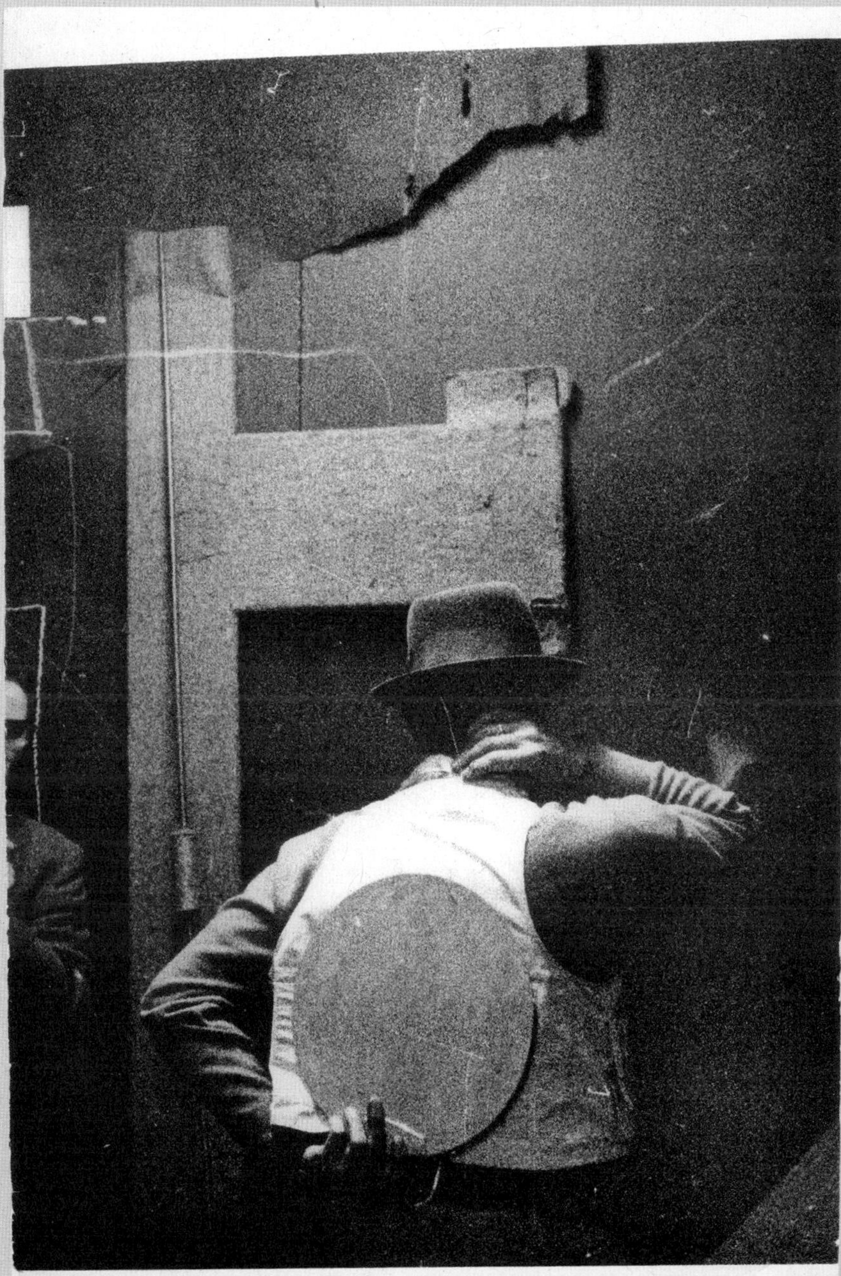

Crackling sparks | from the induction device
Light of sparks |

Hare's ears.

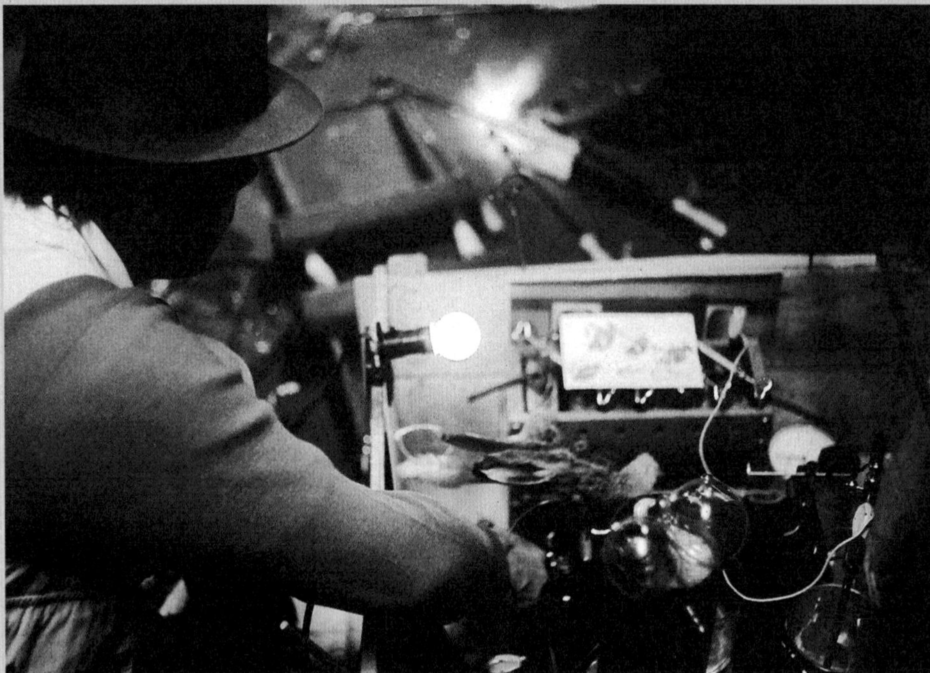

H

I

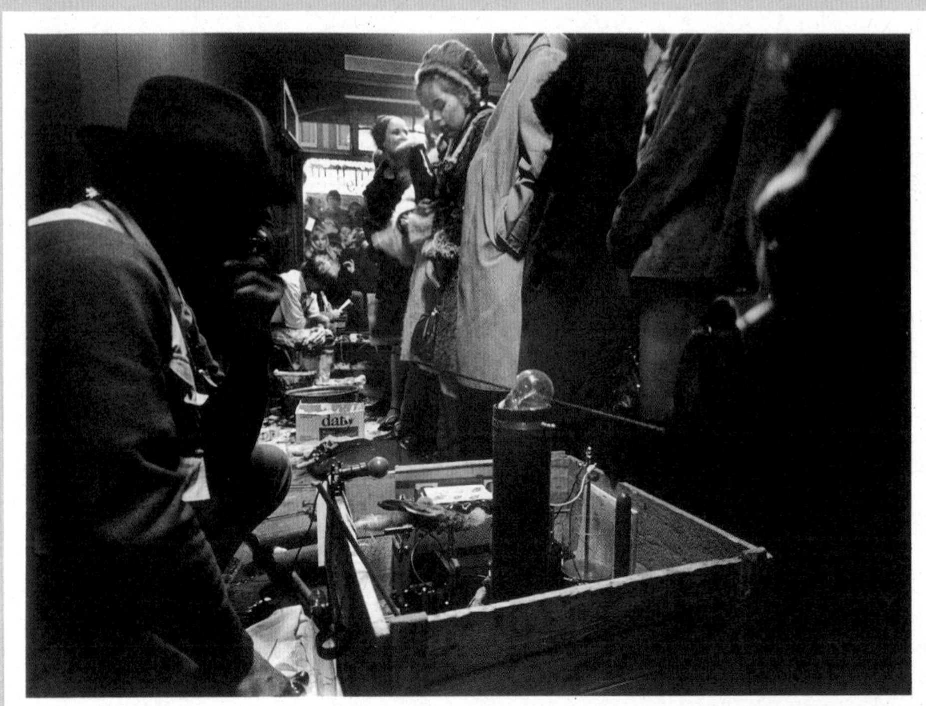

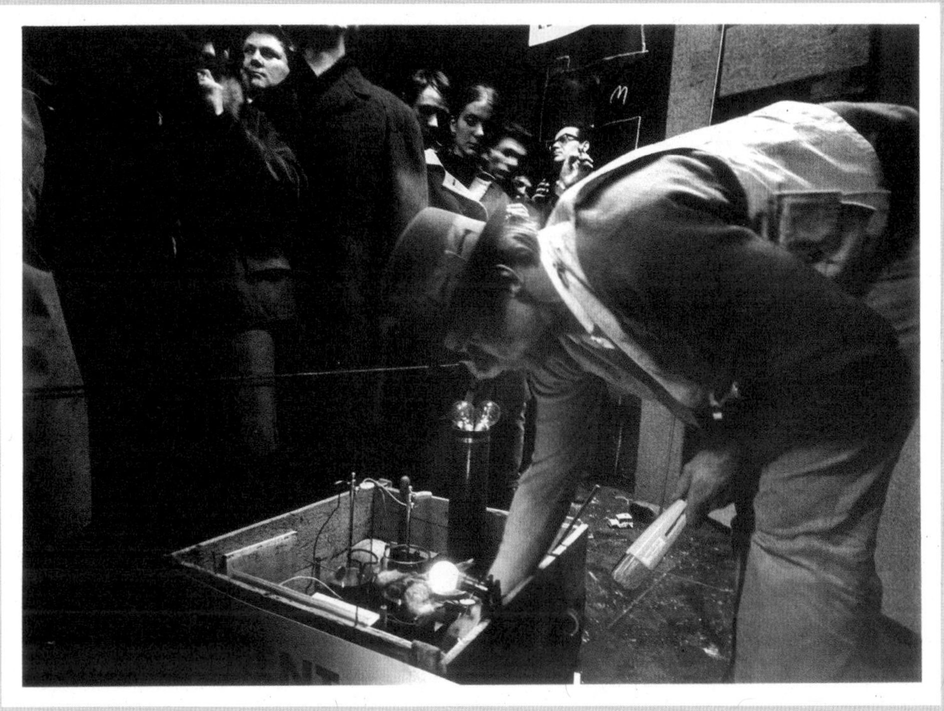

J

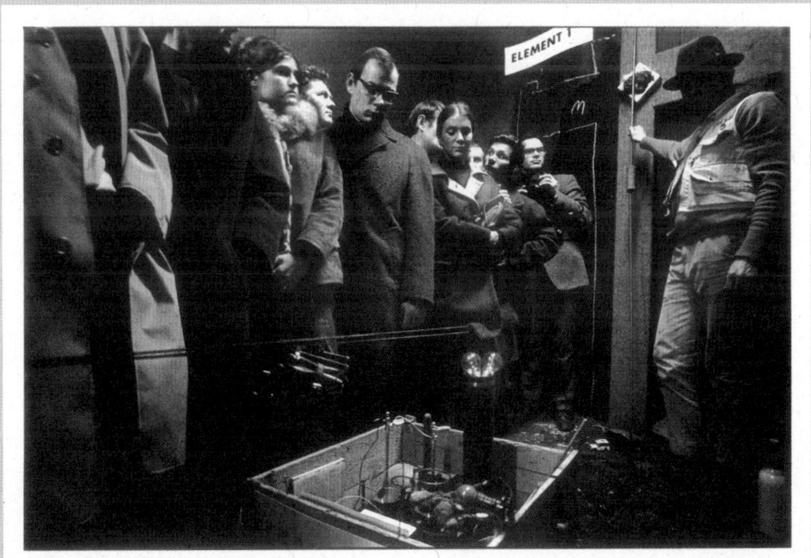

K

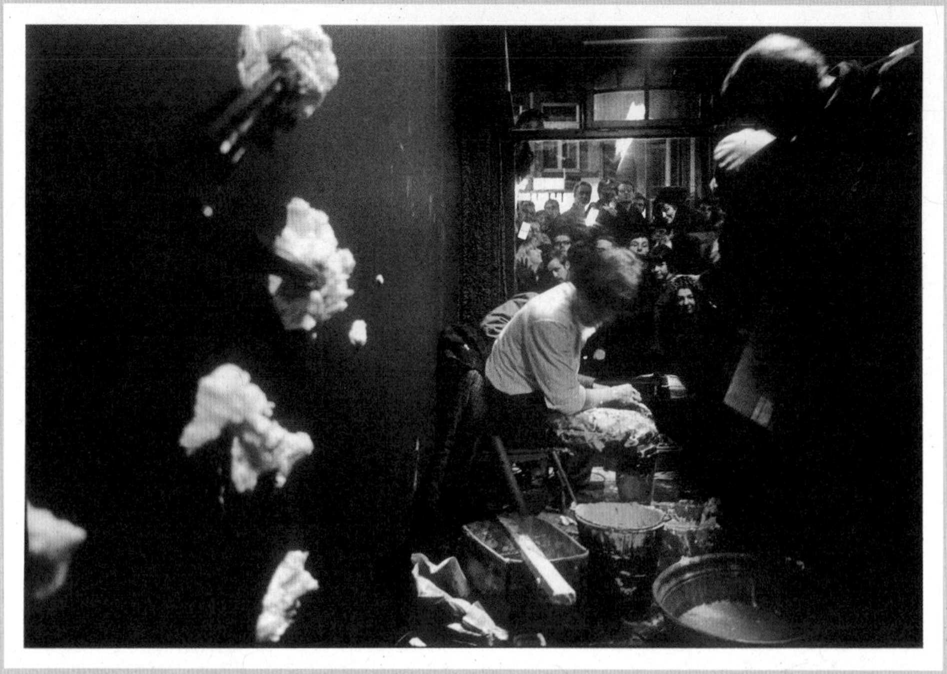

L

B.N.

An arbitrary number of arbitrarily chosen materials is processed and brought into proportion to one's own legs.

–

A 15-cm-high wooden frame is filled with electric bulbs. The frame is covered with a blue cloth, the bulbs are trampled underfoot.

A cube of clay (30 × 30 × 30 cm) covered with blue fabric is slowly pounded into a pillow-shaped mass.

H.C.

from here ⟶ and ⟶ to there
from there ⟶ and ⟶ to here
Coffee ⟶ Cup

Hand ↗
Sound ⟵ Teaspoon
↙ Hand

J.B.

Electrifies the golden rabbit - it glows.
Look at the hare's innards.
Rubbing the Geissler tube - short, long.

Where is Element three?

Kinderambulancemilitär[3]
fährtmitseinemkreuzbeschwertumher[4]

Where is Element three?

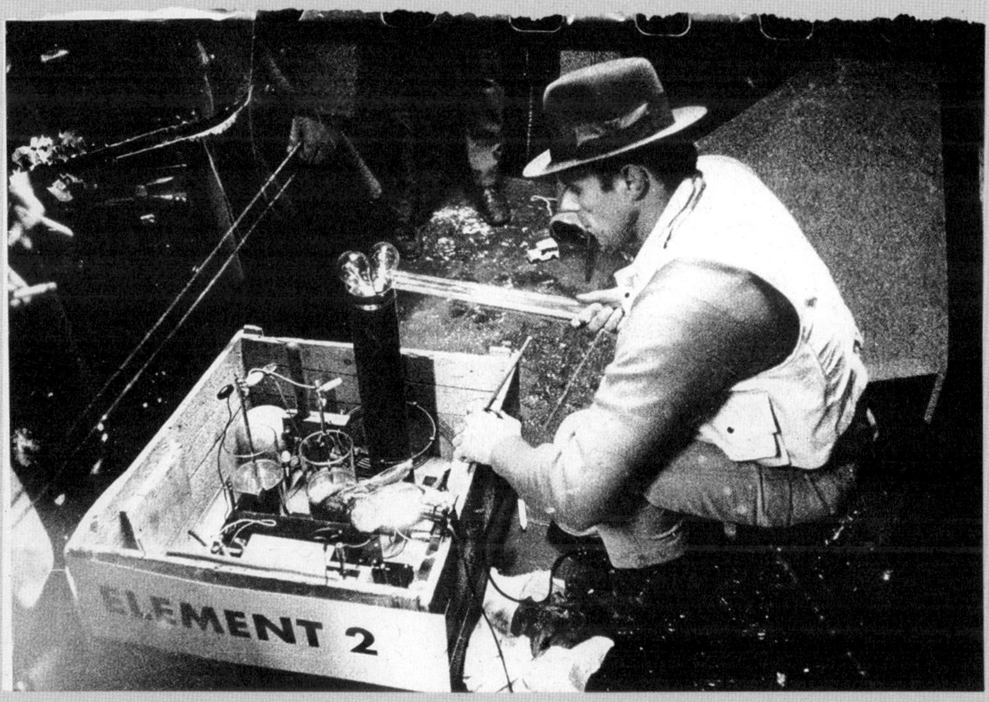

M

H.C.

ikke ikke   ikke   ikke   ikke ikke   ikkeikkeikke ikke
  ikke ikke ikke   ikke   ikke ikke
ikke   ikke   ikkeikkeikke   ikke   ikke

B.N.

A steel wire mesh is stretched on the same wooden frame. With rocking and bouncing movements the net is destroyed.

A large lump of brown soap is crushed on a hard, Masonite board. Sliding feet spread it out over the entire surface.

N

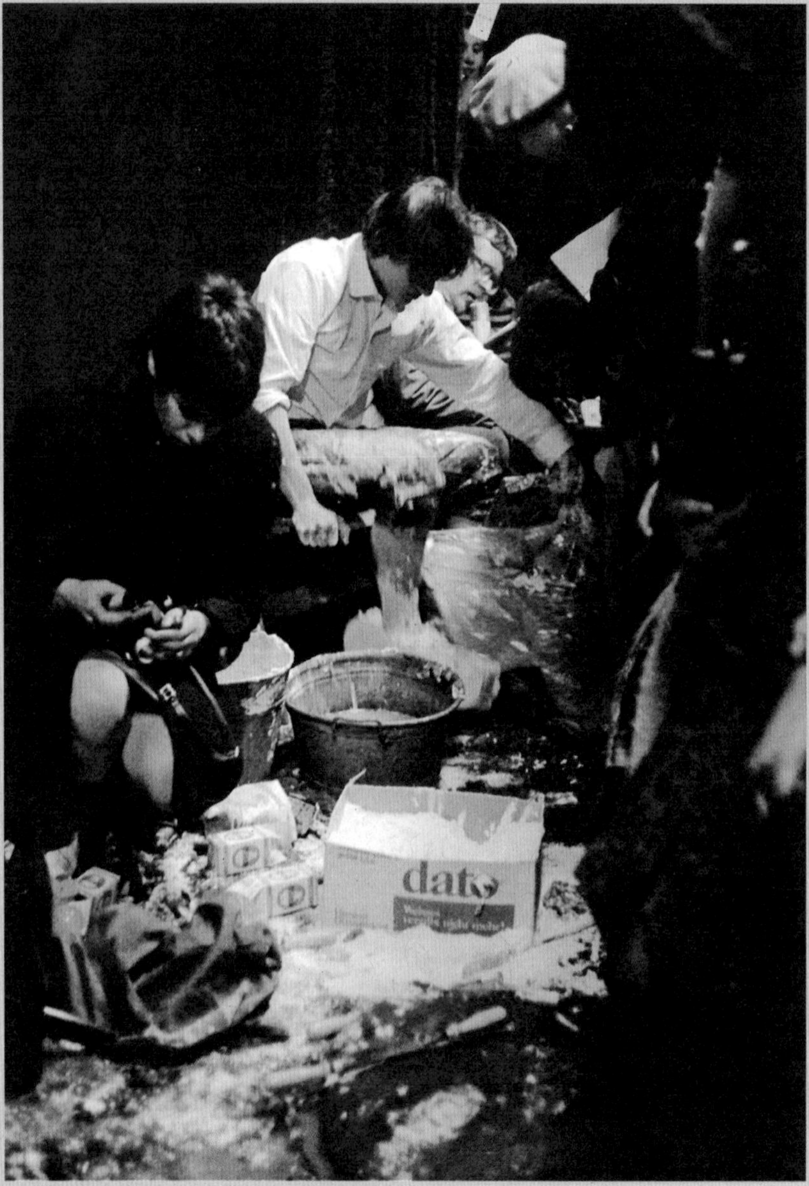

He stands in a cardboard box. Slowly fills it with flour. He moves his feet and legs incessantly.

J.B.

A bottle with milk
A bottle of lead

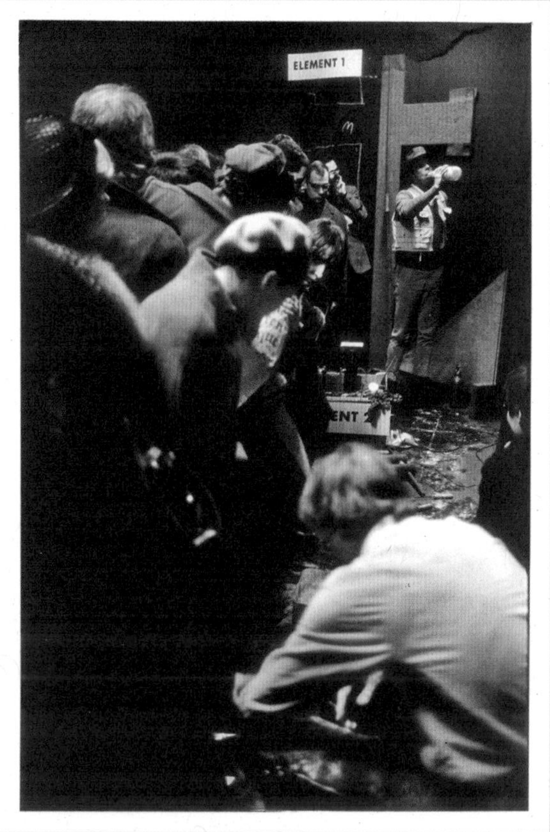

O

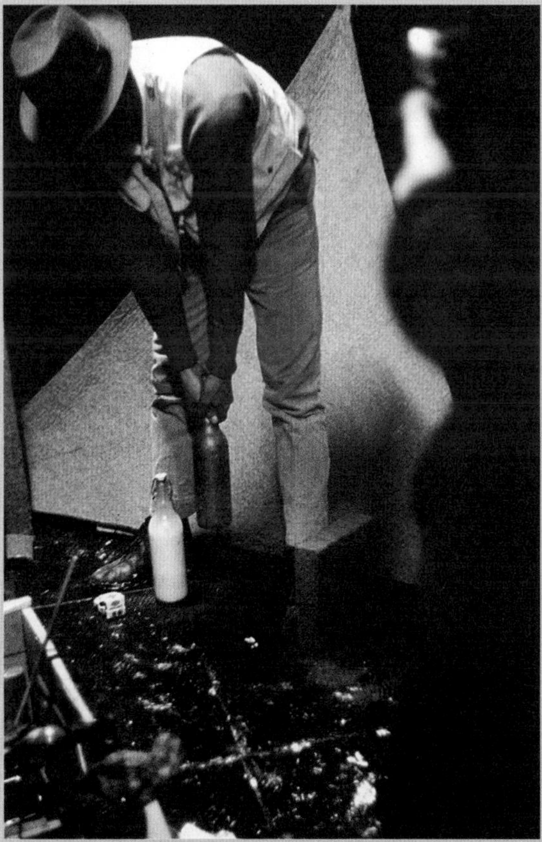

P

Q

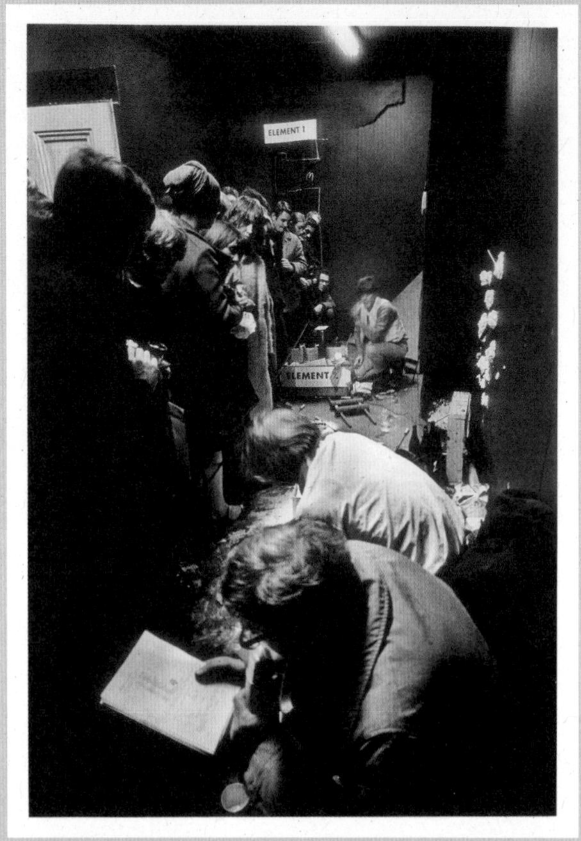

H.C.

kann kann kann kann kann kann kann kann
kann kann kann

kann kannkann kann kann kann kann kann
kann kann

B.N.

Lots of brown soap is dissolved in a container of water.
Splashing with legs.

Each foot is cast in its plaster block.

THE TAPE RECORDER REPEATS SOLDIERS' GREETINGS FROM DANISH NATIONAL RADIO, such as: 789 Jensen sends a
greeting to Karen in Samsø.

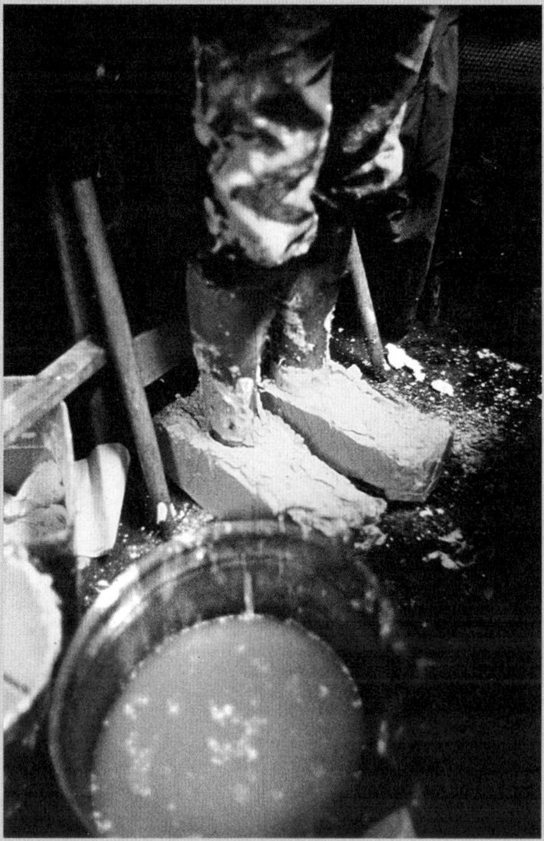

R

H.C.

.... and his energy plan .... Joseph Beuys .... Joseph Beuys is a professor at the Düssel .... Quote is central .... COUNTER SPACE .... The warm cake is placed in the middle of the stage and spills its contents . .. Beuys tries to encircle .... showed Beuys .... a normal walking stick .... extended with .... Beuys also with the yellow ...... Beuys is dressed in ..... that Beuys is a mystic .... Anti-nature ...... body heat is what separates ..... Beuys with his feet ..... Professor Beuys's chair ..... The Berlin wall 5cm ...... bash it down

listed for German listeners.

J.B.

Two iron blocks connected with gauze.

Where is Element three?

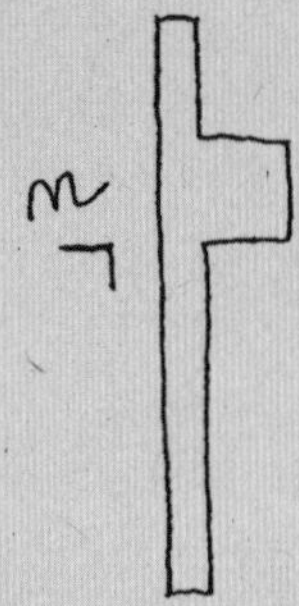

The dividing of the cross
makes it possible to transport
the original Christian message

The halved cross is leant against the wall. The other half is indicated with chalk and n is added.

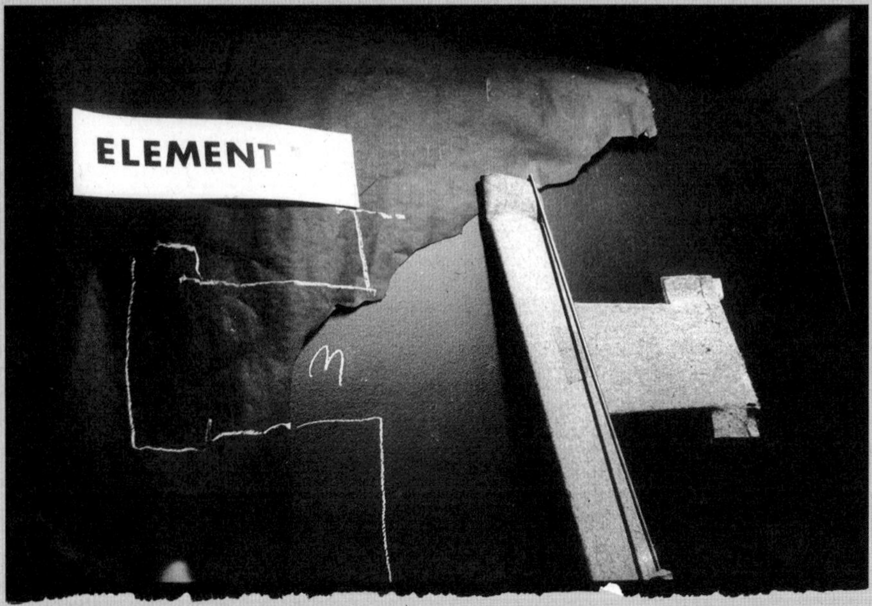

S

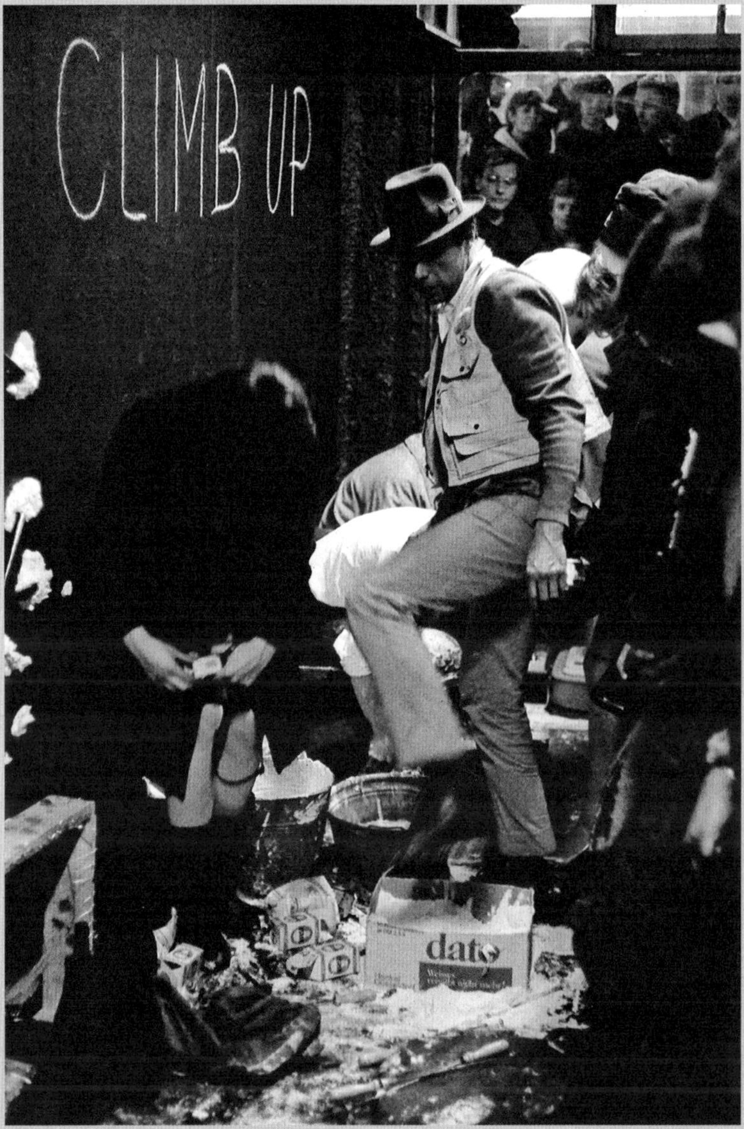

T

H.C.

Climb up is written with chalk on the wall

kann ikke
kann kann ikke
kann kann kann ikke
kann kann kann kann ikke
kann kann kann kann kann
kann kann kann kann kann kann
ikke ikke ikke ikke ikke ikke
ikke ikke ikke ikke ikke
ikke ikke ikke ikke kann
ikke ikke ikke kann
ikke ikke kann
ikke kann

J.B.

Induction device sparking. Hands hissing and drowning in

H.C.

Powerful columns of sounds from the loudspeakers ....
ON THE LINE (perceptive constructions)

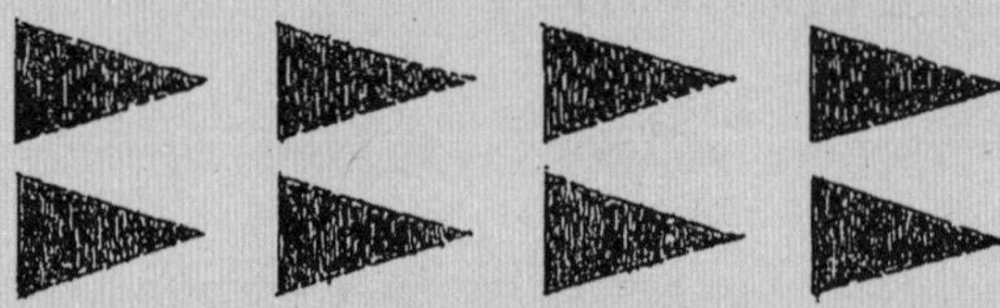

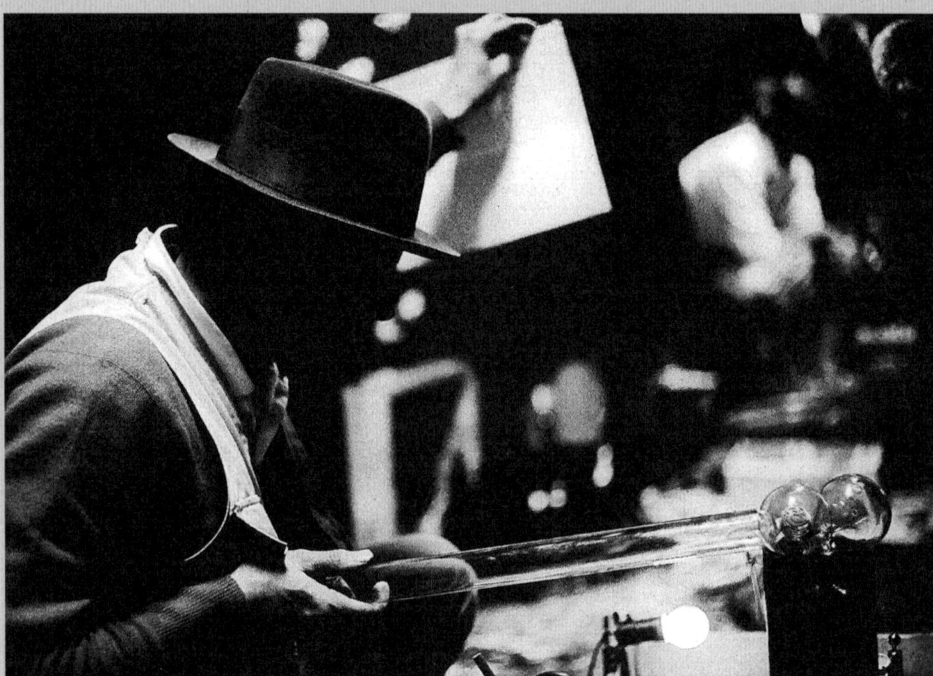

U

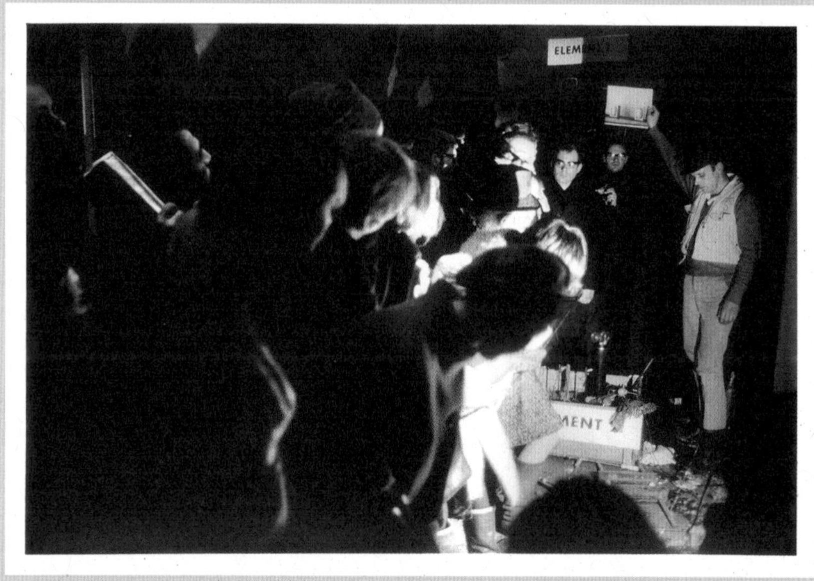

V

W

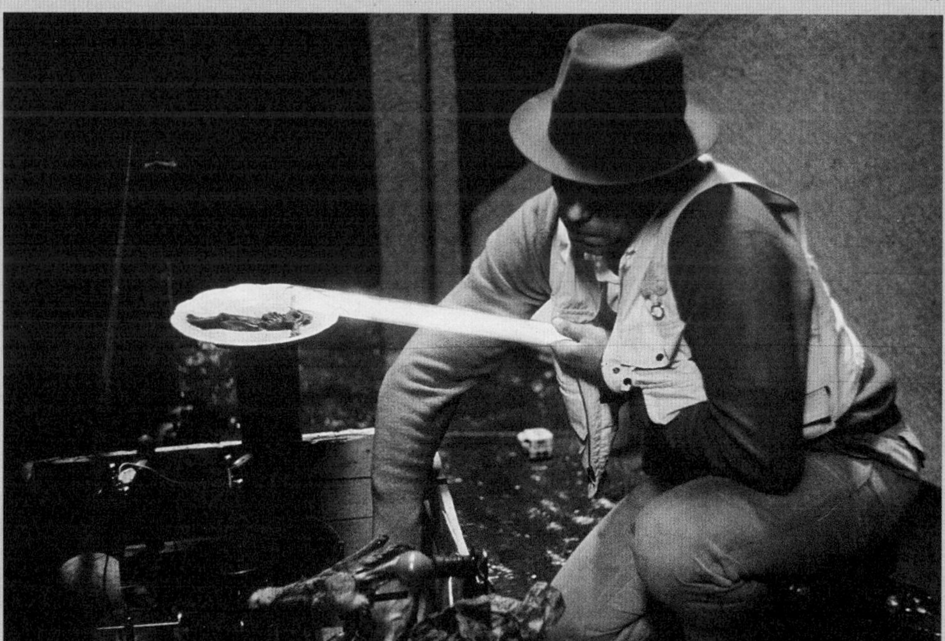

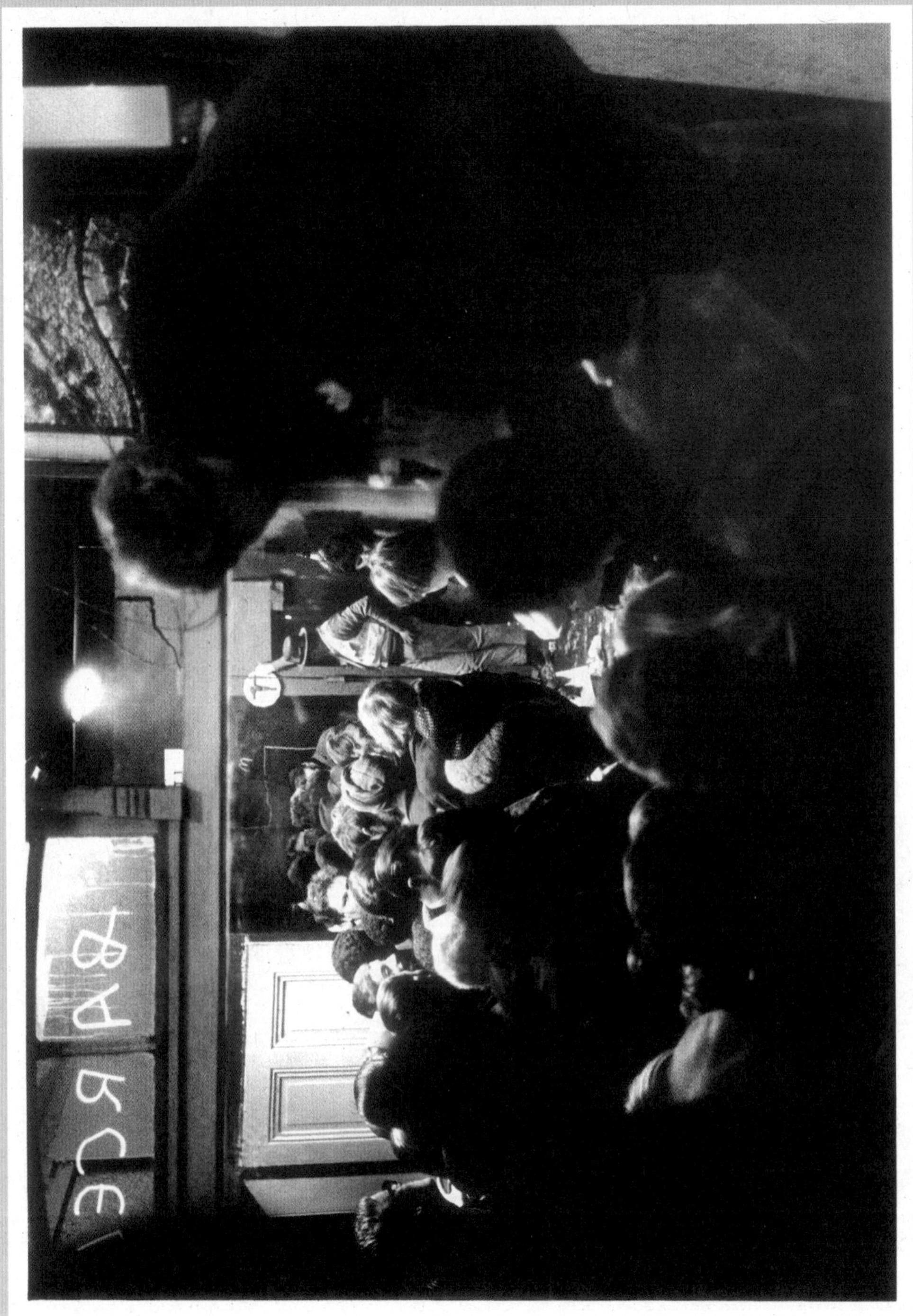

Y

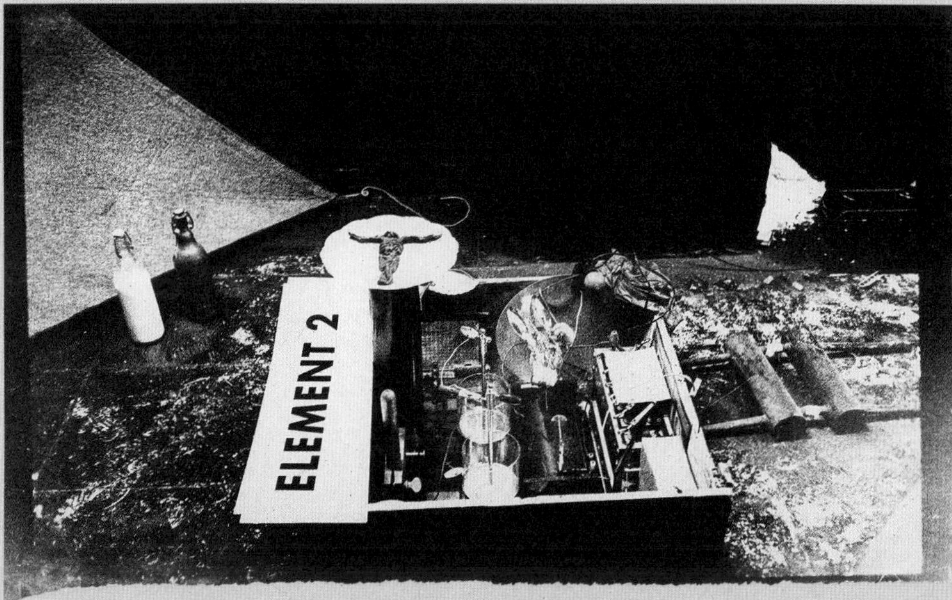

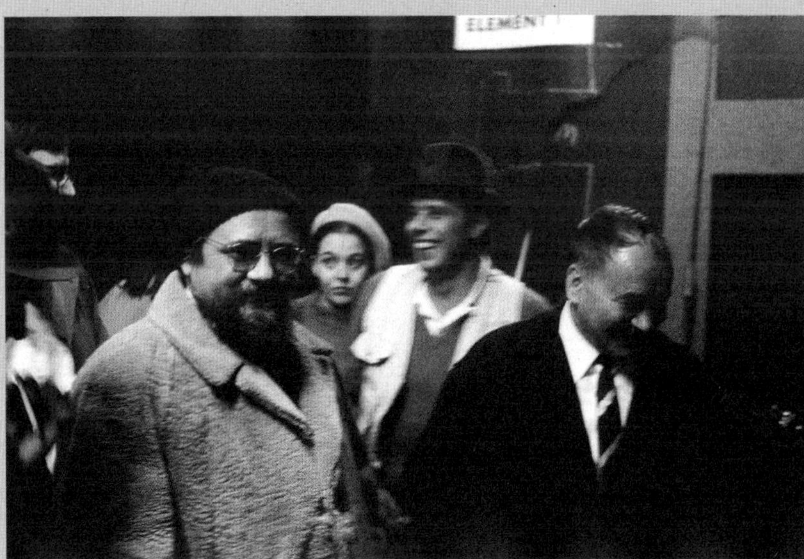

Z

‡ 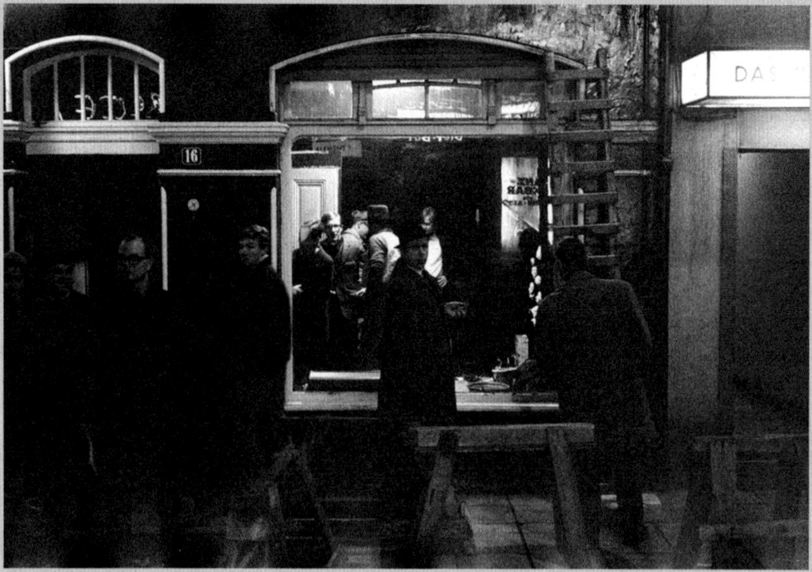

Galerie Schmela after the action. Inside, Henning Christiansen (back turned), Joseph Beuys (back turned) and Bjørn Nørgaard.

Photographies by:
Jörg Boström: A, B, C, E, H, N, T, U
Ute Klophaus: F, G, M, S, Y
Manfred Leve: Z, ‡
Reiner Ruthenbeck: P, R, W
Walter Vogel: D, I, J, K, L, O, Q, V, X

1
Translator's note: *Strahllinie* is the word used in German. It appears to refer to Beuys's concept that he was 'a transmitter' ('ich strahle aus') (e.g. *The Chief*, 1963–64), as well as various art objects to which he gave this title.

2
Translator's note: Henning Christiansen, who played these words via tape during the performance, is saying 'I – can – not' (in Danish). See also Friedhelm Mennekes' description of the action MANRESA in this book, p. 82.

3
Translator's note: literally translates as 'childrensmilitaryambulance'.

4
Translator's note: literally translates as 'drivesaroundburdenedbyitscross'.

A Monika Schmela, Joseph Beuys and Henning Christiansen before the public arrived.

B Joseph Beuys at the start of the action.

C The box of Element 2 with the induction device, the dead hare, the toy bird and the drawing *2×3 Goldhasen* (2×3 Golden Hares).

D Beuys lifts an unidentified object to the centre of the halved cross, now with the other half of the cross drawn with chalk on the wall, and the letter 'n'.

E Joseph Beuys lifts the copper staff with the felt handle.

F Beuys raises the plate with the crucifix to the centre of the cross.

G Joseph Beuys with the solar disk on his back.

H Joseph Beuys electrifies the hare, while in the box we see the drawing *2×3 Goldhasen* (2×3 Golden Hares).

I Joseph Beuys looks thoughtfully at the box of Element 2.

J Joseph Beuys continues to work with Element 2, with the toy ambulance at the foot of the cross.

K Joseph Beuys activates the copper staff placed in front of the felt cross of Element 1, in an ongoing up and down movement. In the middle of the cross there is a piece of wood with the entrails of a hare, in an attempt to transform energy of biological origin.

L Fat marks on the wall at Galerie Schmela, while some of the bicycle pumps have also remained on the wall. Bjørn Nørgaard has manipulated various materials with his feet, and prepares the cast of his feet in plaster.

M Beuys with the Geissler tube.

N Bjørn Nørgaard seated, raises his right foot, encased in a block of dried plaster. Around him we see lightbulbs, flour and the water basin used during the action.

O Joseph Beuys drinks milk from one of the two bottles with him, with the lead one beside him on the floor.

P Beuys handling the lead bottle.

Q In the foreground, the composer Henning Christiansen, in the middle ground, the sculptor Bjørn Nørgaard and, in the background, Joseph Beuys manipulating the box of Element 2. On the wall, the halved felt cross of Element 1 has shifted.

R Bjørn Nørgaard with his feet bound in plaster blocks.

S The halved cross is leant against the wall. The other half is indicated with chalk and n is added.

T Christiansen has written CLIMB UP in chalk on the wall.

U Beuys showing the image of *Doppelaggregat* (Double Aggregate), 1958–1968, to the public.

V Beuys raising a photography of his work *Doppelaggregat* to the centre of the cross.

W Beuys rubs the Geissler tube, setting up a relationship of light between the plate with the crucifix and his heart, while asking the question “Wo ist Element 3?” (Where is Element 3?).

X On the gallery window the written word BARCELONA is partially seen.

Y Box of Element 2 at the end of the action with the crucifix plate and the dead hare, with the felt corner and the fat corner behind.

Z Alfred Schmela, to the left, after the action.

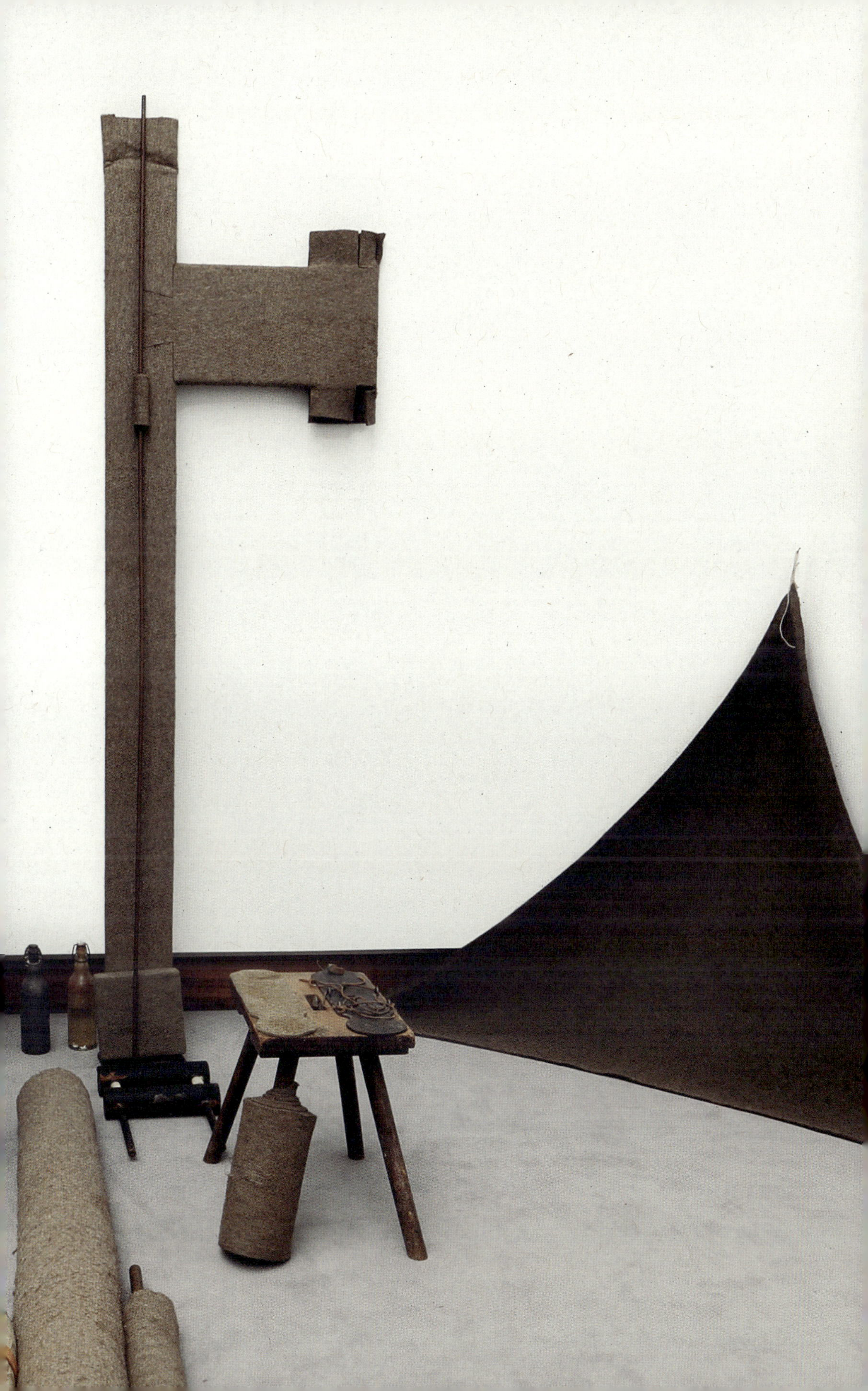

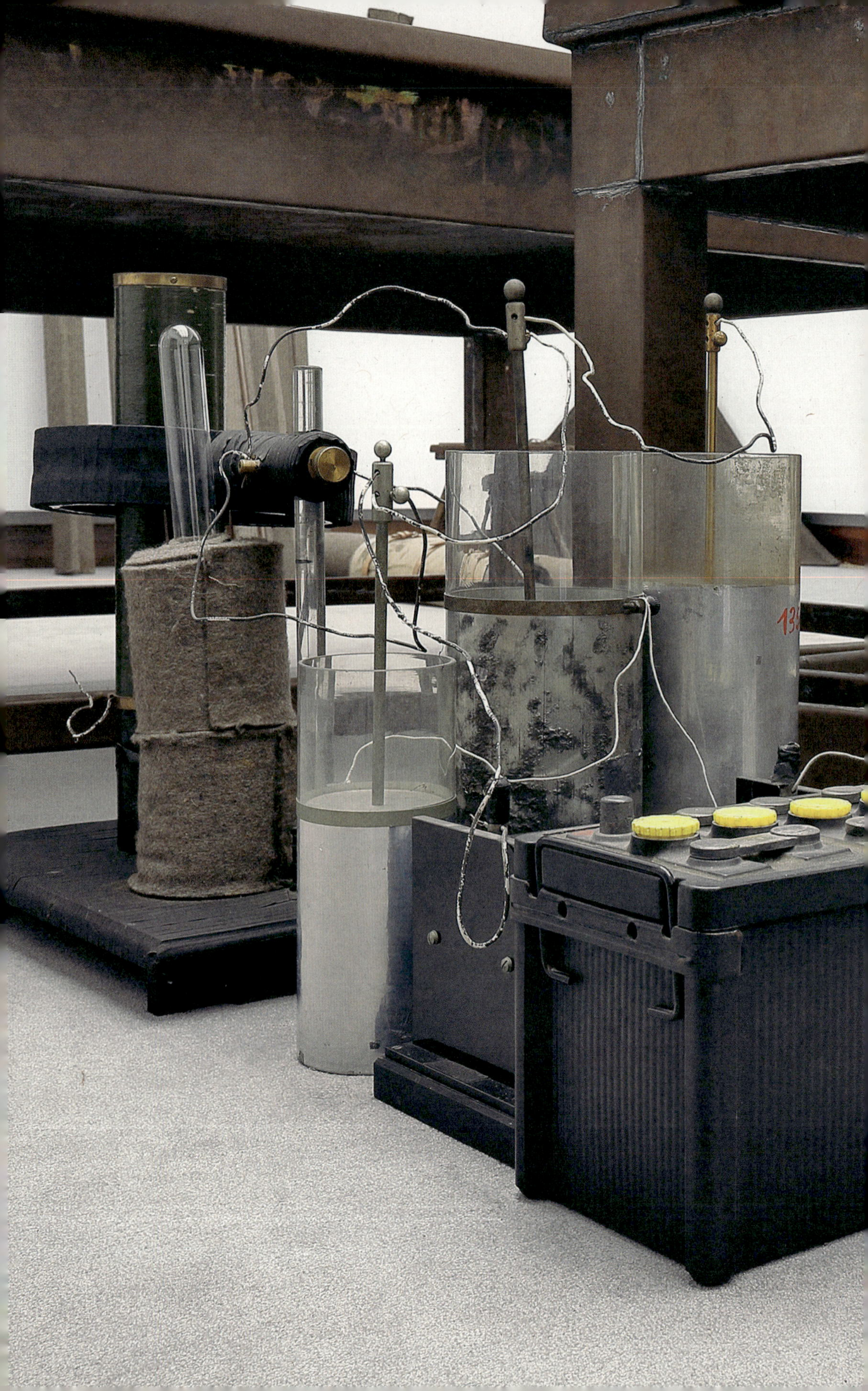

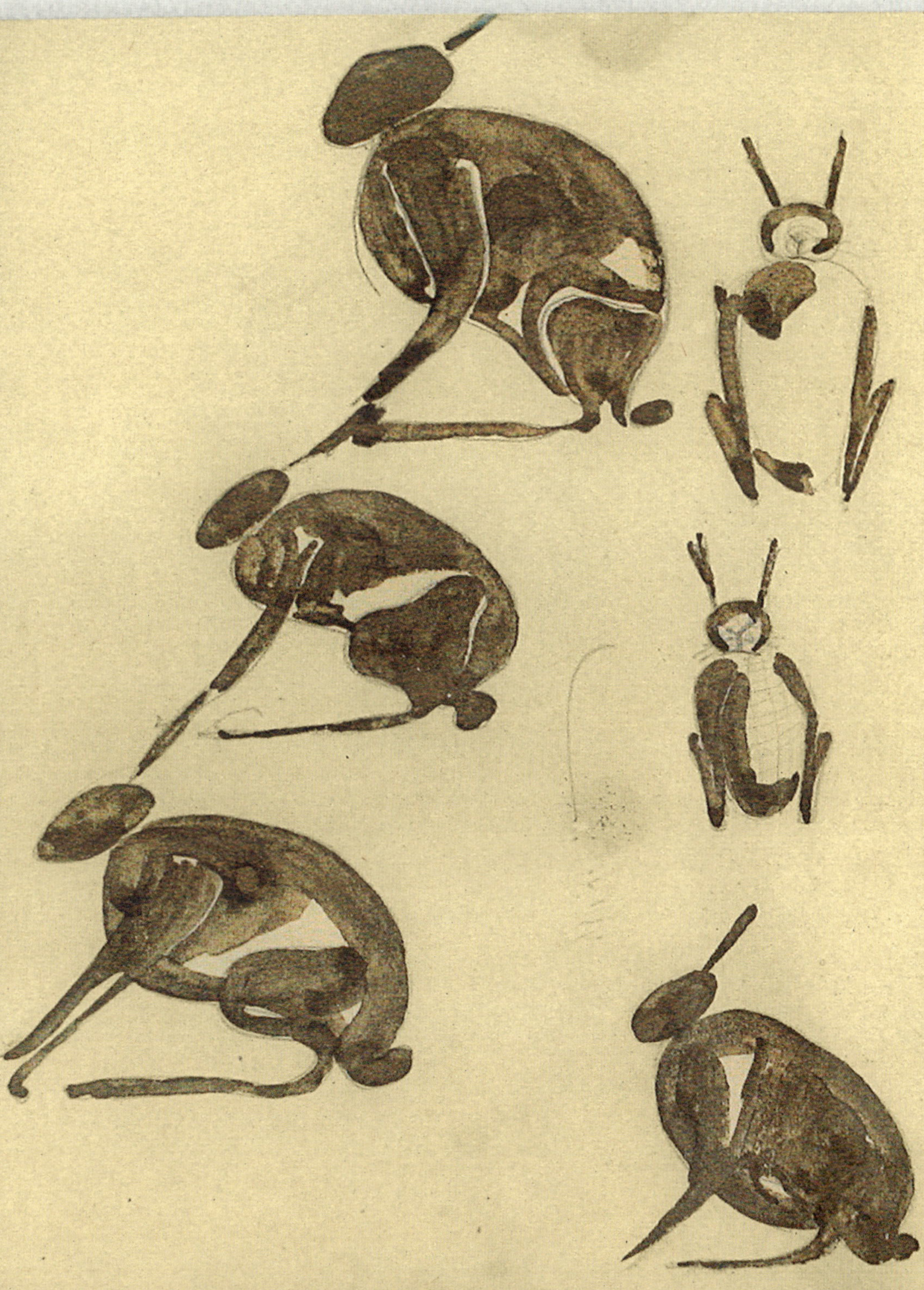

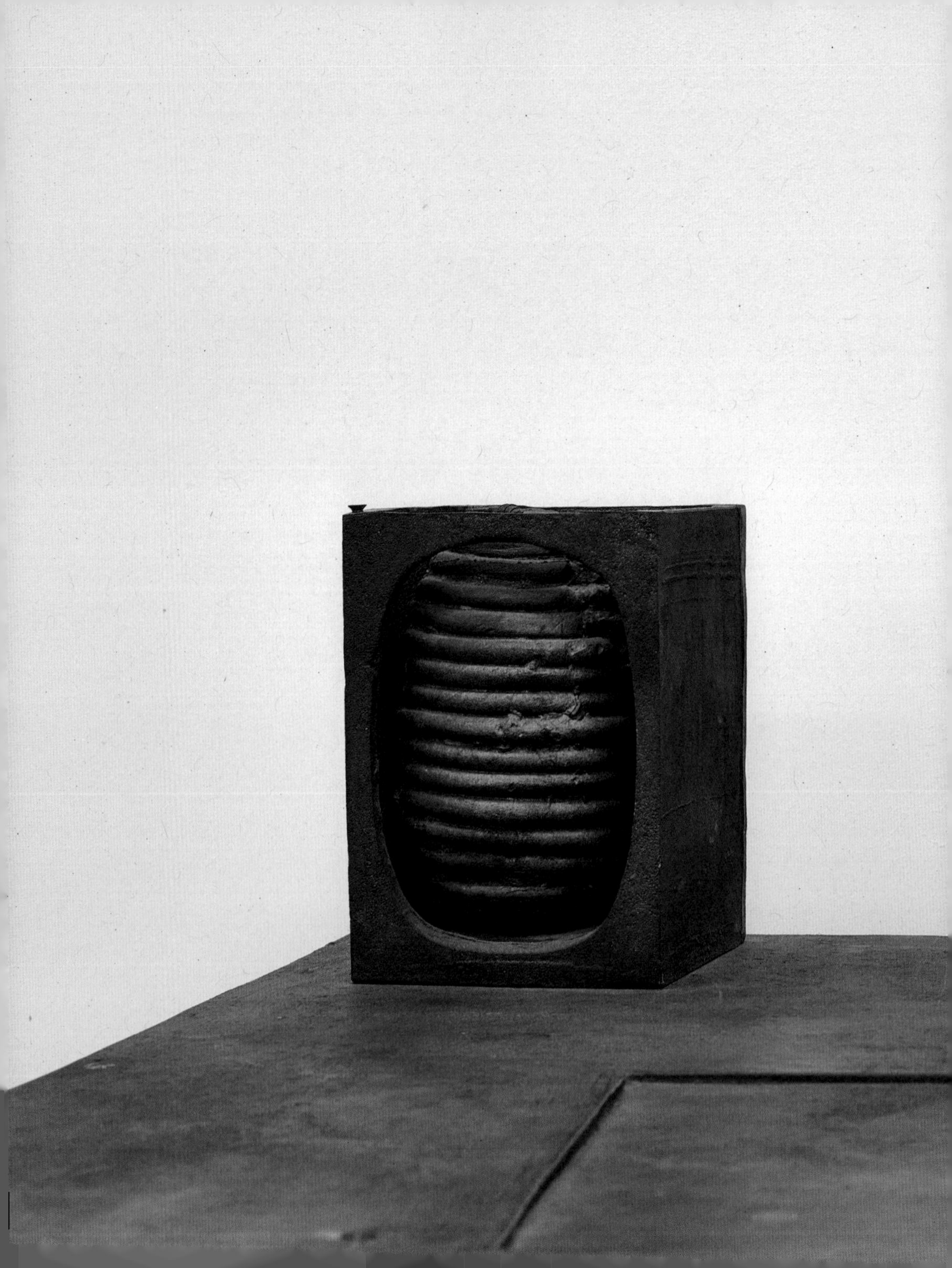

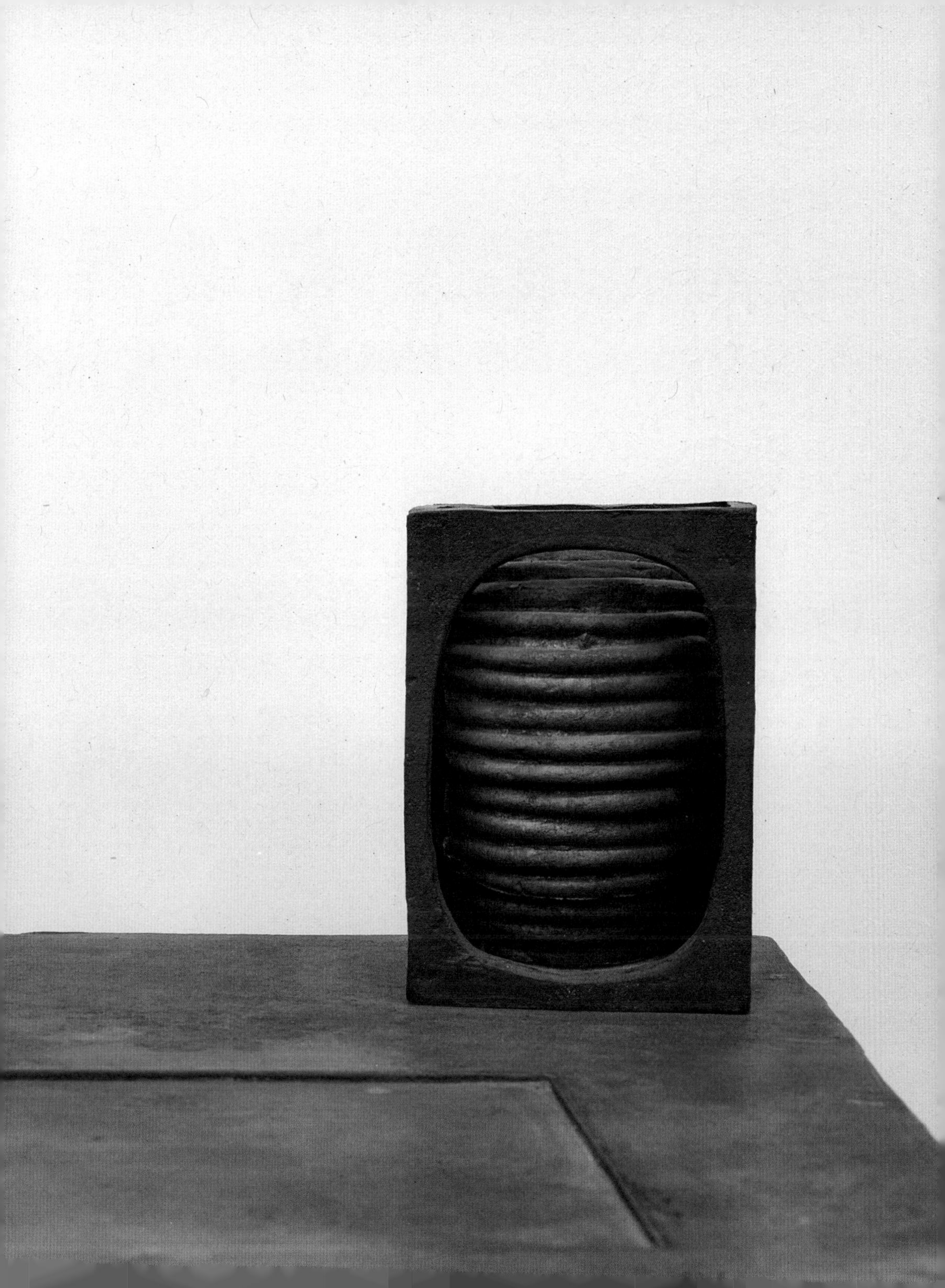

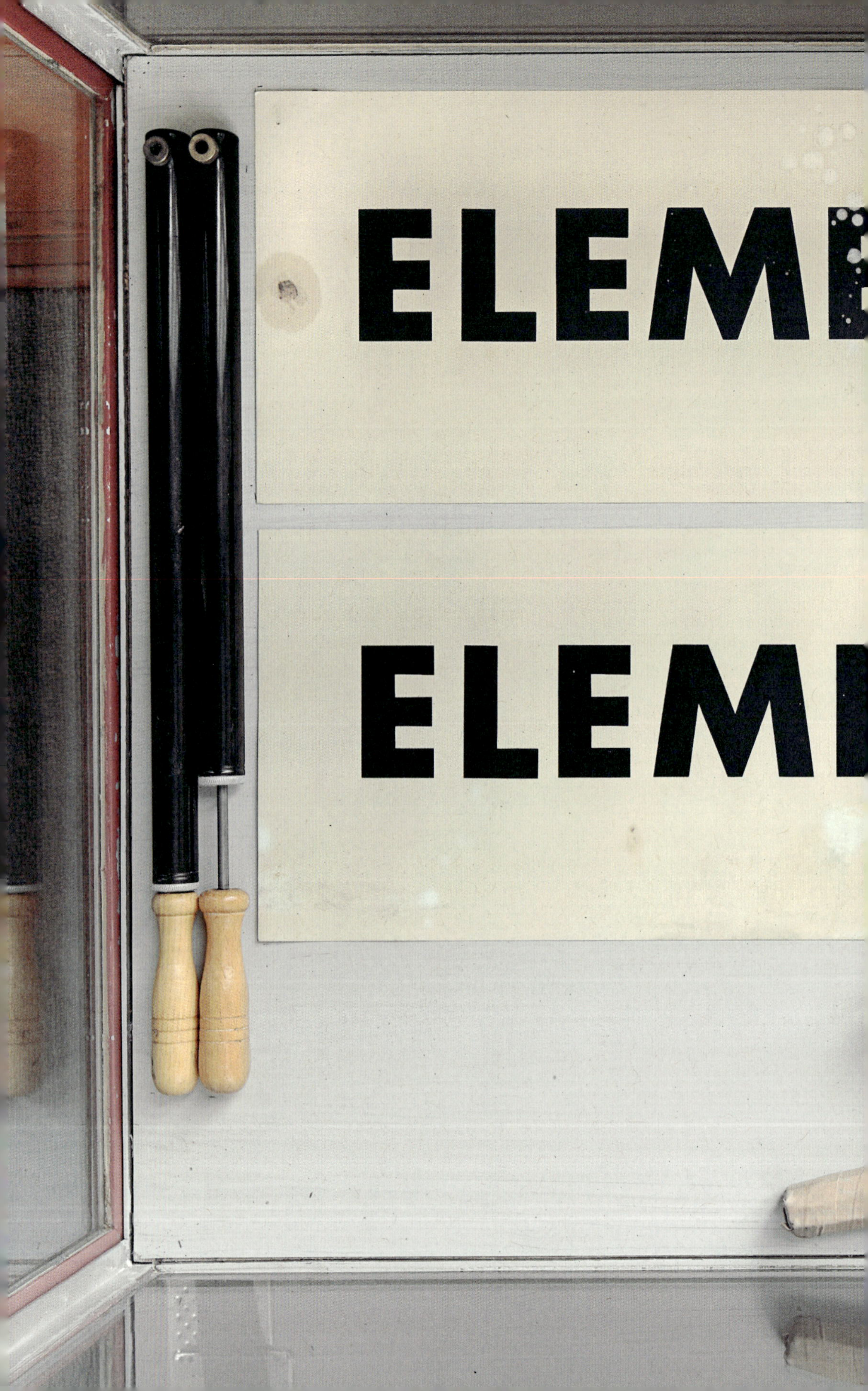

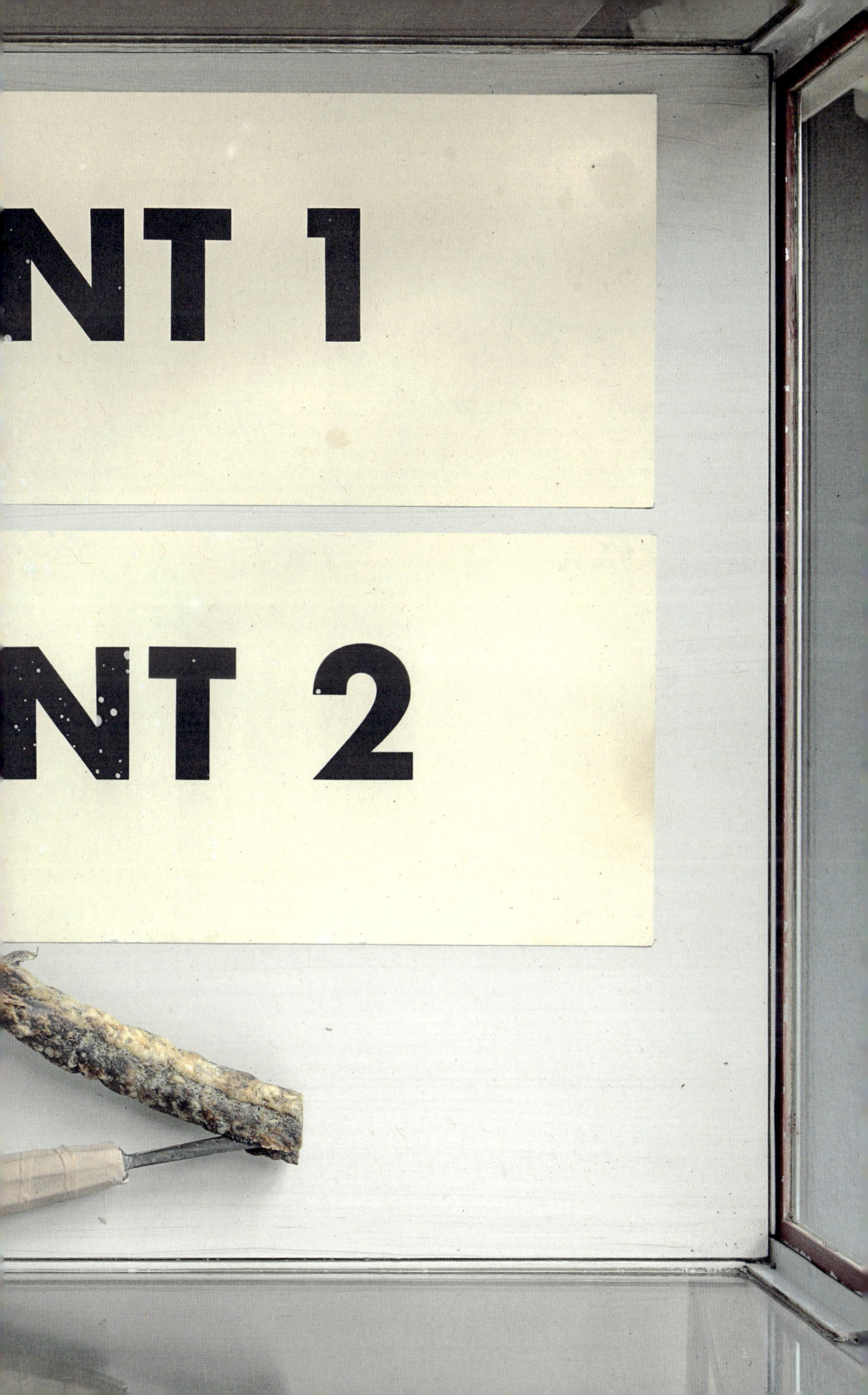
NT 1
NT 2

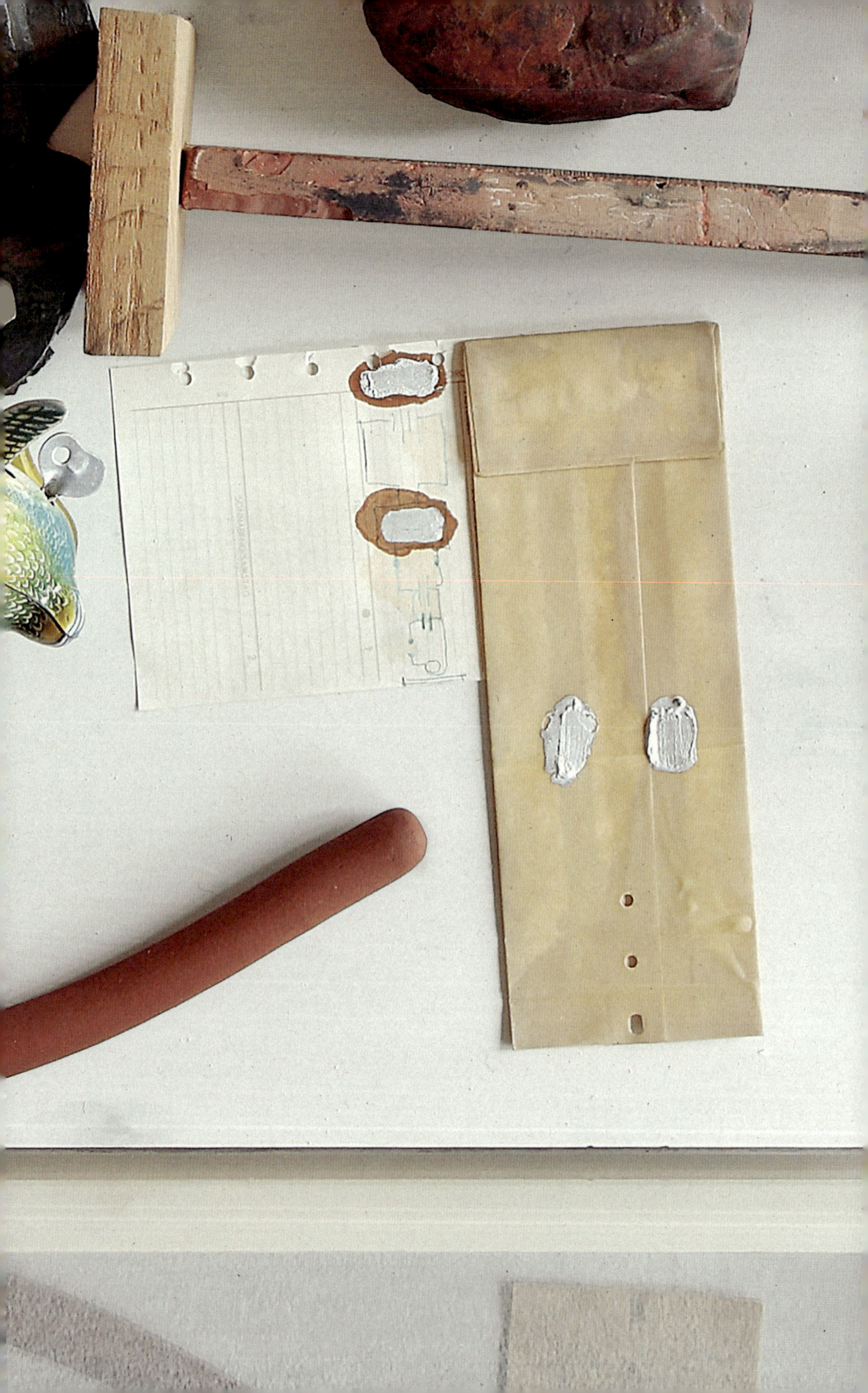

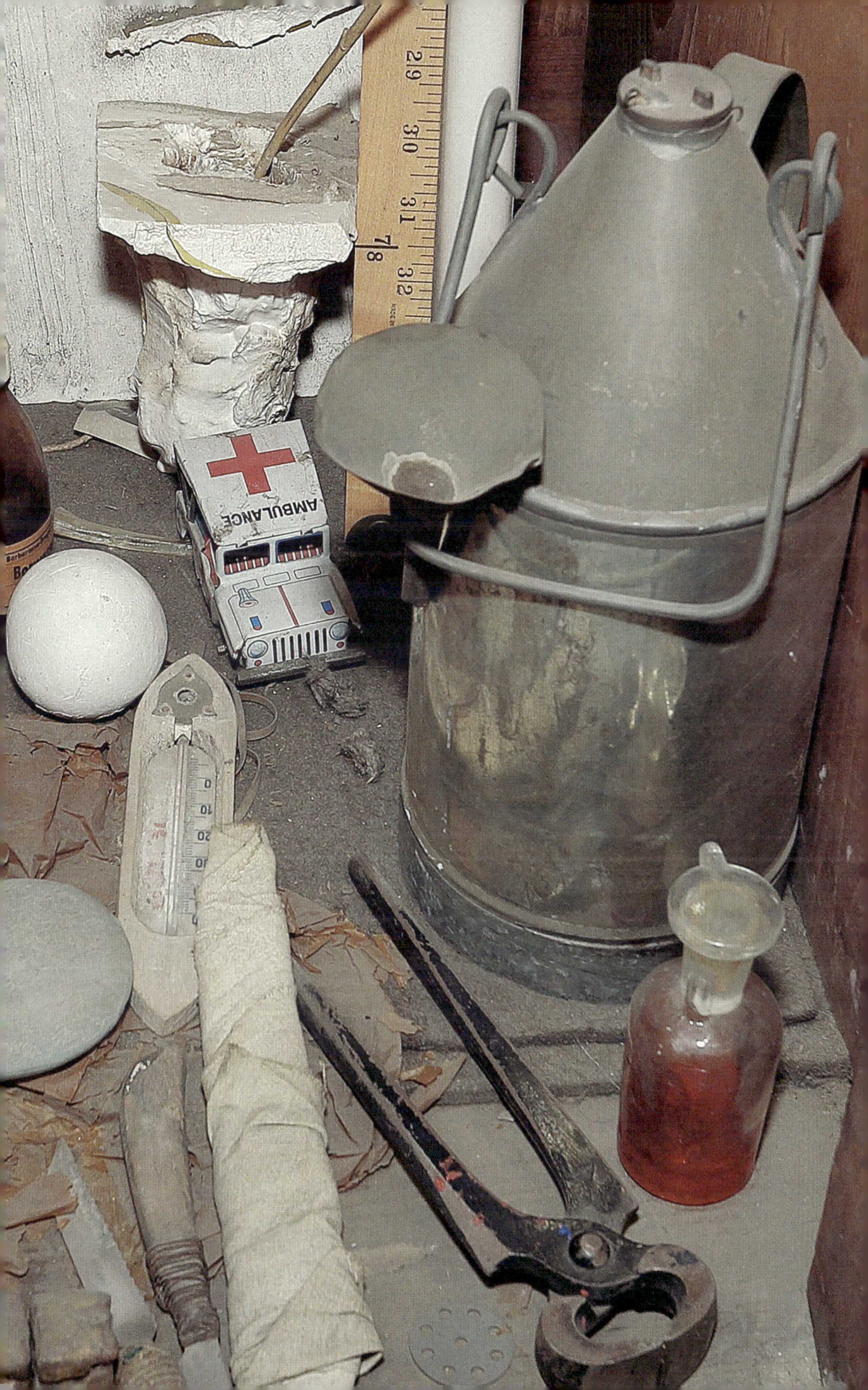
AMBULANCE

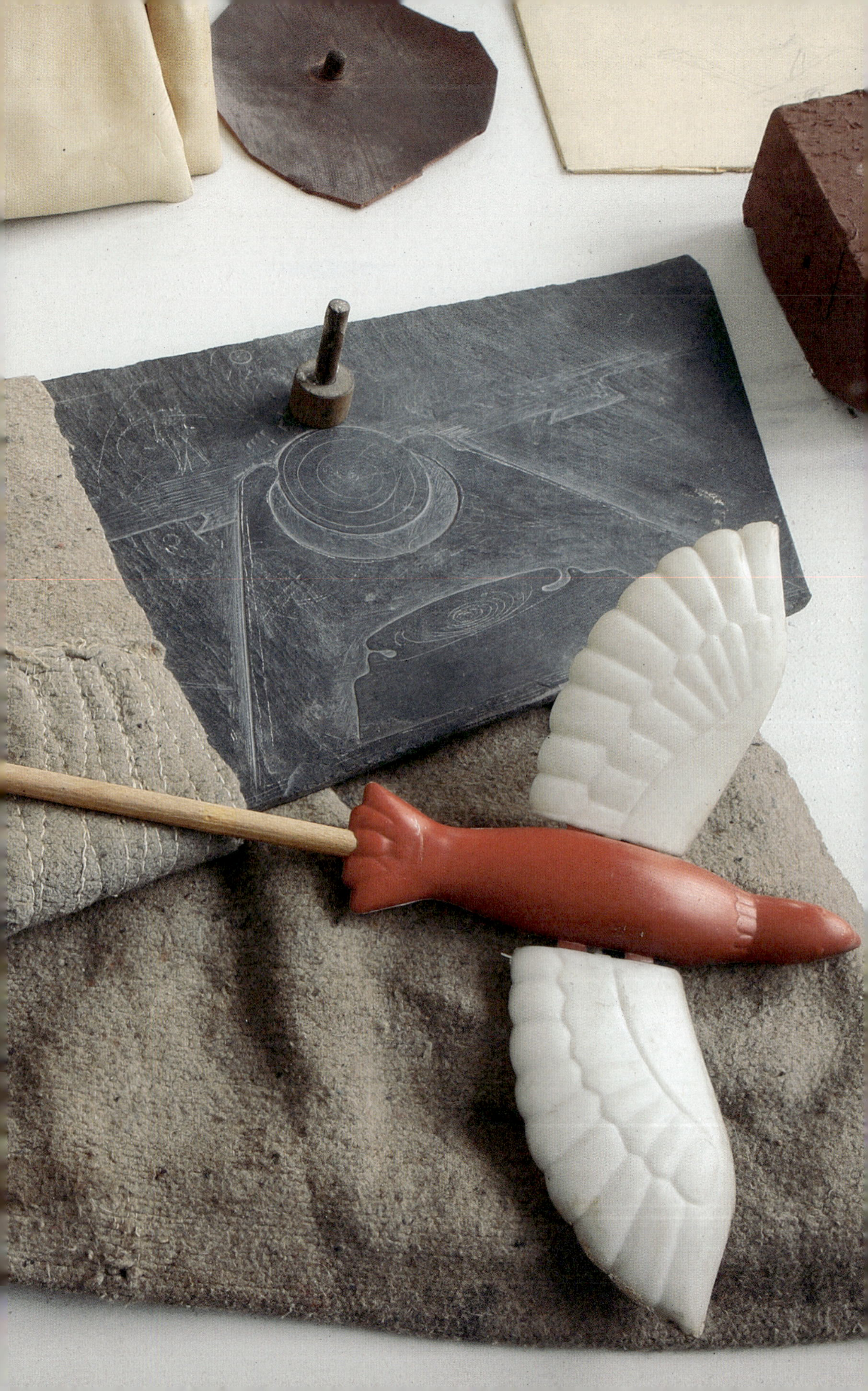

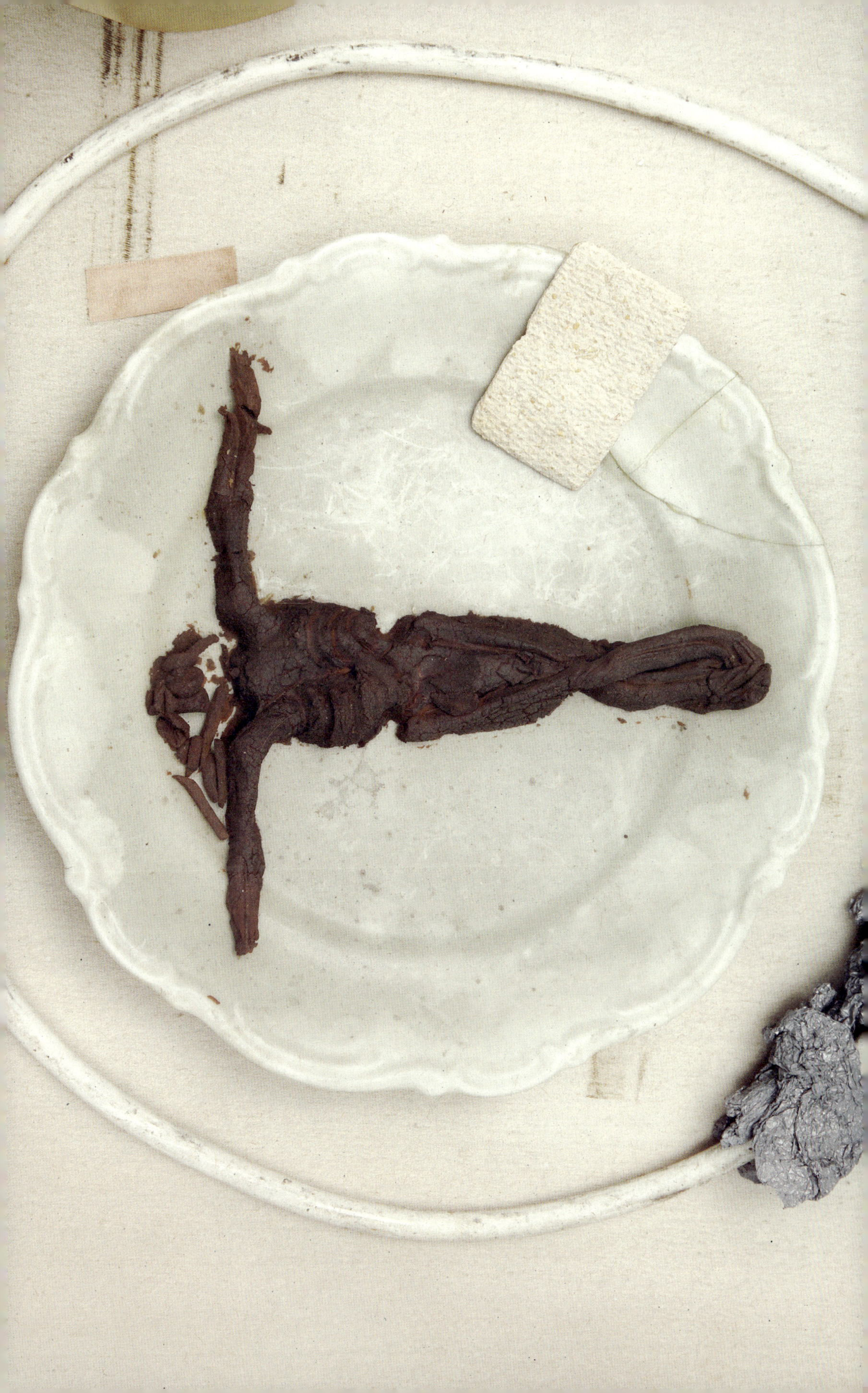

Objects used in the action-demonstration MANRESA, as currently preserved in the Block Beuys at the Hessisches Landesmuseum Darmstadt. Many had been used in previous or later actions.

P. 53 Various components of Element 1: the felt cross with the copper staff leaning on it, two bottles at the base, and the felt corner.
Block Beuys, Gallery 2.

P. 54 Objects that were part of the induction device of Element 2 in the action MANRESA, just as they were reconfigured for the piece *Fond II*, exhibited at the 1968 Kassel documenta.
Block Beuys, Gallery 2.

P. 55 *2×3 Goldhasen* (2×3 Golden Hares), 1949. The hare, a key animal in the work of Beuys, is the biological component of Element 2 in the action MANRESA.
Block Beuys, Gallery 5, display case 9.

P. 56 Detail of the piece *Doppelaggregat* (Double Aggregate), 1958–1968. Beuys showed a photograph of it during the action MANRESA.
Block Beuys, Gallery 5.

P. 58 Paper signs that marked Element 1 and Element 2, shown beside *Comprimed Exhausted*, two of the bicycle pumps used to spray fat during the action MANRESA.
Block Beuys, Gallery 7, display case 1.

P. 60 Electrical plan for the action MANRESA, 1963, belonging to Element 2.
Block Beuys, Gallery 5, display case 3.

P. 61 The toy ambulance appearing in the action MANRESA had been part of the piece *Szenen aus der Hirschjagd* [Scenes from the Deer Hunt], 1961.
Block Beuys, Gallery 5.

P. 62 Toy bird with moving wings, used by Beuys to fly towards the cross while he asked the question 'Wo ist Element 3?' (Where is Element 3?).
Block Beuys, Gallery 5, display case 9.

P. 63 *Kreuz* (Cross), 1957. Plate with crucifix used by Beuys in the action MANRESA. It had been part of *Auschwitz-Demonstration*, 1956–1964.
Block Beuys, Gallery 5, display case 4.

FRIEDHELM MENNEKES, S.J.

BEUYS IN MANRESA

'All questions of humanity can only be questions of design,' said Joseph Beuys in a 1975 conversation with the artists Bernhard Johannes Blume and Heinz Günther Prager. 'That is the totalised definition of art. This draws on everyone's basic capacity to be a creative being [*schöpferisches Wesen*], and [draws] on the questions of the social whole.'[1]

The cross as a form of movement

THIS NOTION that humans are themselves creative beings finds its artistic form in Joseph Beuys's actions. Here, the artist conceives of movement as the central reference point for his art. And he views the internal prime mover (*movens*) of that movement, according to Rudolf Steiner's anthroposophy, as the 'Christ impulse'. This is why Christianity plays such a central role in his overall body of work, but especially in his actions. In a 1984 interview with the author, he made this crystal clear: 'The form in which the personification of Christ manifests itself in our day is the element of movement itself. The person who is moving.'[2]

In Beuys's work, the external figuration of this element of movement is represented chiefly by the cross, which is omnipresent in his work, but constantly shifting between superficial shapes. After appearing in his early drawings in the classical forms handed down by Christian iconography, the cross would be transformed and generalised, ultimately nullifying itself in an expanded definition of art.

His most significant design impulse is 'The Division of the Cross', and from there his evolving construction of 'The New Cross'. This process played out most prominently across the following actions: *Eurasia*, performed in Copenhagen and Berlin in 1966; MANRESA, performed in Düsseldorf in 1966; *Eurasian Staff*, performed in Vienna in 1967 and in Antwerp in 1968; *Vacuum–Mass*, performed in Cologne in 1968; and *Celtic*, performed in Edinburgh in 1970 and in Basel in 1971.

In the actions *Eurasia* and MANRESA, Beuys used bisections of various crosses. In *Eurasia*, a halved equilateral cross was drawn on a blackboard; in MANRESA, an upright cross, halved lengthways and wrapped in felt, leant against the wall. During these actions, Beuys used dashed lines of chalk to emphasise the original wholeness of these partial shapes.

While the first half-cross, in the context of the action, makes reference to the historically evolved and politically conditioned divisions between East and West — the artificial partition of peoples and cultures — the second one alludes to internal ruptures within humanity and modern society. The original unity is broken apart into factions, creeds, nations and all the other estrangements signified by placelessness and timelessness.

Of course, positive mental/spiritual gains also come into play in this process: foremost is the development of ego-consciousness and an attunement to scientific and technical thought. But this 'success' comes at a high price. It entails the loss of unity and, within that, of mental-spiritual forces that once conveyed a sense of the unity of all things: intuition, religion and all types of spiritual empathy for the objects of life. Under these conditions, humans therefore also lost their attunement to the human and Christian dimensions of the cross.

It is no longer a symbol of humanity, but by now almost only appears in the economic dimensions of plus and minus, the scientific dimensions of a coordinate plane, and the strategic/technical dimensions of a machine gun's crosshairs. '[E]ven today,' Beuys once said in an interview with Elisabeth Pfister, 'many people perceive that a different idea of the cross exists within the coordinate system.'[3]

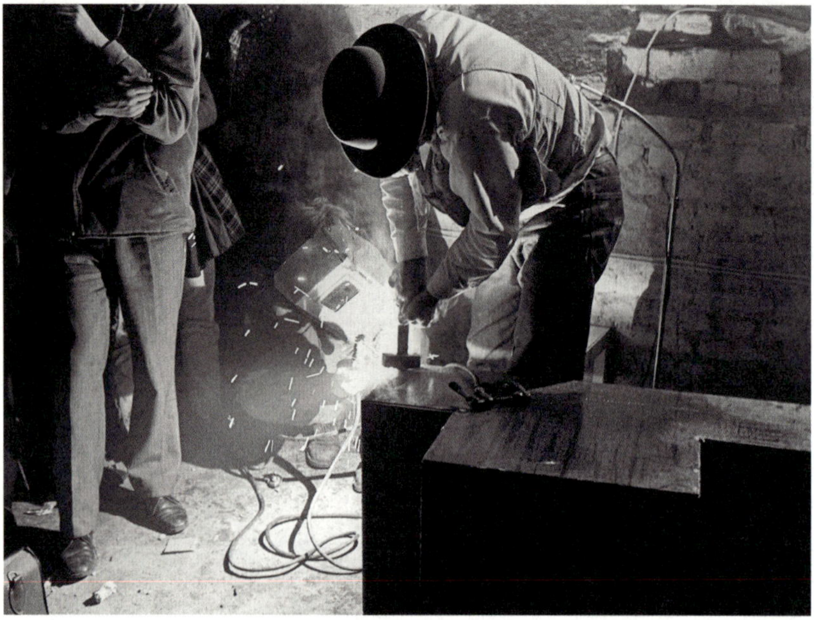

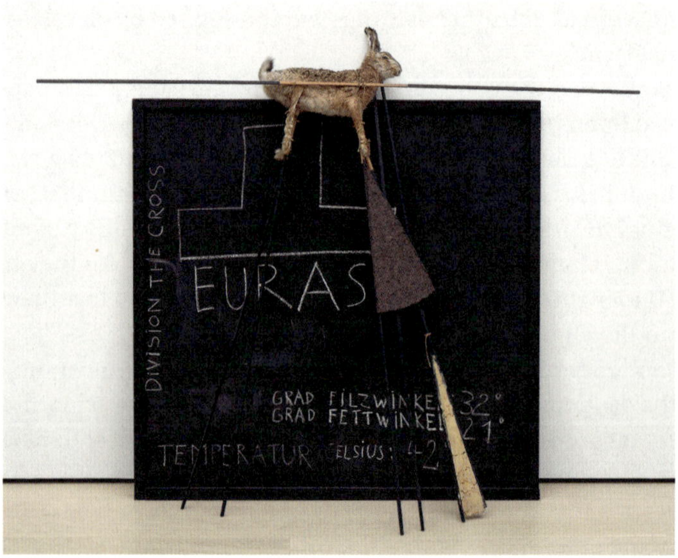

A Beuys handling the cross during the action *Vacuum–Mass*, Galerie Art Intermedia, Cologne, 1968.

B Joseph Beuys, objects used in the action *Eurasia Siberian Symphony 1963*, 1966.

This was the insight that led Beuys to his 'New Cross': a halved cross conveying an impulse to become whole. A spiritually sensitive and living person is able to look at the part and see the whole. In its very title, the action *Eurasia* points to the need for regaining this lost whole: the task of spiritually reuniting Europe and Asia. The Fluxus demonstration MANRESA reveals concrete possibilities for implementing this, both besiegingly and beseechingly. The historical processes of the modern era and the development of the modern consciousness — with its ambivalent, but ultimately lopsided, ramifications — ought to be revised. For Beuys, drawing on the work of Rudolf Steiner, these culminate in the concept of materialism, a word synonymous with a culture that has become mired in its ego-fascination and has lost touch with its roots and its sense of spiritual possibilities. Although the development of 'ego-energies' and logical, deductive reasoning can be very positive, they can grow dangerous in lopsided overabundance:

> If this restricted definition of science [*Wissenschaft*] as a definition of culture becomes binding for the entire culture', he explained to Rainer Rappmann in an interview, 'the culture will collapse because it is the principle of death. Materialism has elaborated the principle of death.[4]

Drawing on Rudolf Steiner, Beuys views this spiritual death-state as a present-day reprise of the 'Mystery of Golgotha'. Hounded by death, humanity strives for the possibilities of redemption, which it can grasp as the 'Christ impulse'. After humanity, like Christ, has 'descended' into the physical circumstances of earth, humanity will 'ascend' in the power of Christ to a new, liberated life.

Rudolf Steiner invokes this train of thought in several places. To quote one example from his writings:

> Because human beings descended deeper into matter [they] made themselves freer and more independent. But they also made their development more flawed than it would otherwise have been. All the things which became flawed in human beings are healed again through the

> Christ impulse. ... Because the Christ impulse is at work in humanity, these characteristics are transformed back in an ascending development. We might say that human beings are being guided back into the spiritual world with these characteristics which they obtained down below.[5]

In view of such perspectives, the halved cross in the MANRESA action appears to be a symbol of humanity today, a symbol in which human beings — deprived of their spiritual development by modern growth — reclaim a spiritual idea of themselves. In the cross, they can become conscious of their situation. In the energy inherent in this symbol, vested in it by Christ, they can recover their selves' lost sensory dimensions. Halving this symbol is a reference to the task of communication, a task that consists of renewing the connections between designed rationality and chaotic intuition, between the conceptually fixed notion of modernity and the flowing substance of the mythic, between the rigidity of Enlightenment and the dynamism of religion. That reconciliation is accomplished in the MANRESA action through the 'Christ impulse', which was reflected in the spiritual experiences of both Ignatius of Loyola and Joseph Beuys.[6]

Manresa as a locus of spiritual experience for Ignatius

Ignatius of Loyola was born in 1491 at his family's castle near Azpeitia, in the Basque country, and originally christened Iñigo López de Loyola. He was the youngest of thirteen children. After his parents nominated him for service at the Spanish court, the Grand Treasurer of Castile, Juán Velásquez de Cuellar, took him in and provided him with an excellent education. Starting in 1517, Iñigo served as an officer under the Duke of Nájera, who had recently been appointed Viceroy of Navarra.

It was a time of political unrest, and military clashes erupted with France. During a siege of the fortress of Pamplona, a cannonball struck Iñigo in the knee, bringing his military career to an abrupt end. A long period of inward and outward struggle set in, during which Iñigo was reborn as Ignatius. The soldier grew into a man of the church; the bellicose warrior blossomed into a figure of great spiritual radiance.

During Ignatius's sunset years, from 1553 to 1555, he dictated his memoirs, *Pilgrim's Journey*, recounting the path and the transformation of his life. After some brief remarks on his childhood and youth, the account delves into detail with the outset of his realignment and seeks to reveal the moments when God's providence and guidance were shown to him. The book embarks on an existential dialogue between God and a seeker who, after many setbacks, leaps of faith and inner crises, finds his way to build a new personality. He would be known to history as a personification of strength, willpower and determination.

'Up to his twenty-sixth year he was a man given to worldly vanities....'[7] Ignatius' third-person report opens, and Polanco, his secretary of many years, phrases these beginnings in his draft of a separate biography of his spiritual father in even more explicit terms: 'He was wanton when playing games, dallying with women, fighting or using weapons.'[8] With this transformation, that cannonball literally shot him into the world. In desperation, the young nobleman attempted to compensate for the resulting wound, which had shortened his leg, by undergoing a series of excruciating operations. These efforts were in vain: there was no way he could continue on his previous life plan.

Outwardly wounded and inwardly battered, the disabled Iñigo spent months bedridden at his family castle. With no other source of entertainment, he eventually immersed himself in reading the *Vita Christi* and the legends of the Saints. These books distracted him, entertained him and stirred up his romantic tendencies. He began having fanciful fever dreams. Suddenly he was seized by the thought of living like those role models from then on. He shifted his former life plan to another level and now saw himself as enlisted in the service of 'higher majesties', a role in which he could continue the fight for fame and honour. But soon enough, uncertainty returned. He vacillated, doubted and fell back into despondency. All manner of thoughts and ideas surfaced, 'and when he grew weary of them he set them aside to think of other matters'.[9] Yet in the midst of this whiplash, he intuited a new level of realities within himself: two alternating but unyielding states of mind: 'consolation' and 'despair'. In their antagonism, they seemed as though directed by different spirits. Somewhat recovered, he finally reached an extraordinary decision: to embark on a pilgrimage to Jerusalem. No

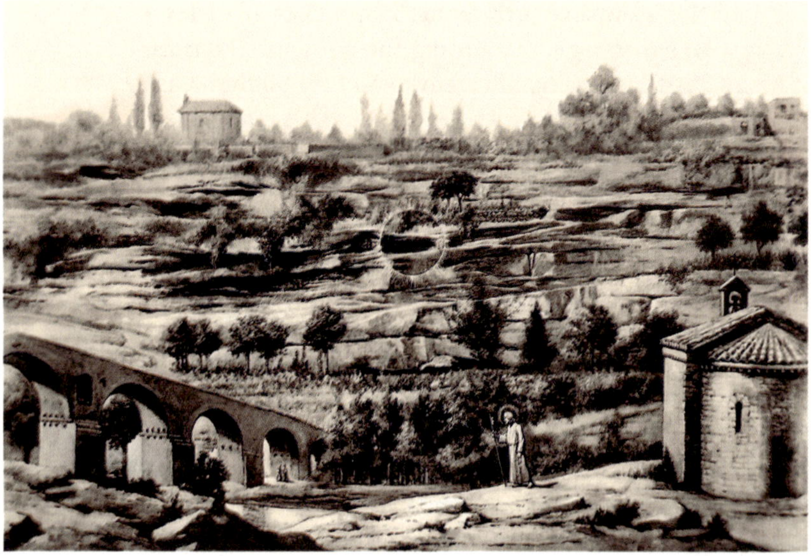

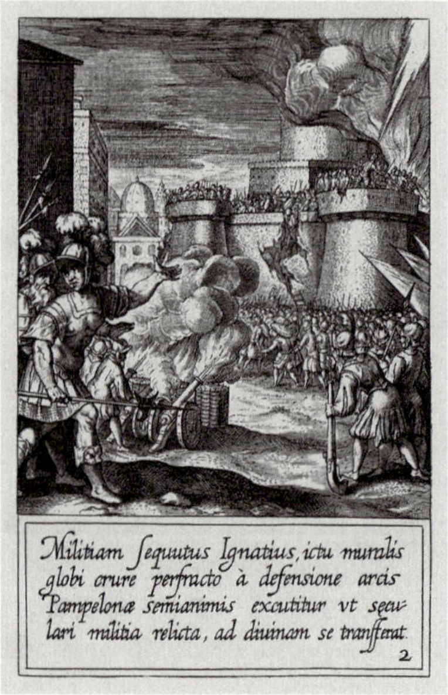

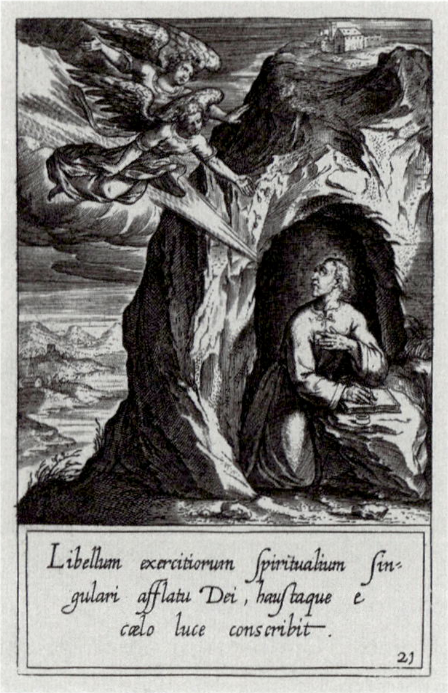

C Reconstruction of the Cardener River landscape in times of Saint Ignatius of Loyola, and the location of the cave where he wrote *Spiritual Exercises*.

D Rubens engravings illustrating the life of Saint Ignatius, 1622.

time to spare. Before long, he was on the road, setting off on an initial pilgrimage to Montserrat. En route from there to Barcelona, he arrived in the town of Manresa, where he decided to rest for a few days and consult a doctor, for his leg was troubling him again. Yet several days turned into many weeks — nearly nine months in all.

His time in Manresa was accompanied by many peculiarities. If we focus on Ignatius' inner development, there are three primary aspects worth highlighting: first, the progression of a severe inner crisis; second, the architecture of its successful resolution; and third, his act of setting off for a new life defined by God's deep pervasiveness. From a bird's eye view, this development follows a visible arc that graduated from a rather quixotic phase, driven by facile enthusiasm, to a steady state of religious sentiment.

In Montserrat, he had already attained a certain inner calm and had bidden farewell to his 'old life'. He had roundly rejected former 'vanities' such as propriety of appearance or a gallant demeanour. He had commenced life as a pilgrim. Soon 'people were saying great things about him'[10] but he was little concerned with this. He occasionally had little uplifted moments of euphoria, when he took 'great consolation'.[11] As he later dictated for his memoirs: 'Up to this time he continued undisturbed in the same interior state of great and constant joy without knowing anything about internal spiritual matters.'[12]

Yet he would soon plunge from this first period of psychological welfare back into the depths. The tensions between these opposing poles are clearly defined, but in bouncing between them, he risked overtaxing himself. A phase of bitter spiritual struggles ensued. Joy alternated with listlessness, confidence with doubt, and confusion with clarity, leaving him in a state of utter bewilderment. His days were filled with depression, sadness and anxiety. But with his inborn tenacity, he went on the offensive. He pushed himself to fast, abstained from sleep and prayed for hours on end. Thanks to his naturally fanatical inclinations, he believed he could regain an inner calm by force of will. But, as if self-surrendering, he was still periodically 'tempted to throw himself into a deep hole in his room'.[13] Each time, he stifled these urges by remembering his grim fear that to commit suicide would entail committing a grave sin.

In the midst of all this, however, he gradually arrived at a consoling and hopeful resolution: to give himself utterly to God. He felt awakened, 'as from a dream'.[14] Gradually, he came to distinguish between 'different spirits'[15] and believed he was discovering their effects on his inward moods. Almost overnight, this discovery freed him from his old anxieties and self-doubts, 'and he held it for certain that our Lord had desired to set him free because of His mercy'.[16] This further unleashed a third stage of his transformation: 'the decisive period of genuine mystical grace'.[17] His account, *Pilgrim's Journey*, describes in detail the exact progression of this experience of liberation. The preceding narrative is interrupted, replaced by a systematic explanation of his inner experience. On a very personal level, Ignatius viewed the old fundamental questions of life and traditional frameworks of faith in an entirely new light. He divided his account of them into five points: the Trinity, the Creation, the Eucharist, the incarnation and spiritual illumination.

His remarks begin with a strikingly laconic sentence: 'He was greatly devoted to the Most Holy Trinity.'[18] That is all. The fact of emphasising this spiritual ascent suffices for him. His first companions and early biographers repeatedly stressed his obsession with the mystery of the Trinity, which he saw as the anchor of his spiritual life. This is corroborated by a letter from Diego Láinez, an ally from the earliest days: 'During the year he was in Manresa the Lord revealed so much to him that he was enlightened and consoled by all the mysteries of the faith and particularly the mystery of the Trinity in which his spirit so delighted that ... he began writing a book about the Holy Trinity.'[19] However, he did not simply see the Christian mystery of the Holy Trinity through the lens of some new dogma. Rather, he perceived it as a kind of 'space' of faith, as a horizon in reference to which it was possible to understand the imitation of Christ in a way that was both personal and transcendent. In the complexity of the divine unity of Father, Son and Holy Spirit, he found an interconnectedness between worldliness and the mysticism of faith.

The second motif of this new spiritual experience is that of the Creation. Ignatius states that, in his eyes, 'Another exceptional mystical grace was to behold how everything in creation proceeded from the

Triune God'.[20] Again there are no further clarifications, although he invokes an image: 'rays stemming from a white object'.[21] Clearly, this vision of faith can be interpreted in light of a cosmological perspective. Ignatius understood everything as having come from God and connected everything back to him. Later, he invokes this connection more clearly, in the 'Foundation' of his book of *Spiritual Exercises*: 'Man is created to praise, reverence, and serve God our Lord, and by this means to save his soul. And the other things on the face of the earth are created for man and that they may help him in prosecuting the end for which he is created.'[22]

His faith's focus on Creation, which becomes clear in this text, is demonstrated even more plainly at the end of *Spiritual Exercises*, in the 'Contemplation to Gain Love', when he calls upon the person performing the exercises 'to look how God dwells in creatures, in the elements, giving them being, in the plants vegetating, in the animals feeling in them, in men giving them to understand'.[23]

Next, the supplicant performing the exercises is asked 'to consider how God works and labours for me in all things created on the face of the earth — that is, behaves like one who labours — as in the heavens, elements, plants, fruits, cattle, etc., giving them being, preserving them, giving them vegetation and sensation, etc.'.[24] Finally, the supplicant is asked to ponder how everything 'descend[s] from above'; in other words, issues forth from God'.[25] Logically, this prompts a reciprocal response from human beings: that they and their lives are in reference to this God and will thus, in grateful devotion, ascend back to him. This spiritual cosmology is a plea for an orientation towards the world and an empathy — arising from a mystical viewpoint — that encourages a person to participate in all things.

The third point of his summarised recollections is intricately linked to the proceeding points. In Creation, all things are united with God. This view is distilled in the Blessed Sacrament. Ignatius 'understood how our Lord is present in that Sacrament'.[26] This cosmic sacredness of all things — i.e., the ability to view the Creator within his creation, to view the Holy Spirit in the material world, this capacity to *see through* the ordinary into the transcendent — is most profoundly revealed in the Sacrament of the divine Incarnation in the mortal world.

The Eucharist is the palpable essence of Christ arisen; it is a kind of primordial exercise of faith, the 'greatest mark'[27] of divine love. And when Christ says, 'Take, eat; this is my body' (Matthew 26:26), Ignatius undergoes the believer's identification with Christ. This is, at once, a setting off away from spiritual union and on to mission and deed.

The fourth point stresses Christ's humanity. Ignatius recounts looking upon the figure of Jesus, his corporeal, earthly figure. He attributes the unwavering certainty of his faith to this moment of contact with the earthly living form of Jesus; this is what he resolved to die for.[28] In his exercises, which he began writing in those months in Manresa,[29] he never tires of urging the supplicants, over and over, to behold the earthly Jesus with all the powers of their senses. The exercises 'The Incarnation' and 'Of the Birth of Christ Our Lord'[30] clearly reinforce this. This is a question of mobilising all one's 'spiritual senses': sight, hearing, smell, taste and touch. The focus here is on a holistic notion of knowledge.

After completing these narrative sections, Ignatius dictated to his secretary the nature and content of his actual epiphany. It was a permeating experience of the Divine Spirit, which he received outside Manresa in the valley of the small River Cardoner. This description probably constitutes the most important passage of his autobiography:

> He was once on his way, out of devotion, to a church... The road followed the path of the river, and he was taken up with his devotions; he sat down for a while facing the river flowing far below him. As he sat there the eyes of his understanding were opened, and though he saw no vision, he understood and perceived many things, numerous spiritual things as well as matters touching on faith and learning, and this was with an elucidation so bright that all these things seemed new to him. He cannot expound in detail what he then understood, for there were many things, but he can state that he received such a lucidity in understanding that during the course of his entire life — now having passed his sixty-second year — if he were to gather all the helps he received from God and everything he knew, and

> add them together, he does not think they would add up to all that he received on that one occasion.[31]

This section lays out a matter-of-fact account, virtually a transcript, of Ignatius of Loyola's existential metamorphosis. From that point on, the man's life proceeded with an ever-strengthening robustness. It was not as though everything became clear to him in a single flash, but it was in this rearrangement of his preceding experiences and views of life — in this clarification; in this 'synthetic view'[32] as Pedro de Leturia once put it — that he accomplished a renewal of his spiritual life. By mustering all his spiritual strength, he was able to soar to the heights of a new lease of life. Along the way, he did not receive any instruction from the medieval order-based mind-set that still governed him; he found his path primarily through intensive introspection. In the meantime, he held an inner conviction that God himself wanted to initiate a new movement through him, provided that he fully abandon himself to his spirit and his will. Thus he discovered inside himself the source of a new, utterly authentic life. For him, Manresa became the setting-off point towards a new theology and led him to rearrange everything he previously knew. In the interim, he began seeking like-minded people and companions, who would form the later Society of Jesus (1540). Their mission would be to *diversa loca peragrare* — to constantly roam from place to place.[33]

MANRESA as an artistic approach for resolving existential crises

Beuys's fascination for Ignatius' life story may very well lie in the parallels between the two men's lives. Beuys, too, repeatedly underwent crises, and at least once confronted the complete reorganisation of his entire existence. In the mid-1950s, Beuys had a profound emotional breakdown, upon which he would frequently reflect in later life. This period lasted nearly two years. It began in the autumn of 1955, around a year after he completed his studies, when he experienced a 'deterioration of [his] physical strength'.[34] This experience gave him strong doubts as to his own work, and he found himself becoming a 'depressed man in an exhausted state'.[35] Yet that, in turn, resulted in renewal. He later reflected:

> Illnesses are almost always spiritual crises in life, in which old experiences and phases of thought are cast off in order to permit positive changes.... Such a crisis ... is a decisive challenge; much has to be settled and one must take new directions toward new experiences.[36]

Both Ignatius and Beuys would, during their lifetimes, turn to inwardly unpacking their earlier crises. Overcoming these crises became an inherent principle of their subsequent work. They often reflected on these periods and tried to understand them in various ways. Ignatius went about this by composing his *Spiritual Exercises*; Beuys did so by directly elevating his personal experiences to underpin his actions. For neither of them was this a matter of personal self-insight. Rather, they perceived these experiences as exemplary opportunities for methodically helping others to find themselves and overcome their own personal or social cataclysms. In this regard especially, art and religion prove to be paradigmatic for the subjective experience of life and serve as useful concepts for transcending spiritual crises.

Beuys looked to Ignatius as a great role model and source of inspiration. He considered the saint 'very important... one of the most important figures'[37] in terms of changing his life and achieving a new consciousness. Beuys deepened his general understanding of thought, spiritual development and how to navigate it when he studied Ignatius' *Exercises* in 1966. In Beuys's surviving papers, this study is attested by three manuscript pages and a well-used copy of a book regarding the life and work of this figure in the early modern period. The book is a monograph of self-testimonies and pictorial documentation compiled by Alain Guillermou, first published in 1960 in Paris and then shortly thereafter in German translation. The copy contains twenty pages of marginalia by Joseph Beuys. In conjunction with the separate notes he made while reading, the marginalia demonstrate his particular interest in the *Exercises* and document a thorough contemplation that was not without its measure of scepticism, but still adhered to their overall tone.

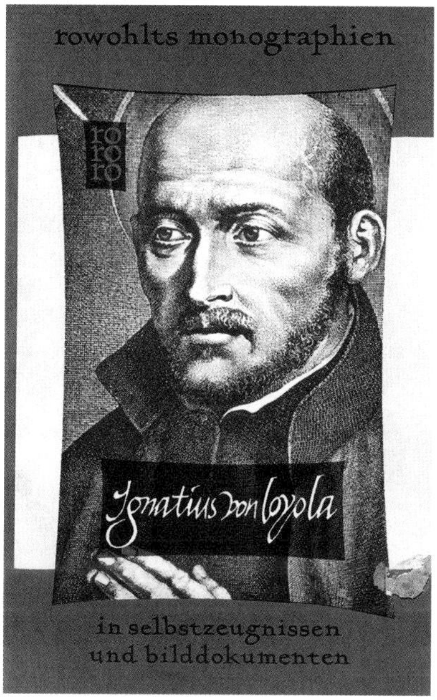

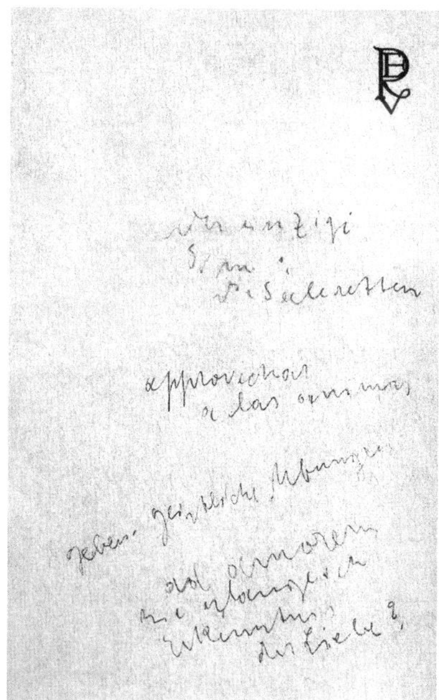

E German translation of the monograph on Saint Ignatius of Loyola, written by Alain Guillermou, published in Paris in 1960, and in 1962 in Hamburg by Rowohlt. This copy belonged to Joseph Beuys and has the artist's personal annotations.

F Annotations by Joseph Beuys in the monograph on Saint Ignatius.

We only have to save the soul

approvechar a las animas
[take advantage of the souls]

Give. Spiritual exercises

ad amorem
How do I get to the understanding of love?

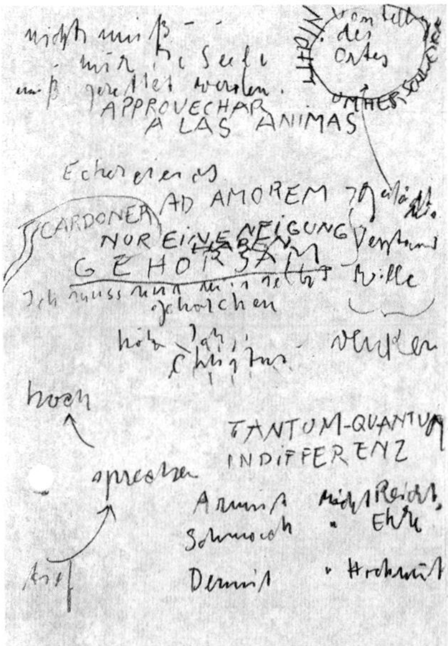

Nothing has to be –
- only the soul
has to be saved.
APPROVECHAR
A LAS ANIMAS
[TAKE ADVANTAGE
OF THE SOULS]

Imagination
of the place
DO NOT WANDER

Echercicios
[Exercises]
AD AMOREM

memory

CARDONER
ONLY HAVE ONE
INCLINATION

reason

OBEDIENCE
Only have to obey
myself

will

higher   I
Christ

think

high

TANTUM-QUANTUM
INDIFFERENCE

speak

low

poverty	not wealth
shame	“ honour
humility	“ arrogance

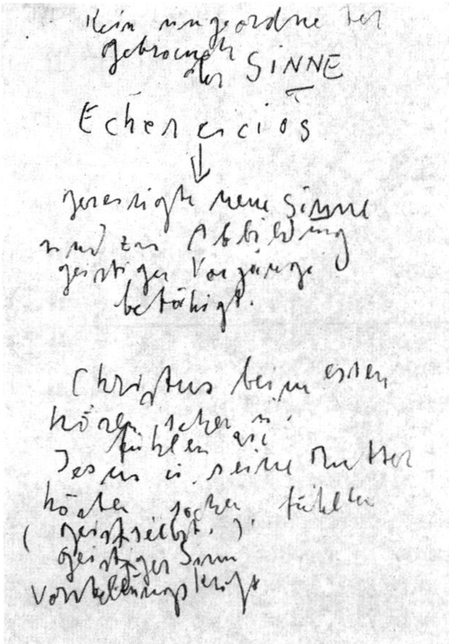

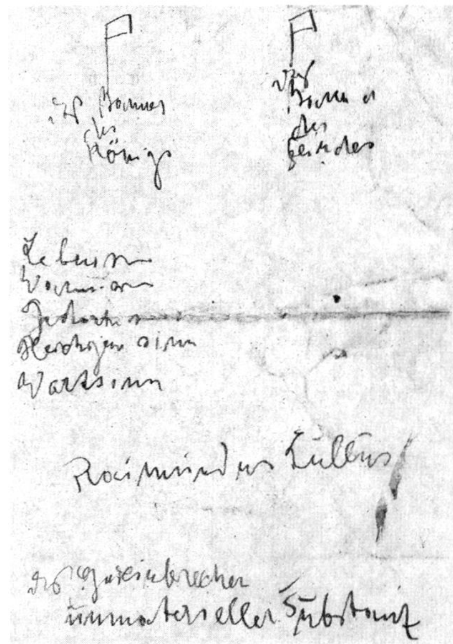

No disordered
use
of the SENSES
Exercises

New purified senses
are able to
do a representation
of spiritual processes.

Hear, see and feel
Christ while eating as
Jesus and his mother
heard, saw and felt
(the spirit as such)
spiritual meaning
strength of imagination

The standard of the king	The standard of the enemy

meaning of life
meaning of perception
meaning of ideas
meaning of balance
meaning of the word

Ramon Llull

The irruption
of immaterial substance

These studies and his reckoning with his own inner development during his years of crisis found their artistic form in the Fluxus demonstration MANRESA, which was performed on 15 December 1966 at the Schmela gallery in Düsseldorf. Unlike later actions, this event was neither filmed nor documented by tape recordings. Neither did any newspaper report on the performance. Thus, the details of what occurred can only be painstakingly reconstructed from artefacts and extant photographs.

Beuys carried out the 'Fluxus demonstration' — as he called his early actions — together with two artists from Copenhagen: the composer Henning Christansen and the sculptor Bjørn Nørgaard. The numerous audience members watched the action attentively, both from inside the gallery and crowded up to an outer window.

In the gallery space, which was painted black, the felt half-cross, Element 1, was leant against the wall. Its other half was drawn on the wall in chalk. In front of it, there was a similarly sized copper staff with a thick felt handle in the middle. 'One [is] sculpture' (*Plastik*) — declared Beuys's pre-recorded text, which Henning Christiansen replayed many times during the action. Later, in a publication about this action, the composer uses the German not-quite synonym *Skulptur*[38] rather than Beuys's *Plastik*, suggesting that this assemblage was no less than a design made of an invisible substance. In all he did, Beuys sought to touch what he termed the *gesamtsubstantiell* — that which is 'totally substantial' — a layered structure ranging all the way from hard realities to a 'supersensory layer'. In this process, as Beuys would later elaborate in more general terms, human beings 'retrieve something from a supersensory realm that changes the circumstances of the earth'.[39]

The halved cross with the copper staff was positioned opposite an Element 2, a lidless wooden box filled with a large assortment of sundry items. The overall impression was of miscellany, but with interesting, vibrant, intriguing details. The items were varied: electrical devices, a plate bearing a crucifix, toys, and other motley objects that would not draw much attention.

'Two [is] potential arithmetic ¶ or one and two integrated', proclaimed Beuys's tape recording. Henning Christiansen later revised this puzzling sentence: 'two potential (potency) arithmetic or both'.[40]

These remarks contain two clues. First, Element 2 ought not to be viewed as fundamentally different from Element 1; second, it has potent characteristics in a philosophical sense. The same substance and the same force hold sway in both elements, but indeed in different forms. Whereas this substance is emphasised as such in Element 1 — albeit in a broken form — it appears to be only indirectly tangible in Element 2, where it is dispersed, fragmented, sloughed off, leaked out, as it were.

An important entry point into the action is via the materials and objects; their interpretation specifically derives from the perception, experience and forms of knowledge that the observer has brought along. This fits a core aim of Fluxus: taking the process of reception seriously, respecting its independence. The individual objects were to be understood both in terms of their material appearance and in terms of the function they take on, both in daily life and in the context of the action. Observers were expected to recognise them while noting how the objects affected them personally, what inner responses the objects elicited. Only through this complex perception could the extended definition be communicated or the impulses emanating from it be creatively relayed. For the sake of concreteness, let us consider two examples: fat and felt.

Among the many objects and materials in the action, fat arguably occupied the most important role. It appeared in MANRESA in various forms: as a 'ball of fat', 'fat corner', 'filter fat corner', flung fat and fat slowly dripping down the wall. By the end, the fat was spread throughout the room. To this day, Monika Schmela recalls with horror how the event space looked after the action: 'The entire gallery was full of fat: the walls, the floor. You couldn't set foot in the gallery.'[41]

In fact, for Beuys and his dynamic notion of art, fat was a common denominator that illustrated his expanded notion of art better than any other material. Fat was an 'energy carrier' and possessed characteristics that, in his view, could cover both poles of sculptural creation. When cold, it was malleable and could be moulded into a ball or a tetrahedron, for example. When heated, the shapes dissolve and the fat liquefies into undirected vagueness. In the 'filter fat corner', it ultimately proves to be a transitory material. Human beings are a product of 'warmth potentials' (*Wärmepotenzen*) such as egg and sperm production, fertilisation, birth and growth; throughout their lives, they are perpetually sensitive and prone to sculptural effects caused by temperature shifts.

For Beuys, fat is the quintessential sculptural element. Via its systematic distribution around the gallery space, it is 'spatial-ised'. Thus, the action occurs 'in the fat', as it were, i.e. within its sculptural dimensions of chaos and form:

- In the corner, it has a set shape, demonstrating its moulded, stored energy: measured, directed, on command.
- On the walls, it drips down, slides, flows, moves; it is undirected 'wild' energy, practically demanding an assertive intervention so as to 'restore order' to the space; in a way, it appeals for the principle of movement.

Therein lie the core tenets of the sculptural theory: that the poles of form and chaos must be perpetually redefined; that a compensatory and directing creative relationship is to be achieved in the constant movement between them. Chaos is the origin of all energies and developments; sculptural enterprise is the source of form, insight; out of them both, evolution ensues. In regard to MANRESA, this occurs through a permanent cycle of 'climbing up' and 'climbing down'. It is between flow and the fixation that the dynamic relationship must be directed in a balanced way. 'That is why you must always think about the polarities ... or about the forces', Beuys warned in a conversation with Volker Harlan. 'Otherwise, you develop a predilection for a certain thing, and predilections are very dangerous'.[42]

Unlike fat, felt is only indirectly connected to energy. Its texture makes it an insulator and gives it the function of insulating and storing heat. This enables the 'heat carrier' (*Wärmeträger*) to regulate its thermal balance and to direct the absorption and release of heat. Felt itself is a pseudo-textile and consists of a 'crushed mass' in which fibres such as animal fur and wool are interwoven without a set pattern. Through the effects of heat, pressure and movement and with the addition of milling agents such as soap, the scaly fibres of wool or hair move towards their root-ends during felting. In the process, they become so tangled together, so interwoven, that they can no longer be separated.

In the action, felt encases the halved cross and a small square wooden frame, the 'filter'. Also, a triangular piece of felt is stretched across a corner, forming a tetrahedron. Its internal structure is energetically charged. Its significance as an insulator constantly points it towards an energy lying beneath or behind it. Based on its form, it can be seen as a 'cold sculpture' (*Kälteplastik*).

Many other objects are discernible in the action: a copper staff; two bottles; iron machinery components. Some other items are not precisely identifiable or attributable within its sequence or are perhaps unaccounted for altogether. That last category includes a small package the size of a musical score (roughly 30 × 20 × 5 cm), which was upright inside the box of Element 2, alongside the car battery.[43] There are also unresolved questions about salt and sulphur, a cake and a copy of the Danish art magazine *Hvedekorn* — all items listed on the organising score 'Nine to sixteen'. Later textual references to MANRESA also mention rosemary.

The spear/staff features frequently in Beuys's work: as a walking stick and a shepherd's staff, as a crutch, as a weapon, as a staff that guides and measures everything, and as an insignia. The staff in front of the halved cross is a copper rod roughly the width of a finger. Copper is a strong and very quick conductor of both heat and electricity. Henning Christiansen's notes refer to the rod as a spear. It had a vertical shape. The felt handle suggest insulation from the energy currents that flow through the staff. The staff would later evolve into the *Eurasian Staff*.

Two bottles sat on the floor near the felt corner. One was made of cast lead; the other was filled with milk. It may be significant to note that Beuys used two bottles for another, nearly concurrent project: the empty blood-donation flasks for *Crucifixion* (1962–63) at Staatsgalerie Stuttgart. There, they have a clear iconographic link to the two supporting figures in classic portrayals of the Crucifixion, Mary and John; here in MANRESA, they are positioned at an angle to and at a slight remove from the cross. One of the bottles is made of lead — that is, transformed into a meaningful material — and the other is filled with milk, a substance that transforms into energy after being imbibed.

In the garden behind Beuys's studio, he grew rosemary in a wooden planter. The story went that Beuys had brought the rosemary back from his trip to Manresa, Spain.[44] But as Eva Beuys clarified in a letter, this story grew out of a misunderstanding. The plant came 'from MANRESA', she writes: that is, from the MANRESA action.[45] Beuys propped it up on a sculpting stand and placed a compass on top of it. In connection with the sculptural environment *Lightning with Stag in Its Glare*, Beuys said that the little side work *Boothia felix* represents a 'little closed cosmos' that takes the shape of that mysterious plant's roots and that 'affects things' both physically and psychologically 'by generating and maintaining them'.[46] Thus, Manresa's impulse to activate and transform cancelled itself out in this, Beuys's last major work, which extended both the ideas and the impulse of MANRESA.[47]

The action includes three strands of activity: that of each participating artist. Fully in keeping with Fluxus, these strands scarcely have anything to do with one another. Each of the participants acts more or less according to his whim. There are no rehearsals, only loose consultations. The 'interplay' draws on the subconscious, on the atmosphere. As Henning Christiansen would later recall, neither of the Danes knew about the Ignatian aspect of the action. Being conversant in Swedish, they thought the action had something to do with a journey. *Man reest* sounded to them like the Swedish words for 'man travels'; humans are always in motion. A man on a journey. They would later learn that Ignatius was a man on a lifelong, never-ending journey. Unfortunately, Beuys had not told them much about the meaning of the action, yet it was somehow clear to them that it had to do with journeying, Henning Christiansen later stated.[48]

Henning Christiansen's part primarily consisted of playing taped voice recordings, including one by Joseph Beuys and another by Bjørn Nørgaard. This is supplemented by spoken and gestural elements of a musical nature. This includes a rhythmic 'Coffee Cup Piece' and staccato shouts of 'I – can – not' (*Ikke kann*) that lent compelling drama throughout the action. In addition, Christiansen would occasionally give a professorial-sounding lecture in which he verbosely and associatively held forth on Professor Beuys's artistic oeuvre. Inspired by the proceedings of the action, he then spontaneously wrote the following in chalk on the wall (in English): 'Climb up'.[49]

During the action, Bjørn Nørgaard was primarily occupied with a variety of footwork: limping, hopping, swaying, stomping, etc. He filled a wooden frame with electric light bulbs, covered them with a cloth and smashed them with his feet. He also trampled a conical lump of clay inside a pillow.

He then launched into his most important contribution by splashing his bare feet around a tub of water, whereupon he lathered his feet with soap and placed them in two empty shoe boxes, which he filled with liquid plaster that rapidly hardened. Finally, he removed the boxes and began walking laboriously with the hardened blocks of plaster on his legs. This was accompanied by Christiansen's staccato cries: 'I – can – not'.[50]

Beuys crouched down in front of Element 2, pulled a photograph out of a two-part device and carried it over to Element 1, where he held the photo up to of the two halves of the cross, identifying them as energy sources. Next, he returned to the box and took out a cardboard disk, which he strung around his neck with string and hung down his back, wearing the circle as a symbol of the bygone wholeness of separated parts.

Finally, he held up the variation of this round shape — a plate bearing a crucifix figurine — in the same spot, as if to suggest that the separated pieces can only be reassembled with pain and sacrifice and at risk of death.

Beuys then filled a series of bicycle air pumps with runny fat from the 'fat corner' and hurled it flat against the wall. The fat gradually slid and dripped down the wall shapelessly.

Out of the box, Beuys next took a toy bird on a stick with mechanically manipulable wings. Beuys made the bird 'flutter' over to the cross — a symbol of movement, of setting off. At various moments, he shouted the mysterious sentence 'Where is Element 3?'

Soon thereafter, for the first time, Beuys started up the high-frequency, high-voltage generator, which changed the electricity from a lorry battery from 12 volts to 50,000. Subjected to this voltage in the dark, the copper wires gave off sparks from their open ends, each spark audibly crackling. Using this teaching aid from a school physics class, Beuys thus demonstrated the presence of invisible energies in the surrounding space.

He then took some hare's ears out of the box and touched them to the generator, symbolically charging them. In this, he was clearly staging a perception of invisible, but genuinely present energies in order to trigger 'action impulses'.

Beuys then walked over to the bottles that were standing alongside the box. He opened the milk bottle and took a sip. The first bottle was heavy and stuck to the floor, the second one light and filled with liquid. With this, he was drawing vital energy from nature in order to transform it into meaningful activity.

The intestines of a hare were arrayed on a small board in the box. Beuys took this assemblage and affixed it to the middle of the two cross halves of Element 1 using the copper rod. With this, he incorporated biological energy transformers, alongside the electronic power converted, into his meditative activities.

Next, he removed a 'Geissler tube' — a glass tube filled with neon gas — from the box and rubbed some fabric on one of its ends. This initiated a flow of electrons and made the gas light up. Finally, Beuys connected the plate crucifix to his heart using the light. Again, he shouted: 'Where is Element 3?'

Next, Beuys reached into the box and pulled out a small toy: a tiny military ambulance with a red cross on the roof. This relates to childish imagination, to sensitivity, empathy and a playfully inventive creativity possessing the knowledge to overcome 'hard' realities and to live by new, imagined perspectives and ideas. The cross on the ambulance roof resembles the cross of first aid; the ambulance itself symbolises the rescuers carrying the cross; Simon of Cyrene and Christ are both identified.

Beuys's work includes many allusions to medicine and healing: thermometers, syringes, ampules and pharmaceutical drugs. In light of numerous works by Beuys, Axel Hinrich Murken concludes that, like Matthias Grünewald, Beuys expressly links endangerment and vulnerability to revitalisation, rescue and metaphysicality.[51] This is the same therapeutic aspect of his work that has already been mentioned elsewhere. When asked whether the medical allusions in his work signified the search for a panacea, Beuys responded: 'That's right. A therapy whose objective, shall we say, has in mind nothing but making man into what he must be made into: a spiritual creature who gradually lifts himself out of physical dependencies'.[52]

Beuys positioned the toy vehicle near two identical-looking iron components from a machine, which were both resting outside the box. Each of the two cylindrical or conical parts had two tips protruding from their ends. He placed them side by side so that they mirrored each other and connected them at their contact points using a gauze bandage. The stark contrast was palpable when viewing the heavy iron pistons, which were paradoxically connected by two small gauze bandages, a gentle juxtaposition of the bulky with the delicate. Again, he shouted 'Where is Element 3?' This paradoxically initiated the healing process, allowing them to grow back together.

Time after time, sparks were produced by the generator; other elements were ritually repeated. At regular intervals, Beuys's prerecorded voice resounded:

> Now? Has Element 2 climbed up to Element 1?
> Now? Has Element 1 climbed down to Element 2?
> Where is Element 3?[53]

What does Element 1 designate? The answer is crucial for any interpretation of the 'action'. In Beuys's eyes, all objects in this world are awaiting activation, which can be achieved through cognitive intelligence and through the act of returning them to their vibrant and manifest context. In other words, they await art. This resolves the search for the meaning of Element 3, which is only present in the 'action' in the form of a question. It solely exists in the symbol of its absence, yet it is shaped and demonstrated by example: in the 'action' and by means of it, that is, via the individuals enacting it.

A central notion of Ignatian theology is that God, as the Creator, is concealed in the world. For this reason, God cannot be directly experienced except for through the mediation of the objects he created.

And he shows himself in Christ, in the cross: because the world is in a transitional state, in an 'interim period'. It has yet to complete its development via the energy that flowed out of Christ. With this in mind, in MANRESA, human beings are called upon to fill in the gap through physical deeds. Human beings, like Christ, must overcome the estrangements of the world and of history. That this can be achieved, according to Beuys, is indicated by the staff set down in front of the half-cross. Being made of copper, it embodies an energy conductor; with its vertical orientation, it embodies the form and direction of movement, the source and the content of that energy, in and through which those estrangements can be defeated. Only: human beings must take hold of that staff and align it in order to mobilise the upper energy so that it 'climbs down'. This energy takes effect in creatures, in elements, the animals, plants and human beings when God gives them existence. Humans, too, receive everything in energy 'from above', as Ignatius will articulate in his *Exercises*. Only in and from God does the being (*Sein*) of the world become transparent to humans as existence-giving, creative energy. God himself is present in objects, truly present, because he indicates his permanent presence to them within his creation and incarnation and because this presence is perpetually gaining intensity.[54]

Beuys was clearly engaged with this aspect of energetic activation. For Ignatius, it was grounded in his vision at Manresa: he saw how God had created the world, he experienced it auditorily 'under the aspect of three keys on a musical instrument',[55] in the image of 'white rays coming from above'[56] and in the inner experience of 'Christ's humanity', which he understood with the opened 'eyes of his understanding'.[57]

For Beuys, this clarity arrived with the development of his definition of art. In his question about Element 3, he calls upon people who take responsibility in the world in the sense of these functions, people who contribute precisely what we so urgently lack today: 'the open invitation to experience that and thus the chance for a total change to take place within the person.'[58]

I will conclude the discussion of this aspect with a quotation from Beuys:

> There are secrets enchanted within Nature that can only be found if you give yourself permission not to make scientific premises (which is not necessary for this) but to intuit which of them are the deeper secrets of Nature, which extends all around us.[59]

The reality described here cannot be perceived through the external senses, however. It requires the 'purified new senses that are empowered to depict spiritual processes', as Beuys wrote in his notes while reading Ignatius; it requires an 'inner eye' that perceives the 'invisible substance' and understands that Christ himself flows through 'every individual room and every individual temporal element substantially'.[60]

With this 'inner eye', humanity transcends the physical spatial/temporal relationship and arrives at a perspective of counter-space and super-time. In the context of MANRESA, these are the brown spaces: the Thorvaldsen Museum and Manresa.

These counter-spaces are evident in the colour brown. It might be happenstance that the main exhibition room of the Thorvaldsen Museum in Copenhagen is dominated by deep-brown wall hangings and brown patterned tiles, and that the 'beautiful Manresa valley' glows brown, especially in the light of the late afternoon. For Beuys, the colour brown certainly symbolises the earth, the material of both becoming and decay.

In the scores for MANRESA, the abstract significance of the upward and downward movement is not merely inhabited by the sculptural concepts such as 'material', 'moulded', 'chaotic', 'substantial' and 'potential'. It is also inhabited geographically, historically and sociologically via the symbols of Northern and Southern Europe. The north is represented by the Scandinavian countries, and the south by two cities: Rome and Manresa.

In Rome, the nineteenth-century Danish sculptor Bertel Thorvaldsen deeply embedded formal ideas from Antiquity into his own classicist work, fruitfully cross-pollinating Mediterranean and Nordic formal sensibilities. The humanistic ideas of Erasmus, who came from Rotterdam, were very present in Manresa during Ignatius' lifetime, transmitted by the nearby Benedictine monastery. This allowed the saint to liberate himself from the collective bonds of individual consciousness and to cultivate a subjective, egocentric, modern consciousness known as *devotio moderna*. As such, northern European reflection was conveyed with a southern emphasis and Spanish militancy. Beuys was fascinated by Ignatius' radical ideas and the practical conclusions he drew from his insights, even if the artist did not apply this stringency to a life in the church, but instead brought it to bear more generally in the spiritual and mental realms:

> The entire militant discipline must apply to the person himself. It must be an inner war ... an argument for the attainment of this consciousness. And this cannot be reached without discipline, and without this militancy.[61]

In the MANRESA action, the copper staff — with its vertical alignment — plays a symbolic role as a sign of both clerical pastoralism ('shepherding' the 'flock') and shamanism alike. In the subsequent action *Eurasia Staff*, the vertical marking and the geographical application complement each other, as they are drawn on the map from north to south and horizontally from east to west. In early sketches for MANRESA, this staff spans a map from East Asia to the West, all the way to 'Ostend', Belgium — literally the end of the East, exemplifying the West — an idea that would later be 'demonstrated' in the subsequent action *Eurasian Staff*. Together with the north/south axis from MANRESA, the staff forms the 'New Cross' with its east/west axis. In sensory terms, Beuys marks this 'New Cross' twofold: once with the Eurasia staff and then with the criss-crossed bases made of iron and felt in the subsequent action *Eurasian Staff*.

Near the end of this symphonic action, Beuys kneaded margarine into the backs of his knees, then bent his legs, squeezing the fat deep into his joints and causing some to spill out the sides under the pressure. Then he took hold of the Eurasian staff, held it up four times vertically at the corners of the previously installed floor-to-ceiling felt corners (*Filzwinkel*) and finally swung it to and fro horizontally — while standing on one leg, making a cross shape — as he slowly probed the four cardinal directions.

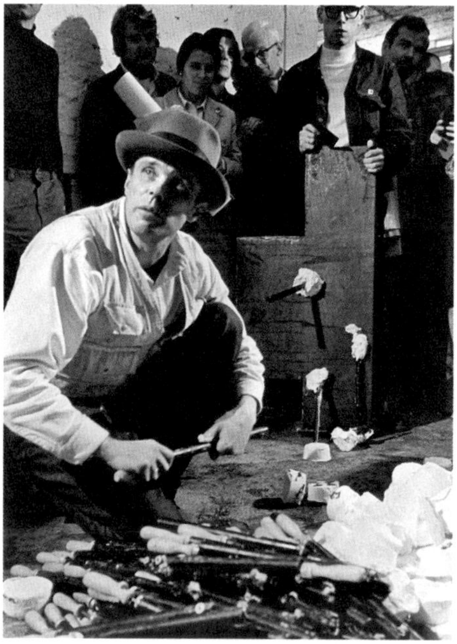

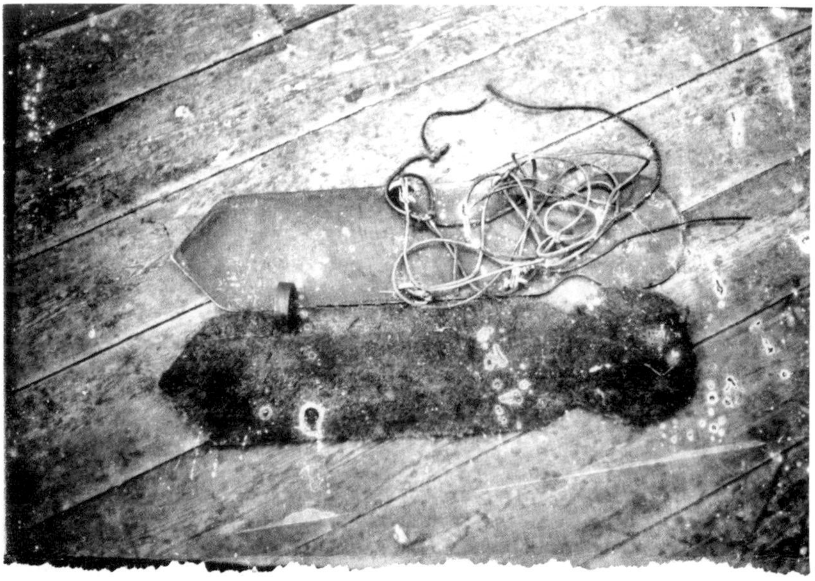

G *Vacuum–Mass*, Galerie Art Intermedia, Cologne, 1968.
H Sole-like bases made of iron and felt, used by Beuys in the subsequent action *Eurasian Staff*, Vienna, 1967.

The shoe-sole cross consisted of one sole made of iron with a small magnet on top, and a second sole made of felt. These two shapes played a role in many of his actions. They first appeared in the action *How to Explain Paintings to a Dead Hare* (1965) and appeared the final time in *Vacuum–Mass* (1968). In fact, the purpose of the cross of shoe soles is to make unseen connections apparent. In the action *Eurasian Staff* (1967), Beuys hovers the iron sole, which is tied to his own human foot, at various distances above and beside the felt shoe-sole on the floor. He performs this ceremonial procedure for quite a while before finally resting the iron sole upon the felt sole at a right angle, forming a cross. For Beuys, the felt sole functions as an insulator of energy from the earth, which in turn can be interpreted, based on Steiner, as the body of Christ. From the way the iron sole interacts with the felt sole, it can be interpreted as an energy conductor for activity in accordance with an expanded consciousness. Transmission and reception are thus thematically addressed by both soles. Crossing them is an activity from the 'Christ impulse': 'it is the basis upon which a person sees, upon which a person develops all other things'.[62]

Manresa: Crossroads and setting-off point

The 'New Cross', as it emerged from the MANRESA and *Eurasian Staff* actions, serves as a symbol of activation, as an impulse to convey historical and cultural opposites: 'Therefore the cross has thoroughly become part of culture', he later told Elisabeth Pfister in retrospect.[63] In these artistic creations and spiritual exercises, Beuys connects separations, links disparities, reconciles divorces, and annuls opposites. In the cross, the Ignatian metaphysical acts of setting off are united with Rudolf Steiner's social and political ones.

As a wanderer with a walking stick, Beuys had once set off as an artist. Later in life, he would repeatedly pose for photographs in such guises: as a 'leader of stags', as a nomad, as a demonstrator in the desert of Western society — always on a quest for lost economic, mental, spiritual and cultural energies. For him, this quest was always a practice, a *Plastik* or sculpture. It was also a setting off and an escape from old comfort zones, from anything crystalline or with a fixed shape; it was like an artistic grasping at the amorphousness in this world, of which humans consciously take hold in their image-making hands. This is the artistic act of humanity: a mental-spiritual movement, a *Plastik* that arises out of a traveller's everlasting quest, a traveller who will not cease his incarnating search until he has found the resurrection of a new humanity and a new world as 'social sculpture' (*soziale Plastik*), or, in Joseph Beuys's own words:

> In the deepness of the night, in the deepness of isolation, in the complete isolation from the spiritual, a mystery takes place in a person ... Only if one has become an entirely new person will one be capable of doing things that have appeared impossible to achieve for man up to now. ... This time Resurrection must instead be experienced by each person himself. ... One somehow must come to terms with his God. One must meet certain conditions, make certain efforts in order to come in contact with himself. And that is the true scientific sense of the word "creativity". ... [I]ncarnation of the being of Christ amidst the physical conditions of the earth. A real mystery, a cosmic event, has thus taken place rather than just a historical one. A flow of energy in absolutely realistic terms has occurred. And thus a metamorphosis takes place within the person which is very difficult to achieve. Very difficult. It is exceedingly difficult for one to really activate this self-determination through one's own efforts. It is extremely difficult. A person would rather accept something that is given, like receiving a gift. However, in that case, one doesn't receive anymore. One doesn't receive anything at all, not from any God, not from any Christ. And yet this energy presents itself and wants to come about with force, but on the condition that the person comes to terms with himself.[64]

1
Joseph Beuys, *Documenta 6*, Kassel: Documenta-Verlag, p. 156 [Exh. cat.]. Translation by translator.

2
Friedhelm Mennekes, *Beuys on Christ: A Position in Dialogue*, [bilingual edition] Lesa Mason and Jon Boles (trans.), Stuttgart: Verlag Katholisches Bibelwerk, 1989, p. 59.

3
Mennekes, *Beuys on Christ*, p. 130.

4
Volker Harlan, Rainer Rappmann and Peter Schata, *Soziale Plastik* [3rd ed.], Achberg: Achberger Verlag, 1984, p. 17. Translation by translator.

5
Rudolf Steiner, *The Christ Impulse: and the Development of Ego-Consciousness*, Christian von Arnim (trans.), Forest Row, UK: Rudolf Steiner Press, 2014, pp. 46–47.

6
Friedhelm Mennekes, *Joseph Beuys. MANRESA: Eine Aktion als geistliche Übung nach Ignatius von Loyola*, Frankfurt am Main and Leipzig: Insel Verlag, 1992, pp. 93–123. Translation by translator.

7
Saint Ignatius of Loyola, *A Pilgrim's Journey: The Autobiography of Ignatius of Loyola*, Joseph N. Tylenda, S.J. (trans.), San Francisco: Ignatius Press, 2001. Section 1. *A Pilgrim's Journey* is divided into numbered sections; this and subsequent citations from it are by section number, not page number.

8
Burkhard Schneider, 'Ignatius von Loyola', *Die Heiligen*, Peter Manns (ed.), Mainz: Grünewald, 1976, p. 457. Translation by translator.

9
Loyola, *Pilgrim's Journey*, section 7.

10
Ibid., section 18.

11
Ibid., section 19.

12
Ibid., section 20.

13
Ibid., section 24.

14
Ibid., section 25.

15
Idem.

16
Idem.

17
Hugo Rahner, *Ignatius von Loyola und das geschichtliche Werden seiner Frömmigkeit*, Vienna: Herder, 1949, p. 55. Translation by translator.

18
Loyola, *Pilgrim's Journey*, section 28.

19
Quoted in Joan Segarra Pijuan, S.J., *Manresa and Saint Ignatius of Loyola*, Patricia Mathews (trans.), Manresa: Ajuntament de Manresa, 1992, p. 66.

20
Loyola, *Pilgrim's Journey*, section 29.

21
Idem.

22
Ignatius of Loyola, *The Spiritual Exercises*, Father Elder Mullan, S.J. (trans.), New York: P.J. Kennedy & Sons, 1914, p. 24. Page numbers cited from PDF version with Library of Congress call number BX2179. L7, downloaded from the Christian Classics Ethereal Library www.ccel.org/ccel/ignatius/exercises.html. [access: 26 October 2020].

23
Ibid., p. 48.

24
Idem.

25
Ibid., p. 49.

26
Loyola, *Pilgrim's Journey*, section 29.

27
Loyola, *Spiritual Exercises*, p. 61.

28
Loyola, *Pilgrim's Journey*, section 29.

29
Many scholars of Ignatius agree that not only did the 'pilgrim' have his first ground-breaking experiences in Manresa, but also made the first notes that would later culminate in the *Spiritual Exercises*. Ignatius' stay in Manresa amounted to his own exercises. In addition to Hugo Rahner, *Ignatius von Loyola*, cited above, this is corroborated by the following articles: R. Cantin, 'L'illumination du Cardoner', *Sciences Ecclésiastiques* no. 7, 1955, pp. 23–56; L.R. Silos, 'Cardoner in the Life of the Saint Ignatius of Loyola', *Archivum Historicum Societatis Iesu*, no. 33, 1964, pp. 3–43.

30
Loyola, *Spiritual Exercises*, p. 29–30 (Incarnation) and p. 53–54 (Birth of Christ) respectively.

31
Loyola, *Pilgrim's Journey*, section 30.

32
Pedro de Leturia, 'Genesis de los Ejercicios', *Archivum Historicum Societatis Iesu*, no. 10, 1941, p. 26. Translated by the translator from the German.

33
Hugo Rahner, *Ignatius von Loyola*, p. 54; J. Calveras, 'La ilustración del Cardoner y el instituto de la Compania de Jesús según el P. Nadal', *Archivum Historicum Societatis Iesu*, no. 25, 1956, pp. 27–54.

34
Götz Adriani, Winfried Konnertz and Karin Thomas, *Joseph Beuys: Life and Works*, Patricia Lech (trans.), New York: Barron's Educational Series, 1979, p. 54.

35
Joseph Beuys, quoted in Adriani et al., *Joseph Beuys*, p. 54.

36
Joseph Beuys, quoted in Adriani et al., *Joseph Beuys*, pp. 56–59.

37
Mennekes, *Beuys on Christ*, p. 25.

38
Mennekes, *Joseph Beuys. MANRESA*, p. 136.

39
Joseph Beuys, 'Selbstdarstellung', *Selbstdarstellungen: Künstler über sich*. Wulf Herzogenrath (ed.). Düsseldorf: Droste Verlag, p. 29. Translation by translator.

40
Mennekes, *Joseph Beuys. MANRESA*, p. 119. Translation by translator.

41
Ibid., p. 102. Translation by translator.

42
Volker Harlan, *Was ist Kunst? Werkstattgespräch mit Beuys*. Munich: Urachhaus, 1986, p. 60. Translation by translator.

43
Eva Beuys does not think that this package contained the cake mentioned on the list. Rather, she suspects that it held one of the two 'Graves', 1949, in the wax form that is now on display in the sixth vitrine of room 6 at Hessisches Landesmuseum Darmstadt. See *Block-Beuys*, p. 242.

44
According to Heiner Bastian in *Joseph Beuys: Blitzschlag mit Lichtschein auf Hirsch, 1958–1985*, Bern: Benteli, 1986, p. 18. Franz Joseph van der Grinten corroborated this in an interview, MS 11.

45
Letter to the author dated 24 July 1989. For a corroborating account, see also Johannes Stüttgen, 'Hirschdenkmäler' in *Zeitstau: Im Kraftfeld des erweiterten Kunstbegriffs von Joseph Beuys*, Munich: FIU, 1988, p. 180.

46
Wenzel Beuys, *Blitzschlag mit Lichtschein auf Hirsch, 1958–1985: Von Joseph Beuys*, Heidelberg: Edition Staeck, 1987, p. 11.

47
Documenta 8, Kassel: Documenta-Verlag, 1987, vol. II, p. 24ff [Exh. cat.].

48
Henning Christiansen, unpublished interview with author, 1990; see Mennekes, *Joseph Beuys. MANRESA*, p. 95.

49
Mennekes, *Joseph Beuys. MANRESA*, p. 101.

50
Idem.

51
Axel Hinrich Murken, *Joseph Beuys und die Medizin*, Münster: Coppenrath, 1979, p. 38.

52
Ibid., p. 37.

53
Mennekes, *Joseph Beuys. MANRESA*, p. 96.

54
Beuys in Mennekes, *Beuys on Christ*, pp. 17, 19.

55
Loyola, *Pilgrim's Journey*, section 28.

56
Loyola, *Pilgrim's Journey*, section 29.

57
Loyola, *Pilgrim's Journey*, section 30.

58
Beuys on Christ, p. 57.

59
Transcript of a handwritten text by Beuys, in *Block-Beuys*, p. 247. Translation by translator.

60
Beuys on Christ, p. 57.

61
Beuys in Mennekes, *Beuys on Christ*, p. 25.

62
Adriani, *Joseph Beuys*, p. 216.

63
Beuys in Mennekes, *Beuys on Christ*, p. 129.

64
Beuys in Mennekes, *Beuys on Christ*, pp. 27, 29, 31.

HARALD SZEEMANN

'WHERE IS ELEMENT 3?'

Reflections on the concept of the *Gesamtkunstwerk* (total work of art) concerning MANRESA, with reference to a saint, a plant, a revolutionary and a prophecy, that come together in Beuys's *Hauptstrom*, 1977.

IT'S 15 DECEMBER 1966. The hare's heart has been exposed; the symphony has evoked poverty, birth and resurrection; clay and sound have been expressed non-visually (*Siberian Symphony, First Movement*, 1963); the definition of Fluxus has been expanded; mechanical children's toys have chimed (*Composition for 2 Musicians*, 1963); the last word in sculptural intervention and sound quality have been wrested from a grand piano by destroying it (*Piano Action*, 1963); the transformative character of fat has been demonstrated, chocolate handed out, aggression countered by Christianity, the crucifix raised in an appellative manner (20 July, 1964). The claim *'I am a transmitter. I transmit!'* has been embodied (*The Chief*, 1964); cold Duchamp banished into a warm 'fat corner' (*The Silence of Marcel Duchamp Is Overrated*, 1964); theories on heat (*Wärme*), the afterlife, overtime (*Überzeit*) and counter space (*Gegenraum*) have been proclaimed; an 'energy plan' embodied (*and in us... beneath us... land under*, 1965); pictures have been explained to a dead hare (1965), suffering has been declared indispensable for the development of new qualities (*Infiltration-Homogen for Grand Piano. The Greatest Contemporary Composer is the Thalidomide Child.*, 1966); information has been filtered (*Felt TV*, 1966); intuition and rationality, Eurasia, the overcoming of separation and the division of the cross have all been evoked (*Eurasia*, 1966). The range of Beuysian actions is enormous: their subjects have been expanded, their visions sparkle and purification is called for in spiritual exercises of 'inner necessity.'

MANRESA. Beuys must have liked the word. *Man* + *resa*. Humanity and complete devoutness, even delivery, unite in the name of the city, where a particular man and soldier, who later became a saint, devoted himself unconditionally to religious faith.

This man, Ignatius of Loyola, was admired by Beuys for his militancy, his total dedication to the human inner struggle and to the process of becoming aware and conscious. In Christianity, Beuys found 'quintessence' — which, in Paracelsus' world, was not a fifth element above all others, but an element in its own right: 'Man is the fifth element and a microcosm and the son of the whole world'; indeed he considered it 'like nature, strengthened beyond its level'[1] — the quintessence of spirituality; and in Ignatius, he found the disciplinary model to understand and break down the mystery of the Holy Trinity, the threefold figure of God in one, the spirit of three essences, which all religions have in common; a spiritual union between the Orient and Occident, as sought by Richard Wagner, the originator of the term *Gesamtkunstwerk* (total work of art), which he sought to achieve in *Parsifal*.

For his MANRESA action, Beuys noted: 'Pater physis. earth Atman father, Filius, ethereal movement, Buddha, son, spiritus Sanctus, soul, manas, Holy Spirit'.[2] It was equivalent to Rudolf Steiner's dimensions of the 'spiritual human/spiritual figure filled with life, and Buddha as the "non-deluded" being who appeared for the salvation and blessing of this world, the spirit/ego'.

Beuys's MANRESA action on 15 December 1966, which will not be discussed here in detail, was also an 'act of love' (Bjørn Nørgaard) for the living, namely for Monika and Alfred Schmela, who closed their gallery on Hunsrückstrasse 16 and moved to a new building on Mutter-Ey-Strasse 5. These gallerists' names, to whom Beuys paid homage for their pioneering work, are also concealed in the title of the action. And Beuys, who admired Erik Satie and James Joyce, must have been delighted to notice this:

MonikA uNd AlfREd SchmelA

Relocation, change, transformation and transubstantiation were therefore present on all levels in Beuys's repeated question, 'Where is Element 3?'

The notion of cyclical processes or infinite recurrence exists in MANRESA in the form of a rosemary plant, which Beuys brought back from Manresa either in 1964 (according to Bastian) or in 1966 (according to Mennekes) and planted in the garden of his studio on Drakeplatz in Düsseldorf; first as part of his action, then in the 'Boothia Felix' section of the sculptural ensemble *Lightning with Stag in its Glare* (1958–85) complete with soil, roots and shards.[3]

Rosemary, *ros marinus* or 'dew of the sea', which grows wild in the maquis scrublands of Mediterranean countries, has been cultivated as a cooking herb, decorative shrub and medicinal plant since ancient times. It has greyish, felt-like, decussate (i.e. cross-formed) leaves, and flowers that range from blue to purple. Both its leaves and flowers contain essential oil of rosemary, which is used for denaturing olive oil and spirits to make soap fragrances and eau de cologne. Ovid paid homage to the plant by creating the poetic name *ros maris*. It has medicinal, healing and cosmetic properties in Weleda's range of anthroposophic remedies; it is used in decorations, wreaths and incense. It is applied in love and fertility magic, is the symbol of Aphrodite in the south and consecrated to Freya in the north. It is the cherished food of bees. Its aroma expels diseases, calamity and evil spirits. But it is also associated with death, so it appears not only at baptisms and marriages, but also funerals. Rosemary was lain on

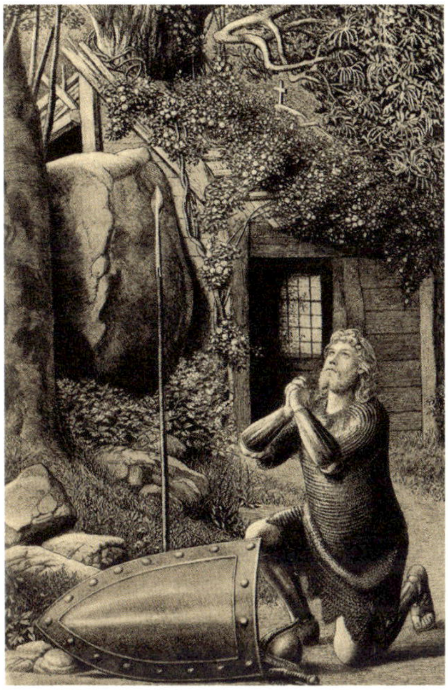

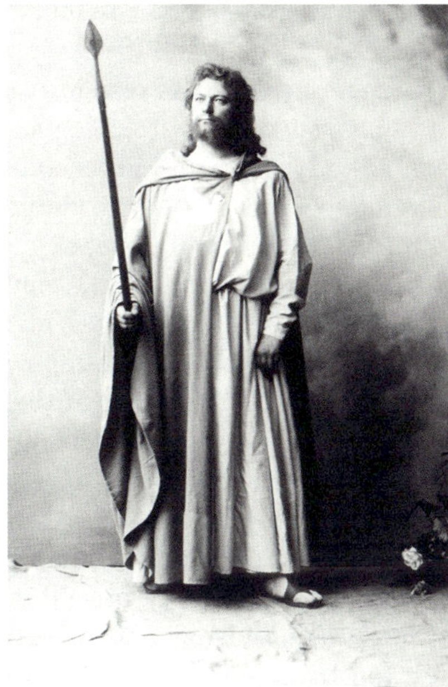

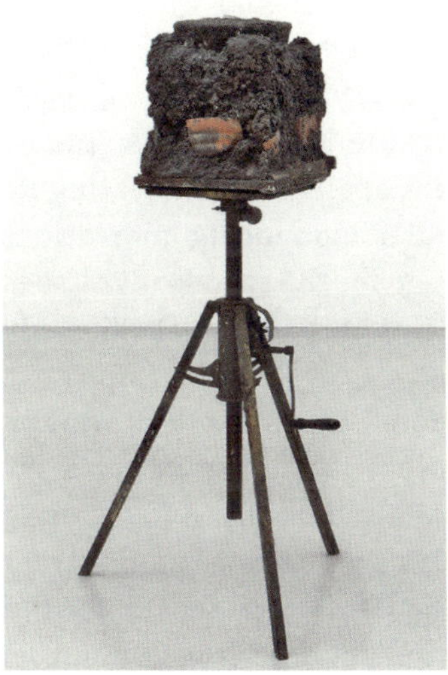

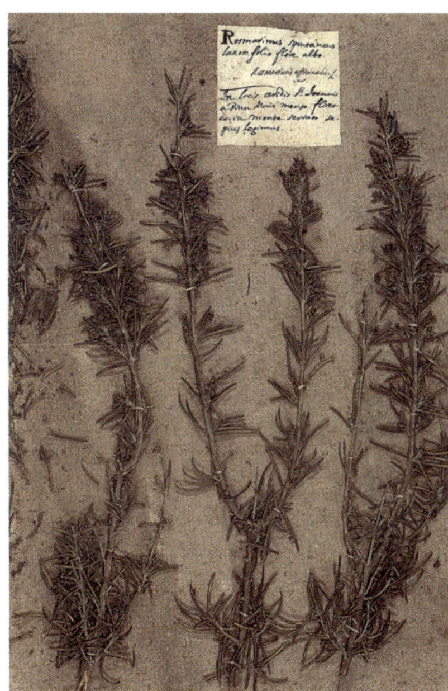

A Parsifal, in the moment he embraces a spiritual path.

B Parsifal represented as a warrior.

C *Boothia Felix*, 1958/1982. Metal tripod, terracotta shards, earth, rosemary roots, compass. Galerie Thaddaeus Ropac, Paris.

D Flowering rosemary from Montserrat, catalogued by Herbari Salvador (17th C), the oldest plant collection in Spain.

Ophelia's grave. It can be found in Hungary water, a distilled product made of alcohol and the leaves and flowers of rosemary, which later became a solution of rosemary oil in wine spirit, was used against 'the Hungarian disease' (the Plague), and was appreciated by the Sun King, Louis XIV, as an all-purpose medicine. Sexologist Magnus Hirschfeld ranked it as a fertility medicine 'in combination with mastic herbs'.[4] Mastic, the resin of the eponymous shrub, leads us straight to Egypt, where rosemary was used to embalm corpses, clean pearls and remove script from papyrus leaves. Mastic is also a fixative for wound dressings, chewing agents, tooth powder and facial care products.

Thus, Element 2 of the MANRESA action alludes not only to Egypt, antiquity, the Middle Ages, modern times, birth, marriage and death, south and north, west and east, but also to the Thorvaldsen Museum with its classicist, formally strict, 'male' principle, and it is lent a 'female', Danish element via the rosemary on Ophelia's grave.

Typical Beuys: everything is present and included. He knew the composition, history and effect of every material he used. And although when writing about this action, Schneede uses the word 'apparently' in connection with rosemary, he goes on to call it by name in a footnote,[5] and although Bastian refers to a specific plant, it is sufficiently significant to allow this herb — a *Gesamtkunstwerk* in itself — to appear as a protagonist in more detail. I am not overly preoccupied with where it came from: whether Beuys brought it back from Manresa or, as Eva Beuys implied, it was 'the rosemary from Manresa', i.e. that was used in the MANRESA action.[6] Just as the Bayreuth Festspielhaus appears as the sacred church of ancient opera, with its seating arrangements for a classless society, its acoustic-enhancing innovations in opera-house architecture and rising stage for the spectacular appearance of the operatic gods, so rosemary seems here to me to be the substance of elements, times and epochs.

In Beuys's sequence of 'actions', MANRESA/*ros maris* could be seen as a private purification process performed for a small audience in a small room with a window looking in for those on the outside, but nevertheless with Beuys's usual total commitment and participants with ascribed roles. The (Beuysian) search for the other half of the cross was first evoked in his action *Eurasia* and pre-dates the connection of sculptural and acoustic elements featured in his *Hauptstrom* action in Darmstadt. These realities, evoked to overcome oppositional fields, are part of Joseph Beuys's *Gesamtkunstwerk*: the union of intuition, imagination and inspiration in thought. Hans Richter's description of Kurt Schwitters, when he said, 'In reality, *he*, Kurt Schwitters, was the *Gesamtkunstwerk*'[7] also applies to Beuys, but on a different level. Despite all the sources of inspiration that Beuys owes to Schwitters — for example, the light-hearted use of heterogeneous material in combination with visual, verbal and acoustic expression as found in Beuys's 'sculptural images' (*plastische Bilder*) from 1961 to 1970, which included the insight that:

> ... art includes art and anti-art. The expression emerged as soon as musicians, painters and poets attacked non-art (Schwitters). For me, space and the inadequate, vague concept of time developed so far — our life between birth and death — calls for the exploration of counter space (*Gegenraum*), heat and time, the immortal essence of man and life after death. It depends on our insight in this context (anti-art) whether we obtain reliable possibilities for controls and measures concerning what we do in space and time.[8]

Despite all this, Beuys's *Gesamtkunstwerk* took a Christological, existentialist and emancipatory course via ego-consciousness to the education of the people, people as social beings, as sculpture.

The propulsive thrust of Element 3 aimed even higher. Beuys, whose own militancy propelled him forward at breakneck speed, founded the German Student Party on 22 June 1967, almost seven months after MANRESA. His inspiration was a modern incarnation of Loyola:

> A pale forehead, over which falls a shock of raven-black hair, a chin dotted with stubble, dark eyes alight with excitement under bushy brows, a wide-open mouth, deep-set into lean cheeks, as he gives a strained speech... The

revolution wears jumpers — loose-stitched knitwear in garish patterns. The coloured stripes across his chest and biceps indicate a rebel's attitude. His rolled-up sleeves suggest getting down to business. His upper body rocks back and forth as he delivers his speech. His fist is clenched, resting on the lectern, thumbs raised. His forearms: bent at the elbows, taking up space as is only expected in the choreography of a worker's cantata...

And when he speaks of revolution, he adopts a grim, shouting expression... He speaks in a strained, monotonous tone — a torpor-inducing litany if it weren't for the challenging thoughts. He speaks with artificial intonation and reveals the laborious work his tongue and brain have to do. He excessively emphasises the consonants, stretches vowels to the extreme: I-I-I- th-i-i-i-ink. What he thinks: revolution, counter-revolution, obstruction, production, reproduction, subsumption, integration, transformation, abstraction, repression, manifestation, manipulation.

Hardly anyone understands what he's saying, but he's the talk of Germany. On cue, tired parties become lively, lukewarm politicians loud. Someone who moves minds in such a way has become a rare thing in Germany. For months he has been the inspiration for leading articles in national newspapers: an 'anti-authoritarian anarchist' according to the *Süddeutsche Zeitung*, an 'ideological wandering preacher' according to *Die Zeit*, and a revolutionary boss man with a 'misanthropic chip on his shoulder' according to the *BZ* ... Some find him repellent; others, noble-minded... The *FAZ* identifies him as the conscience of extra-parliamentary opposition. His 'monk-like face' (*Die Zeit*) is seen with greater frequency on German screens. He's in demand... His performances — a mix of earthy proletarianism and highbrow sociology seminar — attract thousands of students to lecture halls in Frankfurt, Berlin and Hamburg. And the lively intellects in society which he wants to turn upside down, hurry to watch the

> spectacle with opera glasses. Fascinated and confused in equal measure, the audience gets whiff of a demagogic talent. He holds a bright promise: never before has the possibility of the Garden of Eden been 'so great' — the fantastic fulfilment of 'humanity's' age-old dream. His goal: 'We want a conscious, mature society'.[9]

This is a childlike vision of an Elysium without bureaucracy and military, without war and misery — the eternal longing for an ideal world. Now, in a highly industrialised world, it can be fulfilled at last, as long as the people disempower the powerful ('the deconstruction of people's domination over each other'), as long as the 'system of manipulation' is broken by direct action and provocation ('the unmasking of authoritarian structures'), as long as people become aware of themselves and their historical possibilities: 'The material conditions for the feasibility of our history exist.'

This is why he radically rejects everything that exists: the political parties (which for him do not represent the true interests of the population), the entire parliamentary system (which for him is a mere stock exchange of interests), universities (which in their current form are for him merely poorly rationalised factories for the production of narrow-minded boffins), the economic system, the press and every other institution that 'manipulates' citizens. He demands better people, who are aware of themselves and their possibilities (...) He has discovered the philosophy of his own movement in a Marxism imbued with religious overtones and eschatological goals. His vocabulary gives it away. He hardly ever describes conditions; instead, almost always movement. This involves 'transformation', 'manipulation', 'centring', 'tending', 'making impossible', 'unsettling', 'targeting' and 'revolutionising'.

Reality only appears as a place of transition: as a 'point of process' perceived in passing, a moment in a process — for example, the 'process of becoming conscious'. Although the German Federal Republic's 'state capitalism' is not yet authoritarian, it 'tends' to be. The elimination of student opposition has not yet taken place, but there is, paradoxically, a 'tendency towards elimination'. Although the Federal

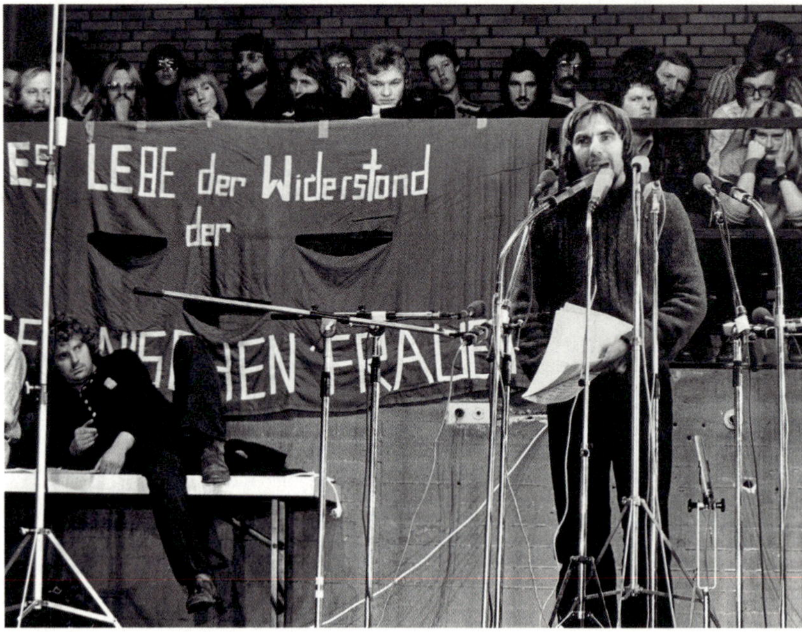

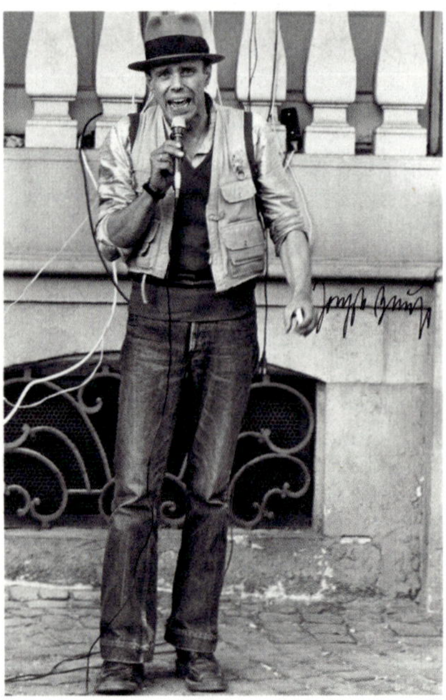

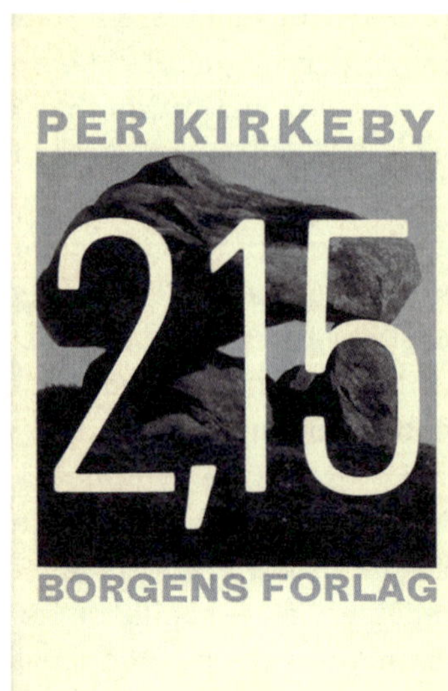

E Rudi Dutschke in a rally against the Franco dictatorship, October 1975.

F Joseph Beuys in an event of the Free International University (FIU), documenta 6, Kassel, 1977.

G Cover of the book *2.15*, by Per Kirkeby, 1965.

Republic of Germany is not yet an 'authoritarian state', it is 'an authoritarian state in the way it wants to assert itself in the years to come.'

The fact that the world and its conditions are mobile, plastic and malleable is one of the basic truths of Marxism as well as Western technology and empiricism. But he turns facts into hypotheses — and hypotheses into absolute truths. He sees the 'feasibility of the historical process' as infinite. Interpreting Marx's 'classless society' as a final state of history is, for him, a 'misunderstanding'. On the contrary, it should be seen as a state in continual flux, of continuous replacement, election and defeat of all leaders, and all 'councils'.

> If it is possible to achieve the total enslavement of today's labour force — dead costs, unused capacities, etc. — it is possible to eliminate this enslavement and, within a few years, perhaps a decade, develop a labour force for production that makes automation the dominant reality of industrialised countries. This is the key to the reduction of work time, the liberation of humankind, its re-sexualisation, and the development of individuality.[10]

This is not a portrait of Beuys, nor are they his demands. This is clear, not only because of the absence of the hat in the descriptions; reams could also be written on the differences between Beuys's position and the above regarding the reality of the revolution and Marxist analysis. A few days before MANRESA, in November 1966, Rudi Dutschke (1940–1979), who is described here so vividly, made his first public speech against the German grand coalition government and became the embodiment and leader of the German student revolution overnight.

Beuys did not meet Dutschke until 1977, but he was familiar with his activities from the turn of 1966/67. He admired Dutschke's anti-authoritarian actions and way of thinking, his activities governed by Rosa Luxemburg's maxim that 'freedom is always the freedom of the dissenter', in which he found his own 'unity in diversity', which implied non-violence and thus the 'long march' towards awareness.

Before we return to this modern Loyola, I would like to draw attention to another chapter that took place in Spain. In bold anticipation, before he had actually met Beuys, the Danish artist Per Kirkeby published his first novel in Copenhagen in early 1966 with the title *2.15*, in which he described Beuys's fictional death in Spain:

> My wife and I went on a summer holiday to Spain with Beuys and his wife. It was in southern Spain, inland, far from any water, in the middle of extensive vineyards with dry and crumbling earth. It was a strangely dusty landscape shimmering with heat. We stayed with some winegrowers who had rented us a farm consisting of a huge complex of different buildings, some of which had either partially or completely fallen into disrepair. The owners, two winegrowers, had moved to the adjacent tract, although, as I said, it was difficult to distinguish the individual parts of these outbuildings. Beuys was in very bad shape because of a chest condition, which is why we had gone here. One day I went to the nearest provincial town and was present during a conversation between the local doctor whom Beuys had consulted and our two winegrowers, who were always together. The doctor said to one of them that if his wife continued to use this device, it could have very harmful consequences for the stranger.
>
> Far from all the houses, far out in the misty and dusty landscape, they had pitched a large tent. One such as Roman generals might inhabit in films for the big screen. Here lay Beuys dying. They were probably afraid of infection. Far away from the tent the winegrowers stood with their wives. One woman was crying and screaming so much that the small group near the tent could hear her: Beuys, who was almost blind, my wife, who had been sobbing for days, and myself. Beuys was lying in the tent with his head more or less outside, as one of the walls of the tent had been opened. His whole body was covered with a sheet, his head partially covered with a paper bag with holes for the eyes, his whole lower face ravaged by the disease, so that only his teeth in his upper jaw, the skin stretched

> tightly across it, stood out. In his mouth were five or six cigars, because he certainly loved cigars. Using only his eyes, he appealed to his wife to come over and raised his head so that she could put her hand underneath it. This was his last act of love.
>
> He said to me with a strange sound, that came from a place at the back of his throat, that his artistic life had been shorter than we had thought, less than a year, and that he was leaving, horrified and paralysed at his fate.[11]

It was the year of the MANRESA action. And, after reading Kirkeby's lines prophesying his illness, Beuys noted in his text *Life Course = Work Course*: 'It is 1966 and this is the end of Beuys's. In fact, it was a very Spanish year for Beuys, who from then on concentrated his energies on Germany: the political, public Beuys was born in 1967.

Moved and stricken by the death of the student Benno Ohnesorg during the anti-Shah demonstration in Berlin on 2 June 1967 and influenced by Rudi Dutschke's body of ideas, which were causing a public stir — the theory of a society of free creative people beyond the violence inherent in the late capitalist system — Beuys was driven to action.

Since students were the driving revolutionary force against the widespread paternalism of thought, he named his German Student Party after this minority driving for change. Filled with the desire to apply his 'expanded definition of art' in a non-violent way as an artistic concept to all humans, he aimed to provide a political platform for student discontent, which he considered justified, and carry out anti-authoritarian 'energy and thought work' for them.

On 22 June 1967 at 4 p.m., due to the ban on public assembly in the institution, the founding of the German Student Party took place on the green in front of the Kunstakademie Düsseldorf. The charter of the new party, whose founders were Joseph Beuys, Bazon Brock and Johannes Stüttgen, was the 'education of all humans towards spiritual maturity'.

As the real basis of its work, the party acknowledged the human rights enshrined in the German constitution in their pure form as being capable of positive, organic-evolutionary transformation. It was an 'educational party' in response to the threat of a general, materialistically oriented, economic and political tendency towards centralisation. The party advocated for the justified feelings of students and all people, because 'each person who is aware of their development and infinite work is a student'. Beuys called for the 'self-governance of autonomous entities such as law, culture and economy'. Only in this way 'would these social sectors be truly operable in relation to each other and, once truly separated, would achieve their essential goal of global effectiveness'. The majority vote, when applied to the election of qualified professionals was, in his opinion, absurd: 'This is in no way incompatible with the idea of a genuine democracy, since democracy means, after all, the genuine, mature, responsible cooperation of all people and — if reduced to purely quantitative, numerical terms — becomes absurd'. Furthermore, his party was in favour of 'cutting back nationalist interests', in other words, against any form of egotism. He also called for complete 'disarmament: the "balance" between world powers does not mean peace (...) but instead a highly anachronistic feat of acrobatics on a keg of dynamite.' Consequently, the party represented conscientious objectors. It was in favour of intellectual reality as an ideological struggle. Every party member would allegedly become greater in their human commitment — a strong, spiritual weapon. The party was therefore against the German Emergency Acts (passed on 30 May 1968). It was in favour of the unity of Europe, and in favour of the world not as a utopia but 'as a reality, and for the end of the East's dependence on the West'. It was committed to:

> the development of new perspectives in teaching, education and research as a foundation for the world economy, world law and world culture. Art, by its nature, is the force that drives away the dilemma, lunacy and schizophrenia of the time, expelling cold and paralysis; its effect, of which all people are capable and must be made capable — all people are artists! — is the real basis for genuine healing and development in all areas of human activity, for progress and intensity in science, technology, in skilled professions

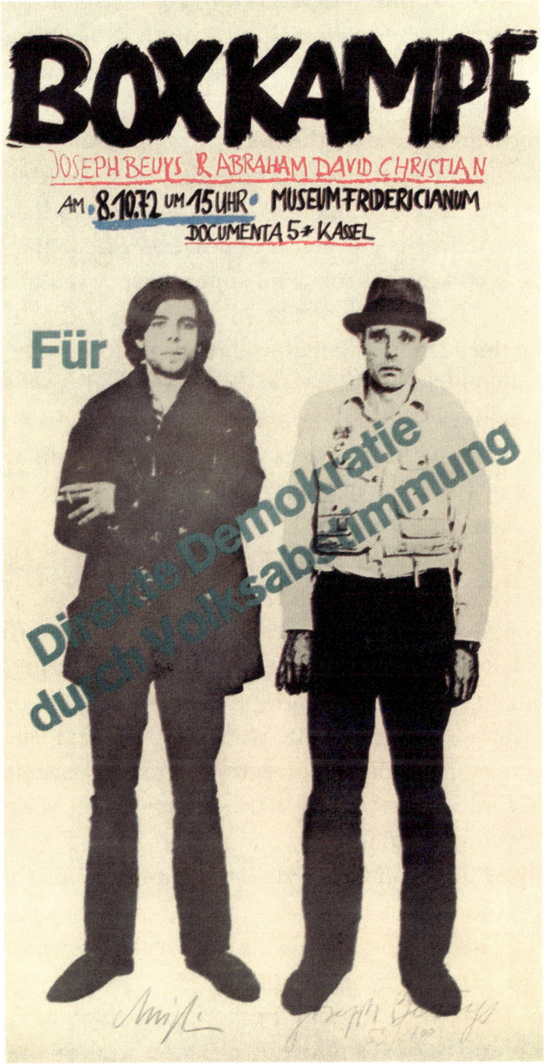

H Beuys Boxes for Direct Democracy, at documenta 5, Kassel, 1972.

> and everyday work. This of course results in a fundamental change in the school and higher education system. The party fights against the restoration of the German education system and the influence of foreign powers on schools.

An essential part of the programme was therefore its constant expansion and concentration, and intensification through differentiation. Human thought and action, which are principally artistic, had to achieve an appropriate awareness. The reality of freedom was proven in the possibilities created and offered by the material. This was — according to Beuys — existence on earth. New forms should be created by being formed; people created everything. It was the party's religious mission to raise awareness in this area. Beuys pointed out the significance of the difference between the sensory and supersensory realms: understanding this was people's greatest desire. All human spiritual information would need a material medium: material required form, after all, to be a medium. Between birth and death — both essential stages in shaping human development — humans had common work to do on Earth. And so, the party would also address the question of life after death, knowledge of which was the natural right and need of every person and everyone's natural duty to work towards.

The connection between Western and Eastern spiritual transmissions, and principles of heat and coldness were particularly important (e.g. in the concepts of Eurasia, incarnation and Element 3); to achieve this confluence (*Hauptstrom*), Germany was the appropriate starting point, not least due to its geographical position, which was not to be considered accidental or beyond a spiritual context, but which was the case for a reason. Such considerations were not occult fantasies or sectarian esotericism, but rather the real inspection of existing material, which was connected to everyone's origins and future.

The party, which was in favour of 'the realisation of a genuinely Christian world' could therefore be elected by everyone, and everyone was invited to participate. Beuys designed a stamp for the German Student Party with a cross, Earth/sun and imperial orb.

German Student Party meetings and discussions also took place in 1968 at the University of Education in Essen and at the

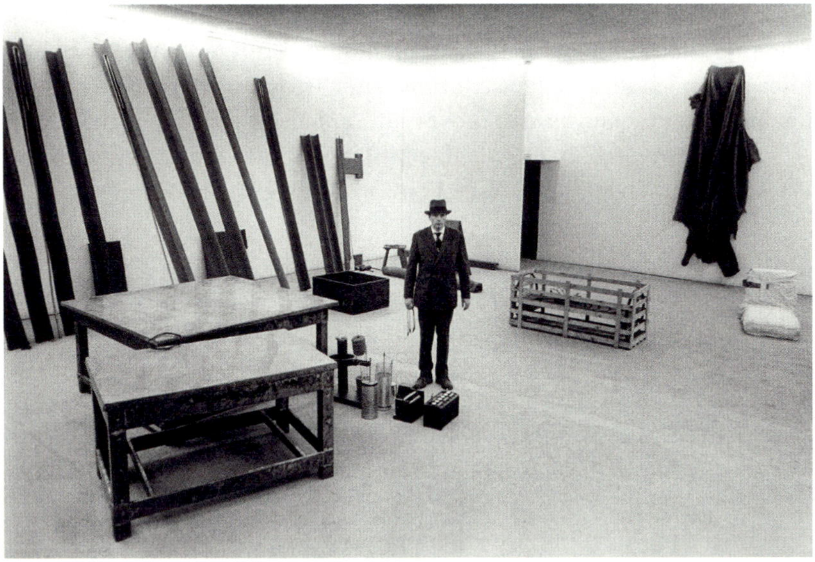

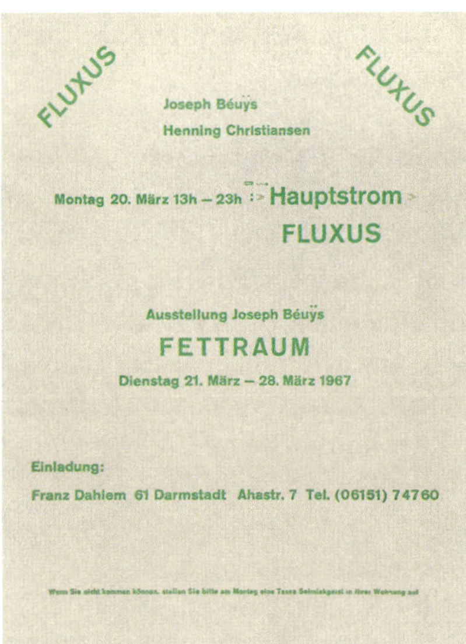

FLUXUS FLUXUS

Joseph Beuys
Henning Christiansen

Montag 20. März 13h – 23h Hauptstrom
FLUXUS

Ausstellung Joseph Beuys
FETTRAUM
Dienstag 21. März – 28. März 1967

Einladung:
Franz Dahlem 61 Darmstadt Ahastr. 7 Tel. (06151) 74760

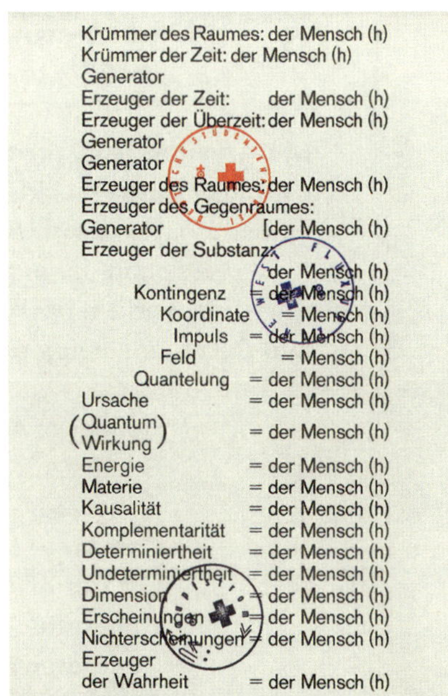

Krümmer des Raumes: der Mensch (h)
Krümmer der Zeit: der Mensch (h)
Generator
Erzeuger der Zeit: der Mensch (h)
Erzeuger der Überzeit: der Mensch (h)
Generator
Generator
Erzeuger des Raumes: der Mensch (h)
Erzeuger des Gegenraumes:
Generator [der Mensch (h)
Erzeuger der Substanz:
der Mensch (h)
Kontingenz = der Mensch (h)
Koordinate = Mensch (h)
Impuls = der Mensch (h)
Feld = Mensch (h)
Quantelung = der Mensch (h)
Ursache = der Mensch (h)
(Quantum Wirkung) = der Mensch (h)
Energie = der Mensch (h)
Materie = der Mensch (h)
Kausalität = der Mensch (h)
Komplementarität = der Mensch (h)
Determiniertheit = der Mensch (h)
Undeterminiertheit = der Mensch (h)
Dimension = der Mensch (h)
Erscheinungen = der Mensch (h)
Nichterscheinungen = der Mensch (h)
Erzeuger
der Wahrheit = der Mensch (h)

I Components used for the actions MANRESA and *Hauptstrom*, amongst others, reconfigured for the installation *Fond II*, documenta 4, Kassel, 1968.

J Invitation to the action *Hauptstrom* in Galerie Franz Dahlem, Darmstadt, 1967.

K Cover of the catalogue to *Krümmer des Raums: der Mensch (h)*... by Joseph Beuys, Kunstmuseum Basel, 1969, with the stamp of the German Student Party, *Fluxus Zone West* and *Hauptstrom*.

Göttingen Centre as 'actions' and discussions with Joseph Beuys, Henning Christiansen (music), and Johannes Stüttgen and Strotmann (discussion leaders). The invitation read: 'Be the missing thing itself/ and fill in for it!/The human is everything/has everything/is the future'.

On November 24 1968, nine professors from the Kunstakademie Düsseldorf published a manifesto of no confidence in Beuys, citing:

> [...] presumptuous political dilettantism, addiction to ideological paternalism, demagogic practice and — in its wake — intolerance, defamation and non-collegial behaviour aim to disrupt the present order, and interfere with artistic and educational areas. With the help of the German Student Party, of which he is the founder, Joseph Beuys has exerted a questionable influence on the reform movement at our university. The student council (...) is increasingly falling prey to utopian and anarchist arguments and is becoming the mouthpiece of this ideology. Conferences turn into pseudo-political gossip and provocative criticism which grow into unrealistic demands, and expose open hostility to parliamentary democracy.

In December 1968, the German Student Party, a meta party, 'the largest party in the world, of which most members are animals', was renamed *Fluxus Zone West*.[12]

Eurasia, incarnation, Element 3, *Hauptstrom*; a genuinely Christian world, a party that addresses the question of life after death, and the human being as a total work of art; after all, he is, for Beuys:[13]

Bender of space:	the human being (h)
Bender of time:	the human being (h)
Generator	
Creator of time:	the human being (h)
Creator of 'overtime':	the human being (h)
Generator	
Generator	
Creator of space:	the human being (h)

Creator of 'counter space':	
Generator	[the human being (h)
Creator of substance:	
	the human being (h)
Contingency	= the human being (h)
Coordinate	= human (h)
Impulse	= the human being (h)
Field	= human (h)
Quantisation	= the human being (h)
Cause	= the human being (h)
(Quantum Effect)	= the human being (h)
Energy	= the human being (h)
Material	= the human being (h)
Causality	= the human being (h)
Complementarity	= the human being (h)
Determination	= the human being (h)
Non-determination	= the human being (h)
Dimension	= the human being (h)
Appearances	= the human being (h)
Non-appearances	= the human being (h)
Creator of truth	= the human being (h)

The question 'Where is Element 3?' filled the entire MANRESA action. It was a call to go on a journey of self-discovery, extended by the public act of founding a party of like-minded people and apostles: the comparison to the apostles immediately comes to mind, as well as the foundation of the Order of Ignatius of Loyola. Element 3 becomes a way of overcoming 'The Division of the Cross', first in the individual, then in others through 'social sculpture'. The 'Christ impulse' (Steiner) is personified in each individual and becomes a living example for fellow humans. Beuys, who had already become a university lecturer, became a teacher of the people; Christian references and iconography became rarer in his work. They merged into his energy equations, whereby drawings became instructions on blackboards; provocation, demonstration and 'actions' became coherent discourse.

Sculpture evolved into *Fond* (material, primary material, battery, storage), *Grond* emerged as multi-layered, fundamental statements in space; words became sculpture, music became sculpture, and multisensory experiences were fed by blood circulating through the central organ, which was no longer just a mechanical pump. But all this was always imbued with a spiritual conviction: 'that there was no other certainty for humanity than to put itself into the role of Christ'[14] — the 'Ignatius Impulse' had now become part of thinking. The rite of passage followed the act. And it was only then that the concept of the *Gesamtkunstwerk* appeared in Beuys's vocabulary — only after the implementation of the breakdown of society into three parts to form the action of life, which he formulated before Rudi Dutschke in a rudimentary way in his lecture *Journey into a Living Being*, (1977): 'I want to try to reconcile three different things: the concept of the living being, that of the revolutionary and that of social sculpture'.[15]

This was the idea of a new, spiritually free person without ideologies blinkering their view and blocking the path to reality. This was a concept of art that co-revolutionised the bourgeois concept of science (materialism, positivism) and which has now become historical just like the religiously active sage. 'Everyone is an artist' who learns from their freedom (because that is the position of freedom which they experience directly) to determine the other position in the *Gesamtkunstwerk* of the Future Organisation of Society. Self-determination and participation in the cultural sphere (freedom), legal structure (democracy) and economic sphere (socialism) exists. Self-government and divestiture (three-part structure) exist as well as Free Democratic Socialism,[16] and:

> I contend that the term 'social sculpture' is a whole new category of art. A new muse is emerging alongside the old muses. This muse was previously unknown, and because it was unknown, well-known errors in thinking have occurred; now the situation has become so critical that some spirits have set out to discover this muse. It carries the future concept of sculpture, which takes precedence over any other concept of sculpture.[17]

In MANRESA, Beuys screams: 'WHERE IS ELEMENT 3?'

Here, too, he screams: 'I even scream: there will be no more usable sculpture if the social organism is not present in the form of living beings. This is the idea of the *Gesamtkunstwerk* in which everyone is an artist.'[18]

Beuys's vision is fused with the original vision of Richard Wagner's *Gesamtkunstwerk*. Both wanted not only the aesthetic union of the arts, but also a new community of individuals, masses and peoples. 'In this work of art, we will be one': this is the people's new capital. In the magnetic field of Beuys's shaping of reality we find: Ignatius' spiritual exercises, Rudi Dutschke's practiced revolutionary spirit and the lived dissolution of the discrepancy between art and anti-art against the backdrop of the cathartic message of the opera in fellow actors, inspirations, role models for a permanent demand to dissolve the boundaries of various artistic fields, as well as between art and life. In six months, Beuys underwent a change from ego-fulfilled spirituality to humanity, to the anthropological dimension: 'So let us change human nature'.[19] MANRESA is part of his will and imagination turned into a *Gesamtkunstwerk*. Element 3 had become articulated energy and spirit.

This text was written in 1994 for the exhibition catalogue *Manresa Hauptbahnhof*, published in Catalan and German.

1
Theophrast von Hohenheim, genannt Paracelsus. *Schriften*, Leipzig: Insel, 1924, p. 472, translated in Walter Pagel, *Paracelsus. An Introduction to Philosophical Medicine in the Era of the Renaissance*, Basel and New York: S. Karger, 1958.

2
Uwe M. Schneede, *Joseph Beuys. Die Aktionen*, Stuttgart: Hatje Cantz, 1993, p. 152.

3
See Schneede, *Joseph Beuys. Die Aktionen*, p. 154, and Friedhelm Mennekes, *Joseph Beuys. MANRESA*, Frankfurt am Main and Leipzig: Insel Verlag, 1992, p. 113f; Heiner Bastian, *Joseph Beuys. Blitzschlag mit Lichtschein auf Hirsch*, Bern: Benteli Verlag, 1986, p. 18.

4
Magnus Hirschfeld and Richard Linsert. *Liebesmittel/Eine Darstellung der geschlechtlichen Reizmittel (Aphrodisiaca)*, Berlin: Man Verlag, 1930, p. 199.

5
Schneede, *Joseph Beuys: Die Aktionen*, p. 148.

6
Schneede, *Joseph Beuys: Die Aktionen*, p. 154; Mennekes, *Joseph Beuys. MANRESA*, p. 113; Bastian, *Blitzschlag*, p. 18.

7
Hans Richter, *Dada – Kunst und Anti-Kunst*, Cologne: M. Dumont Schauberg, 1964, p. 156.

8
Joseph Beuys, 'Krawall in Aachen', 1964, in *Joseph Beuys, Werke aus der Sammlung Karl Ströher*, Kunstmuseum Basel, 1969, p. 12. Cited in Harald Szeemann (ed.), *Der Hang zum Gesamtkunstwerk*, abbreviated from here below to *GKW*, Aarau/Frankfurt am Main: Sauerländer, 1983, p. 422.

9
'Der Lange Marsch' in *Studenten/ Dutschke* [online], *Der Spiegel*, 51, 1967. www.spiegel.de/spiegel/print/d-46209544.html [access: 20 October 2020].

10
Idem.

11
Joseph Beuys, *Werke aus der Sammlung Karl Ströher*, Kunstmuseum Basel, 1969, p. 9 [Exh. cat.].

12
Harald Szeemann, 'Deutsche Studentenpartei', in *Joseph Beuys*, Kunsthaus Zürich, 1993, p. 249.

13
Kunstmuseum Basel, 1969 [Exh. cat.], cover.

14
Dialogue between Joseph Beuys and Elisabeth Pfister (German/English), in Friedhelm Mennekes, 'Homily on Beuys's, in *Beuys zu Christus/ Beuys on Christ*, Stuttgart: Verlach Katholisches Bibelwerk, 1992, p. 125.

15
Joseph Beuys, 'Eintritt in ein Lebewesen', 1977, in *GKW*, p. 424.

16
Joseph Beuys, *Ich durchsuche Feldcharakter*, 1976 in *GKW*, p. 424.

17
Joseph Beuys, *+ – WURST*, in *Zeitgeist*, [Exh. cat.] Berlin 1982, no page number; and *GKW*, p. 426.

18
Idem.

19
Joseph Beuys. Zeichnungen I (Drawings I), Cologne, 1972, in *GKW*, p. 426.

KLAUS-D. POHL

MANRESA, LANGUAGE AND THE ELEMENT OF MOVEMENT:

ON JOSEPH BEUYS'S ROLE IN THE FLUXUS MOVEMENT

THE MANRESA ACTION began with a playback of a voice recording by Joseph Beuys, which opened, according to the score, with the following sentences (originally in German): 'This is Fluxus speaking/ /Fluxus ¶ This is Fluxus speaking/ /Fluxus.' As the placement and tone make clear, this is not merely an ordinary introduction, but a headline that will shape the score and therefore the action. Moreover, the duplications — of the word 'Fluxus' in said headline, of the entire sentence in the recording, and of the recording itself, which was played back multiple times during the proceedings — give it an emphasis that is not merely semantic, but that permeates the senses. The same holds for other sentences in the score, just as the incessant repetition of specific acts constitutes a key element of a Beuysian action. Still, the opening sentences take on a character of their own, as a strongly appellative self-representation and a demonstrative semantic declaration of place. The message of the ensuing sentences and acts seems intended, without question, to elicit an emphatic, unambiguous effect: 'This is Fluxus [as personified by

Joseph Beuys, Henning Christiansen and Bjørn Nørgaard] speaking [at the location of this action] / /Fluxus [an artistic/art-theoretical movement].' Fluxus is making an appearance in space, in time and in person. Fluxus has something to tell us. Fluxus is real.

The Fluxus movement and its connection to Joseph Beuys have been explored and interpreted many times in the literature. The MANRESA action has already been described as explicitly connected to Fluxus, most recently by Friedhelm Mennekes and Uwe M. Schneede.[1] Yet more than any of his other actions of the 1960s, this one exceptionally showcases Fluxus. Fluxus is an incisive aspect of the MANRESA action. The movement therefore merits more elaboration and description with regard to the intersections, particularly against the backdrop of an exhibition that links the spirit of a place with a reappearance by the Fluxus actionists Henning Christiansen and Bjørn Nørgaard, who originally participated in MANRESA.

I

The Fluxus movement was officially born in 1962. Years earlier, its foundations had been laid in the context of contemporary music, spearheaded and set in motion (or rather in movement) by John Cage. His seminars in experimental composition and performance at the New School for Social Research in New York, from 1956 to 1960, and his lectures at the Internationale Ferienkurse für Neue Musik (International Summer School for New Music) in Darmstadt, Germany, brought together the same artists who would go on to represent the Fluxus movement from 1962 onward. Cage's New York students, including George Brecht, Al Hansen, Dick Higgins, Allan Kaprow, Jackson MacLow, La Monte Young and Richard Maxfield, made up the core of the Fluxus movement. In Europe, primarily inspired by the Darmstadt Summer School, they were joined by Henning Christiansen, Eric Andersen and Nam June Paik. Finally, in the spring of 1961, George Maciunas, who was a graphic designer and a New York gallerist, became part of the American contingent. Eager with excitement, he began organising various concert series, exhibitions and lectures featuring the artists. In 1961–62, as a designer for the US Army, he was stationed in Wiesbaden,

Germany. From there he organised Fluxus concerts around Europe, which grew into the legendary Internationale Festspiele Neuester Musik (International Festival of Newest Music). Thus, from 1962 on, the Fluxus movement was centred in Germany. Thanks to the Lithuanian-born Maciunas, Wiesbaden became its base of activities. Maciunas positioned himself as the movement's chief organiser, while Dick Higgins, George Brecht, and others followed him to Germany. He hoped to arrange the Fluxus concerts as world tours and to distribute the artists' works around the world in Fluxus Editions — a global network of a new subversive world art, comprising sounds, words, images and actions. Yet the Fluxus artists — who ultimately included the aforementioned names as well as Ben Patterson, Emmett Williams, Charlotte Moorman, Bazon Brock, Robert Filliou, Arthur Köpcke, Thomas Schmit, Daniel Spoerri, Ben Vautier and Wolf Vostell — never viewed themselves as a clearly structured group armed with agendas or manifestos. In fact, they rejected any efforts to formalise or theorise their work. Thus, what began in 1962 with Maciunas' near-obsessive devotion ended just as quickly, in 1964, with the artists parting ways. The breakup did not imply that the individual artists' works lost their Fluxus characteristics. Quite the contrary. Up to the late eighties, many of the movements' artists held true to them in their actions. The movement's lasting impact, extending to the present, has only recently been rediscovered.[2]

What was Fluxus? The name was devised by George Maciunas, originally as the title for a planned magazine in which to publish works by the aforementioned American artists from the New School for Social Research. Fluxus (from the Latin *fluere*, to flow) sought to express an artistic stance in the Dada tradition that challenged ossified art forms and their modes of both presentation and reception. It was to be flexibly structured, 'a loose and open thing. The audience puts it together the way it wishes or not at all'.[3] Building upon John Cage's expansion of music to include everyday noises, tones and sounds beyond those of conventional instruments and the subsequent breakdown of the traditional musical score with the inclusion of subjective instructions and symbols, a Fluxus action was usually performed by several participants at once and constituted an all-encompassing event combining music (noises), theatrical elements, integrated media and visual art displays.

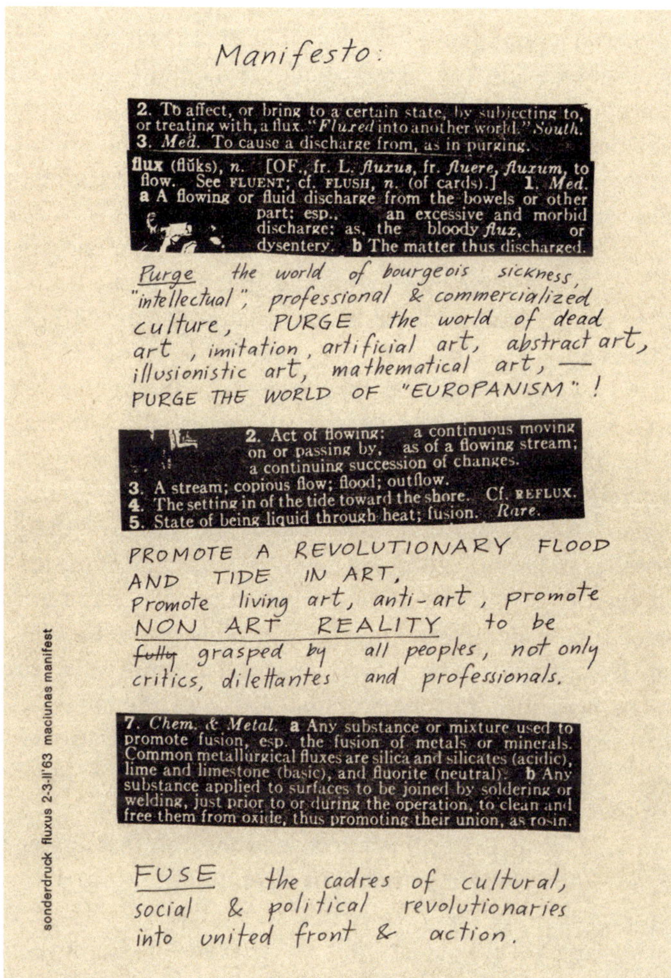

Manifesto:

2. To affect, or bring to a certain state, by subjecting to, or treating with, a flux. "*Fluxed* into another world." *South.*
3. *Med.* To cause a discharge from, as in purging.

flux (flŭks), *n.* [OF., fr. L. *fluxus*, fr. *fluere*, *fluxum*, to flow. See FLUENT; cf. FLUSH, *n.* (of cards).] **1.** *Med.* **a** A flowing or fluid discharge from the bowels or other part; esp., an excessive and morbid discharge; as, the bloody *flux*, or dysentery. **b** The matter thus discharged.

Purge the world of bourgeois sickness, "intellectual", professional & commercialized culture, PURGE the world of dead art, imitation, artificial art, abstract art, illusionistic art, mathematical art, — PURGE THE WORLD OF "EUROPANISM"!

2. Act of flowing: a continuous moving on or passing by, as of a flowing stream; a continuing succession of changes.
3. A stream; copious flow; flood; outflow.
4. The setting in of the tide toward the shore. Cf. REFLUX.
5. State of being liquid through heat; fusion. *Rare.*

PROMOTE A REVOLUTIONARY FLOOD AND TIDE IN ART, Promote living art, anti-art, promote NON ART REALITY to be ~~fully~~ grasped by all peoples, not only critics, dilettantes and professionals.

7. *Chem. & Metal.* **a** Any substance or mixture used to promote fusion, esp. the fusion of metals or minerals. Common metallurgical fluxes are silica and silicates (acidic), lime and limestone (basic), and fluorite (neutral). **b** Any substance applied to surfaces to be joined by soldering or welding, just prior to or during the operation, to clean and free them from oxide, thus promoting their union, as rosin.

FUSE the cadres of cultural, social & political revolutionaries into united front & action.

sonderdruck fluxus 2-3-II'63 maciunas manifest

A George Maciunas, Fluxus Manifesto, 1963.

The participants, materials and timeframes were predetermined, but during a given performance, the individual artists acted and reacted to one other spontaneously, so that the audience could always count on an unexpected and surprising sequence of episodes. In almost anarchic fashion, without a discernible beginning or end, absurd and ordinary elements collided — scraps of reality, associations, movement sequences, objects and sound — forming an overarching composition with no internal logic that was left at the mercy of happenstance and proffered without any symbolic value. In the end, this approach did not generate any kind of recognisable, self-contained and thus accurately reproducible product; the focus was on the process alone; the action was the aim. Performers and recipients were united at last in an 'extended aesthetic attitude'.[4] In the synthesis of ambiguity, concurrence and overt incoherence, they saw the prerequisites for a new type of creation: creation as a process without beginning or end.

The Fluxus movement was founded in the United States and later progressed and was elaborated in Europe. To plot its coordinates within art history, the movement integrated both Romantic and Dadaist theories of art. Natural growth as an open-ended, incomplete process — a notion articulated most prominently by Novalis during the Romantic period — finds some parallels in reflectivity and subjectivity, that is, in the human mind's creative force. Observing nature's process of becoming and decay, humans see mirrored their own embeddedness in the same process, but also their opportunities and, most of all, their freedom. Their knowledge is a revelation of nature, but at the same time it signifies a growing consciousness of their own inexhaustible living minds. The subject's natural and reflective processes converge in an 'infinite bounty of materials and phenomena'.[5] This bounty evokes the fragility of forms, identities and values. Hence, the process necessarily incorporates the destruction that limits any development, but that can also lead to renewal.

Fluxus actionists harnessed the cultural destructiveness of Dada — the Dadaist action had a genuinely anti-artistic (i.e., 'finite') character — as the vehicle of a new artistic method. Provocation — colliding absurd objects and procedures — is employed as a method of its own. They went about this, however, with a plan (per George

Maciunas's strategy) of globally expanding the definition of art. This was not a case of negating the idea of art altogether, as Marcel Duchamp had, but about liberating it — within art itself — from all restrictions or expectations, freeing it for an expanded perception of the living process in its complex interdependencies and, most of all, in its open-endedness. The dismantlement of ossified art forms would lead to 'resurrection', to new creations that gave both artist and audience expanded opportunities for reflection and sensory experiences. Art became process = movement = life.

II

Joseph Beuys immediately spotted the opportunities posed by the Fluxus movement for his own work. After his personal and artistic crisis of 1957–58, he had reached a critical juncture that compelled him to open up to the movement. His artistic evolution — previously expressed mostly in drawings and sculptural objects — had been continually anticipating his future motifs and his cultivation of a new definition of art. In 1961, when he was appointed professor at the Kunstakademie Düsseldorf, the position essentially catapulted him into the public sphere and obliged him to communicate. (He had so far been considered a rather introverted artist.) These combined factors led him almost inexorably to action art. 'All these actions were important in order to expand the old definition of art. To make it as broad, as big as possible, so that it can encompass every human activity.'[6] The Fluxus movement also allowed him to present existing works, many of them controversial, within a safe conceptual package. His second 'barn exhibition', hosted by his friend Hans van der Grinten and titled *Joseph Beuys Fluxus*, mostly consisted of objects, 'sculptural images' (*plastische Bilder*). He wrote the concept of Fluxus into the title. As Hans van der Grinten recalls, Beuys saw this as a 'liberating' opportunity. 'That enabled him to take objects that had already stirred great ire and, to a certain degree, rebaptise them'.[7] Two years before the exhibition, Beuys had first come into direct contact with Fluxus actionists. The matchmaker was the Korean-born Nam June Paik, whom he had met during the *Zero* exhibition at Schmela gallery in Düsseldorf.

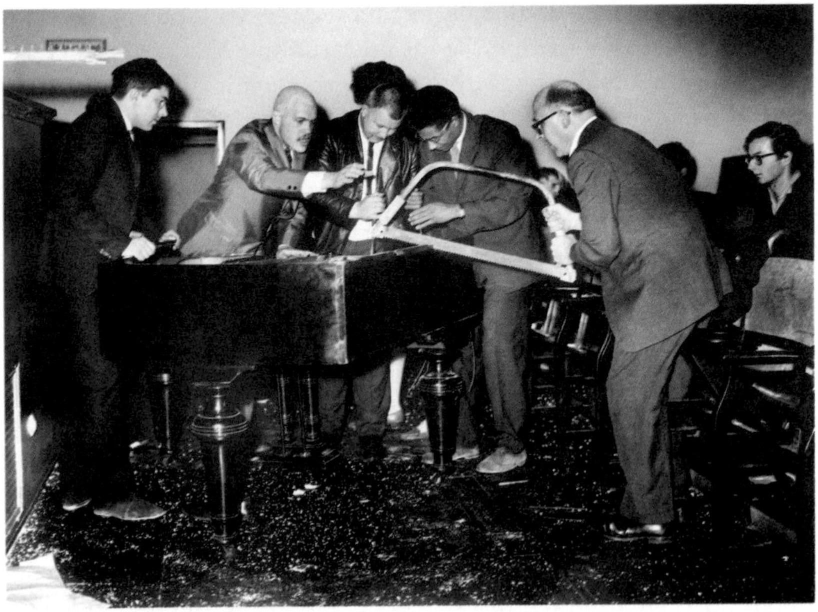

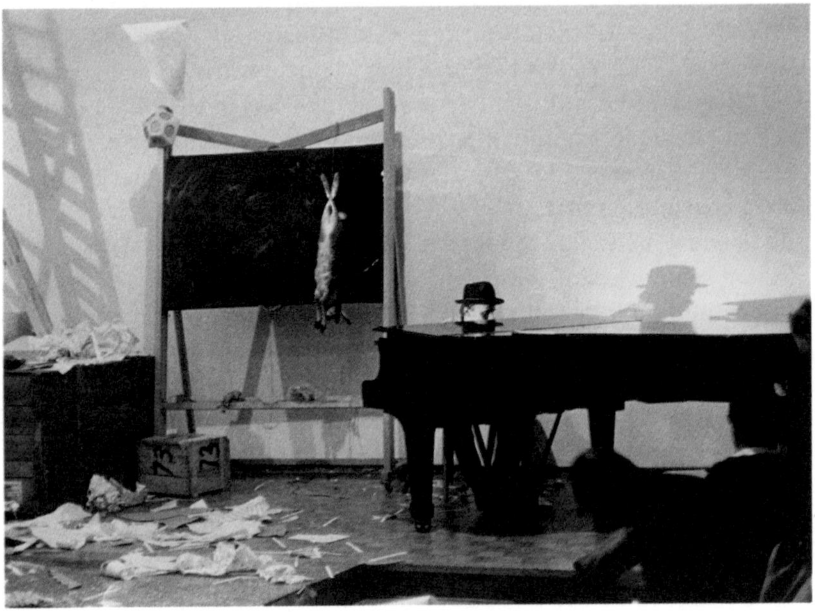

B George Maciunas, Dick Higgins, Wolf Vostell, Benjamin Patterson and Emmett Williams performing Phillip Corner's *Piano Activities*, at the Fluxus Internationale Festival of Newest Music, Wiesbaden, 1 September 1962.

C Beuys at the piano during the action *Siberian Symphony, First Movement*, at the Kunstakademie Düsseldorf (2 February 1963).

With the Fluxus actions of 1962 at Parnass gallery in Wuppertal (*Neo-Dada in New York*), at the Düsseldorf Kammerspiele (Düsseldorf Chamber Festival; *Neo-Dada in Music*) and finally at the four-weekend Fluxus festival titled *Fluxus: Internationale Festspiele Neuester Musik* (Fluxus International Festival of Newest Music) at the Städisches Museum in Wiesbaden, the Fluxus movement began making a name for itself in Germany. George Maciunas started collaborating with Joseph Beuys. In 1963, Maciunas put Beuys in charge of organising *Festum Fluxorum Fluxus – Music and Anti-music – The Instrumental Theatre* at the Kunstakademie Düsseldorf. Beuys struggled to persuade his colleagues at the art academy to give the festival the green light.

In performing among other Fluxus actionists, Beuys was entering a new stage in his own work: his actions. As part of this Fluxus festival, he performed *Siberian Symphony, First Movement* and *Composition for 2 Musicians*. A few months later, to coincide with the opening of Nam June Paik's *Exposition of Music – Electronic Television*, Beuys performed his *Piano-Action* at Wuppertal's Parnass gallery. In 1964, during the large-scale Fluxus festival *ACTIONS/AGIT-POP/DÉ-COLLAGE/HAPPENING/EVENTS/ANTI-ART/L'AUTRISME/ART TOTAL/REFLUXUS: A Festival of New Art* in Aachen, he presented the action *Kukei/akopee-No!/Brown Cross/ Fat Corners/Model Fat Corners*, which caused a sensation and established Beuys's name in the national West German media for the first time. Beuys was attacked by a visitor; his nose bloodied, he demonstratively held aloft a crucifix on a base of chocolate. The same year, in Copenhagen and at Berlin's René Block gallery, he performed his solo action *DER CHEF/THE CHIEF: Fluxus Song Berlin – New York, New York – Berlin*; he also performed the action *The Silence of Marcel Duchamp Is Overrated* at the North Rhine-Westphalia state television studio of public broadcasting channel ZDF. In 1965, at Parnass gallery in Wuppertal, he contributed to the group action *24 Hours* with his own action *and in us... beneath us... land under...* . That November he startled the audience with the action *How to Explain Pictures to a Dead Hare* at Düsseldorf's Schmela gallery on the occasion of the opening of his exhibition *Joseph Beuys ... Any Old*

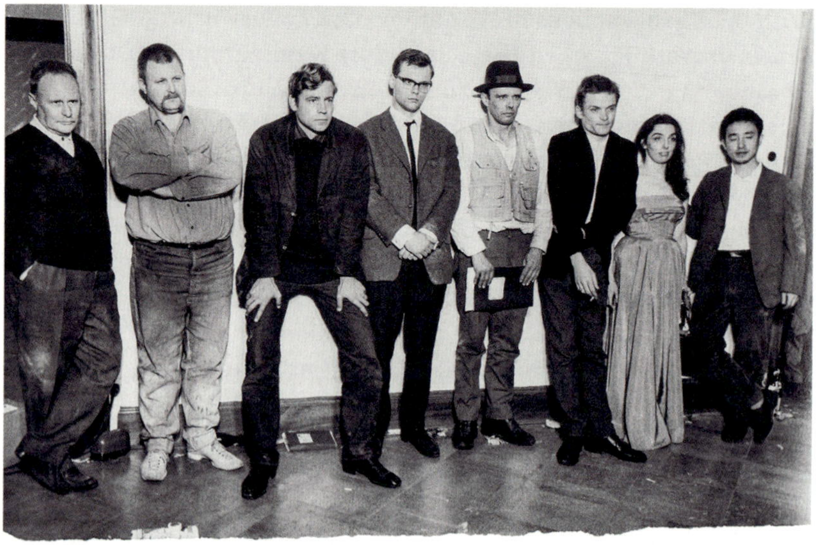

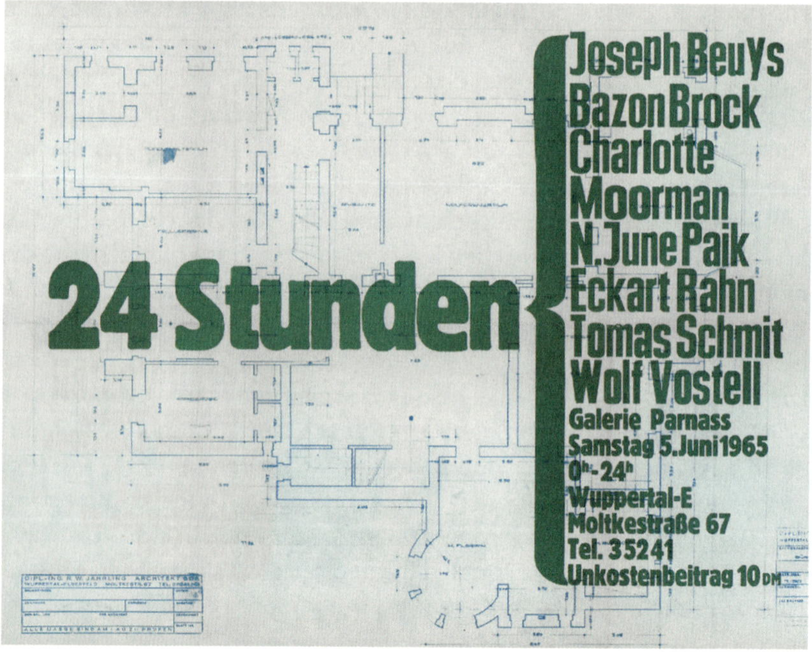

D Rolf Jährling, Wolf Vostell, Bazon Brock, Eckart Rahn, Joseph Beuys, Tomas Schmit, Charlotte Moorman and Nam June Paik in *24 Stunden* (24 Hours), Galerie Parnass, Wuppertal, 5 June 1965.

E Invitation to the group action *24 Hours*, Galerie Parnass, Wuppertal, 5 June 1965.

Noose/with Compliments from FLUXUS. In 1966, as part of a concert by Fluxus artists Charlotte Moorman and Nam June Paik, he proceeded with his next 'action', *Infiltration-Homogen for Grand Piano. The Greatest Contemporary Composer is the Thalidomide Child*. Still in 1966, at Galleri 101 in Copenhagen, Beuys presented the 'actions' *Eurasian Staff*, *Felt TV* and *Eurasia, 32nd Movement of the Siberian Symphony, 1963–Fluxus*. Finally, in December 1966, together with Henning Christiansen and Bjørn Nørgaard, Beuys presented MANRESA at Schmela gallery in Düsseldorf.

In the period leading up to this latter 'action', the relationship between Joseph Beuys and the Fluxus movement had altered significantly. His very first 'action', during the Düsseldorf Festival in 1963, had already featured deviations from typical Fluxus events that would have been noticeable to the other artists. In the words of Beuys, 'This was the first public Fluxus action. My very first. I can still clearly remember how totally surprised Dick Higgins looked; he had understood that this action had absolutely nothing to do with a Dadaistic concept. I believe he had perceived that it concerned itself with something possessing a totally different point of value.'[8] Whereas the Fluxus artists' actions were characterised by spontaneous episodes without particularly conscious semantic or iconographic/symbolic traits, Beuys conceived his action *Siberian Symphony, First Movement* from the outset as a specific procedure performed with dramaturgical precision and concentration using deliberately selected materials and objects that were imbued with meaning, such as lumps of clay (standing in for the material of fat) and a dead hare. These foreshadowed future 'actions' and demonstrated the continuity and concision of his artistic concept. This earnestness contrasted starkly with Maciunas' ideals for Fluxus art, which had the ultimate aim of eliminating so-called 'high art' in favour of an art that was fairly commonplace and could be popularly utilised and produced. (According to Maciunas' ideal vision, Fluxus works would be produced after regular working hours.)

Thus, in Beuys's first collaboration with Fluxus, it was already clear to him that, although he could harness this artistic movement's methods and infrastructure as a vehicle for reaching the public, he would have to accentuate the differences and distance from his own work. What intrigued him about Fluxus was the ease and flexibility of the means, the creative potential of small and seemingly banal objects, the creative energy of a certain dilettantism and the movement's interdisciplinarity, which ultimately could fuel the 'total changeover of human society'.[9] As an artistic method and a sensory representation, the Fluxus action embodied a principle focused on movement. Movement implies changing states, 'Origination and becoming, recognition and education, consciousness-forming and change — in short, all of existence — and to portray it as a sculptural process [*plastisches Prinzip*]'.[10] This conception was implicit in the sequence of a Fluxus action. In Beuys's mind, the actions 'had a value, because they made, along the way, conscious attempts to produce important development'.[11] Yet for Beuys, having an underlying theory beneath the actions was the essential prerequisite for any such further advancement: 'What they [the Fluxus artists] lacked was a real theory, a recognizable underlying structure with a clearly marked goal'.[12] With his own 'clearly marked goal', Beuys was already setting out to develop his 'own Fluxus concept independent of Dadaism or Neo-Dadaism'.[13] The same held equally true for his actions up to 1964, staged in close collaboration with the Fluxus actionists at festivals, and for those that he performed solo or with Henning Christiansen in the later 1960s and early 1970s. His 'prominent Fluxus demonstrations'[14] certainly included the MANRESA action.

III

By 1964, two years before MANRESA, when Beuys performed his action *DER CHEF/THE CHIEF: Fluxus Song*, in which he made sounds and noises while rolled up in felt, the key distinctions between his work and a typical Fluxus action were already coming into focus. There 'took place ... a distinct shift in Beuys's actionist work that pointed outside the direct Fluxus context'.[15] The MANRESA action, whose progression is described elsewhere in this catalogue, likewise exhibits these novel traits:

1. In its sense of time, the action at the Schmela gallery diverges from the Fluxus events, which were usually brief

and led to rapid climaxes. Both the objective and subjective temporalities — the latter manifesting among visitors primarily when they experienced the repetitions or the prolonged static sequences — tested the audience's patience.

2. The distance between performer and spectator was not eliminated — as was often the case with Fluxus — but was in fact distinctly enforced by a barrier in the narrow gallery space.
3. The materials and supplies were limited to the repeated application and use of the same recurring objects and materials, assigned different meanings.
4. Emotional aspects were largely absent from Fluxus. Beuys, however, made sensory and mental states explicit — suffering, crisis, sacrifice, but also pleasurable states — in acts and objects.
5. Accordingly, Beuysian actions had close links not only with his own charismatic personality, but also with biographical references, as has been expressly demonstrated in the case of MANRESA. Other Fluxus actions were abstracted from the artists' or performers' specific individuality.
6. Beuys ultimately viewed himself, his behaviour and his actions as demonstration models for a conceptual apparatus that he called his 'theory of sculpture' [*Plastische Theorie*]'.[16] The integrated texts, the meaningful materials and the meticulously planned procedures contributed to this. Their spiritual charge and mystification necessitated a kind of conceptual explanation that Fluxus had utterly devalued.

A defining feature of Fluxus events was provocativeness in the Neo-Dadaist sense. This was generally successful, but did not leave the spectator with any sense of onward direction. Provocation to what end? Beuys also used provocation as a fundamental artistic tool, but a tool for purposeful movement: 'Movement arises through a provocation, through an induction, through an initiation for the sake of movement. One evokes something, the principle of movement itself.'[17] The structure of the 'actions' and the selection of materials were oriented around this 'principle of movement' — that also holds for the MANRESA action. For Bjørn Nørgaard and Beuys alike, the action with its various behavioural strategies was palpably fixated on the element of movement. This must have been clear from Nørgaard's attempts to walk while encased in plaster, as with Beuys's activities moving between the high-frequency, high-voltage generator (Element 2) and the halved cross on the wall (Element 1). It would have been further underscored by the verbal reinforcement of the movement impulse in the voice recording. Perhaps it was clearer there than in other Beuys actions, even to an uninformed, uninitiated spectator. This was about the principle of movement.

Alongside various of Beuys's typical materials and demonstration objects, such as fat, felt, a hare, a bird and a cross, as well as physical processes such as electricity and light pulses, which illustrate principles of movement and form as synonymous with the Beuysian definition of art, the voice recording must be assigned an especially significant function for this action's didactics, a function that had not been present with such immediate clarity in his previous actions. Although Beuys had previously played audiotapes and recited fragments of text in his 1965 action *and in us... beneath us... land under*, the main text that was important for that action first appeared in the subsequent publication. Not until the action *Infiltration-Homogen for Grand Piano. The Greatest Contemporary Composer is the Thalidomide Child*, performed in July 1966 at the Kunstakademie Düsseldorf, did Beuys employ a school blackboard, previously introduced by the Fluxus artists, 'but now for the first time with the intention of directly integrating that conceptuality that, in his eyes, Fluxus had been lacking. This linguistic portion indicated the direction of the action, and at the same time communicated, through allusion, the conceptual context in which the action was meant to be seen...'.[18] Thanks to Henning Christiansen's collaboration, in the MANRESA action, that purposeful conceptualism — the text that Beuys recorded on tape and repeated various times during the action — attained prominent significance as an auditory element, a semantic focus and a didactic tool all at once.[19] The element of movement, made manifest in activity and material, was thus reinforced verbally. The questions (translated as) 'Now? Has Element 2 climbed up to Element 1? ¶ Now? Has Element 1 climbed down to Element 2?' in conjunction with the question Beuys frequently repeated, 'Where is Element 3?' are not only linguistic applications of the strands of activity. Above all, they indicate the direction of movement: movement between two elements that, for Beuys, correspond to the dichotomies between mind and matter, between spiritual and scientific principles. Yet the movement points beyond this dichotomy to another, yet unknown element that will annul this stubborn stand-off.

In stark contrast to Fluxus, language — or conceptuality — is an integral part of Beuys's artistic process, of his theory of sculpture: 'My path passed though language, peculiar as it is; it did not proceed from a so-called pictorial gift'.[20] As Beuys sees it, the sculptural process starts off with speech and thought, with setting the terms. The inner form of thought, in its immaterial appearance, is the prerequisite and origin of the creative process by way of the linguistic shaping to 'mark the material substance ... as it is present in the work'.[21] During the 1960s, drawing inspiration from James Joyce, Joseph Beuys would make his most poetic verbal statements, before he began emulating Rudolf Steiner's sermon-like style in the 1970s.

However, for Beuys, language always remained embedded in his artistic concept: he integrated all possible variations of it into his activities, or else it served as a comment and interpretation. Either way, he treated it as a 'parallel process' that was equivalent in value to the sensory form. Thus, it seems only logical that he incorporated language into his 'actions', into his own specific understanding and enactment of Fluxus, and that he even gave it pride of place. The sentence 'Here speaks Fluxus /   / Fluxus' therefore opens the sculptural process of the MANRESA action. He demonstrates the prerequisites for, and at the same time the existential possibility of, launching the movement of Element 3.

This text was written in 1994 for the exhibition catalogue *Manresa Hauptbahnhof*, published in Catalan and German.

1
See Friedhelm Mennekes, *Joseph Beuys: MANRESA – Eine Aktion als geistliche Übung zu Ignatius von Loyola*, Frankfurt am Main and Leipzig: Insel Verlag, 1992; Uwe M. Schneede, *Joseph Beuys: Die Aktionen*, Stuttgart: Hatje Cantz, 1993. Translations from both books by translator.

2
FLUXUS VIRUS 1962–1992, Cologne: Galerie Schüppenhauer, 1992 [Exh. cat.].

3
Robert Watts, quoted in John Held Jr., *Small Scale Subversion: Mail Art & Artistamps*, Breda, Netherlands: TAM Publishing, p. 92.

4
Johannes Meinhardt, 'Fluxus und Hauptstrom: Die Ausbildung der Sprache der Aktion bei Joseph Beuys', *Brennpunkt Düsseldorf 1962–1987*, Stephan von Wiese (ed.), Kunsthalle Düsseldorf, 1987, p. 31. [Exh. cat.]. Translation by translator.

5
Ibid., p. 32.

6
Joseph Beuys, quoted in Robert Filliou, *Lehren und Lernen als Aufführungskünste*, Cologne: Verlag Gebrüder König, 1970, p. 161. Translation by translator.

7
Thomas Kellein, 'FLUXUS – eine Internationale des künstlerischen Misslingens', *Europa/Amerika. Die Geschichte einer künstlerischen Faszination seit 1940*, Siegfried Gohr und Rafael Jablonka (eds.), Cologne: Museum Ludwig, 1986, p. 138. [Exh. cat.]. Translation by translator.

8
Joseph Beuys, quoted in Götz Adriani, Winfried Konnertz and Karin Thomas, *Joseph Beuys: Life and Works*, Patricia Lech (trans.), New York: Barron's Educational Series, 1979, p. 92.

9
Joseph Beuys, quoted in Adriani et al., *Joseph Beuys*, p. 79.

10
Adriani et al., *Joseph Beuys*, p. 94–95.

11
Joseph Beuys, quoted in Adriani et al., *Joseph Beuys*, p. 86.

12
Joseph Beuys, quoted in Adriani et al., *Joseph Beuys*, p. 86.

13
Joseph Beuys, quoted in Adriani et al., *Joseph Beuys*, p. 59.

14
Johannes Stüttgen, 'Fluxus', *Joseph Beuys*, Kunsthaus Zürich, 1993, p. 260 [Exh. cat.].

15
Schneede, *Joseph Beuys: Die Aktionen*, p. 73.

16
Ibid., p. 74.

17
Joseph Beuys, as quoted in Friedhelm Mennekes, *Joseph Beuys: MANRESA*, p. 65.

18
Schneede, *Joseph Beuys: Die Aktionen*, p. 114.

19
The spoken text would first be given central pride of place in the 1969 Frankfurt action *Titus/Iphigenia*, but by then without any explicit connection to Fluxus.

20
Joseph Beuys, as quoted in Kunsthaus Zürich, *Joseph Beuys* [Exh. cat.], p. 284.

21
Idem.

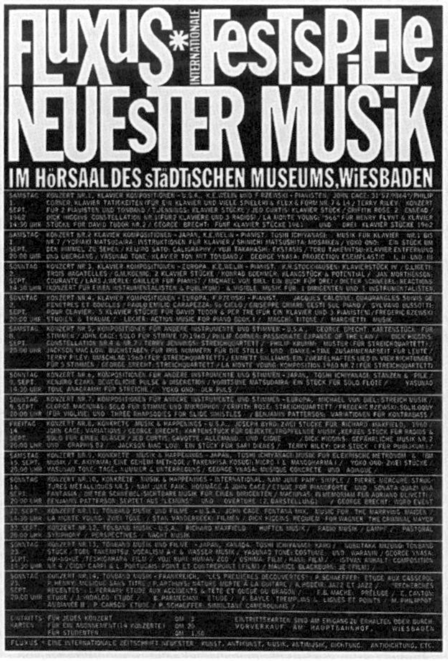

F Programme of the Fluxus International Festival of Newest Music, Wiesbaden, 1962.

PILAR PARCERISAS

'I AM FLYING TO YOU TOO, MANRESA'

'The Valley of Paradise'

MANRESA is part of the underlying mystical geography in the work of Joseph Beuys. Some of his actions from the 1960s could be considered 'travels, visits or incantations' of a ritual character, in proximity to the shamanistic techniques of ecstasy: 'They represent spiritual forays to points of cultural energy that a shaman might have "visited", thanks to his aptitude for magical flight.'[1]

There are three intimately-related actions which were done consecutively, respectively staging initiation journeys (*Eurasia*, 1966), incantations taking place in specific places (MANRESA, 1966) and those in larger territories (namely *Eurasian Staff*, 1967), in the quest for forces for the future.[2]

There is no doubt that the geographical site of Manresa has specific characteristics; in particular it is a focal point of energy, where the water running down the Cardener Valley intersects with the light of Montserrat, the sacred mountain that irradiates in a way that enlivens intuition, to the point of arousing illuminations of a great capacity; there are historical examples of this which have altered the conception of the world. For those of us who were born here, in Manresa, we have always felt that it was like living in a universal centre point.

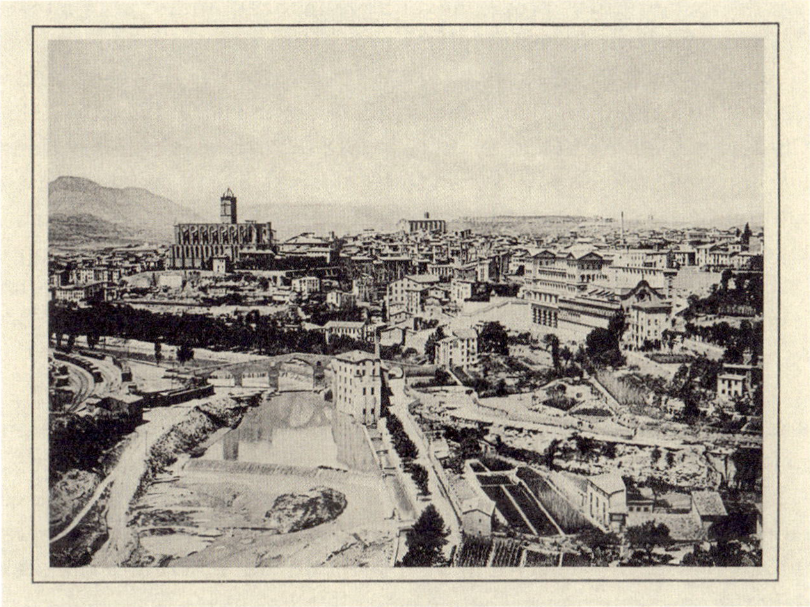

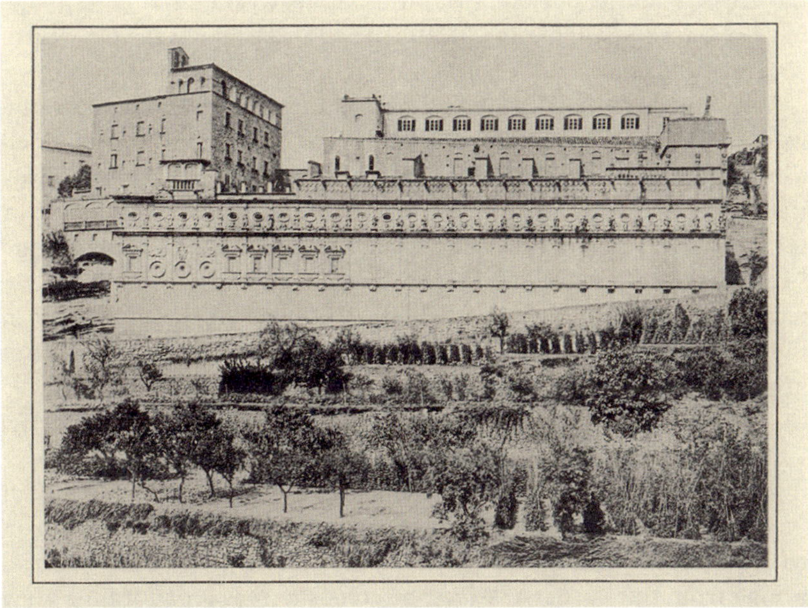

A Manresa, banks of the Cardener River, early 20th century.

Joseph Beuys would never have invoked Manresa in one of his actions of transformation if Saint Ignatius of Loyola had not conceived the draft for his *Spiritual Exercises* there, laying the foundations of his primitive Church during his 11-month stay in the city on the Cardener River. He had gone there in 1522–23 to heal after his serious war injuries, on the tail of a visit to Montserrat, where he had held an all-night vigil and changed his military apparel for the poor and austere clothing of the pilgrim. This would lead him to be known popularly as the *man in the sackcloth*: 'there came to the city of Manresa a man who had come down from Montserrat, dressed in sack-cloth or to say it plainly, sack, wrapped about him with thick cords.'[3]

In Manresa, Ignatius was transformed into a new man through a series of visions and the so-called Cardener Illumination, which 'made all things seem new to him.'[4] Saint Ignatius would not have chosen Manresa if it had not been one of those odd places where the vision of the Holy Trinity would occur right in front of him, at Tort Cross, a limit marker in the form of a cross found just in front of the residence of the same name. A stone medallion has been conserved from the cross from the period of Saint Ignatius, with its sculpted image of Christ accompanying the Jesuits of centuries ago in the Holy Cave, also in Manresa.

The Cardener River, as it passes through Manresa, has left a rather distinguished mark on the landscape. The high waters of olden times covered the low hills that line the valley, shaping them in a way that nowadays they seem to have been run ragged by wind and water. This landscape is eminently visual, as if framed; its colour range features greys, browns and greens, tones likewise inherent to the visual nature of Joseph Beuys's work. It is not unusual, therefore, that in the course of this action, the artist would give MANRESA the value of brown space.[5]

The description the older Ignatian guides make of the Cardener Valley coincide with this visual take. In the album entitled *Manresa Ignasiana*, written by Jaume Nonell and published in 1915, the arrival of a visit to Manresa is traced out with these words: 'As the pilgrim with his entourage rounds the small hill that separates the Rajadel ravine from the Cardener River, he comes across a panoramic view,

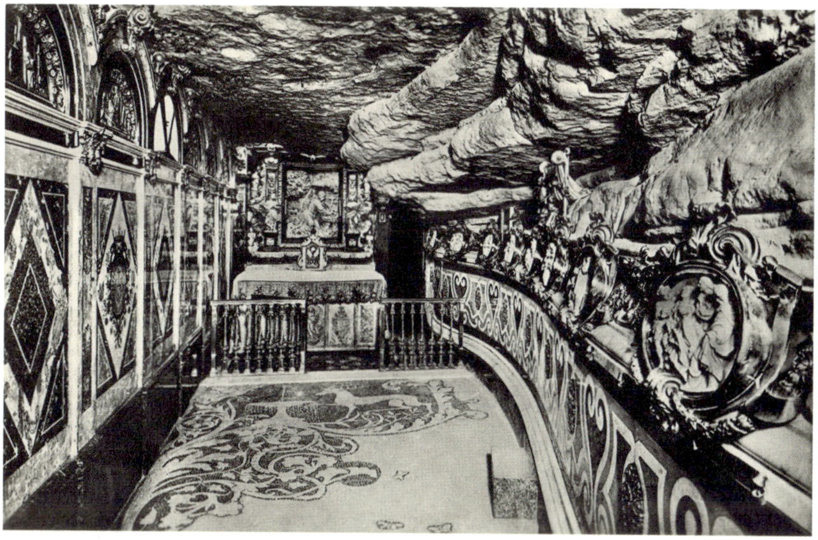

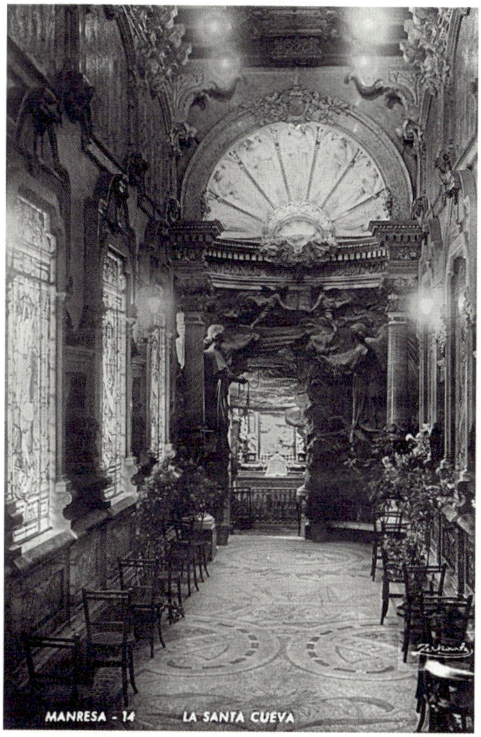

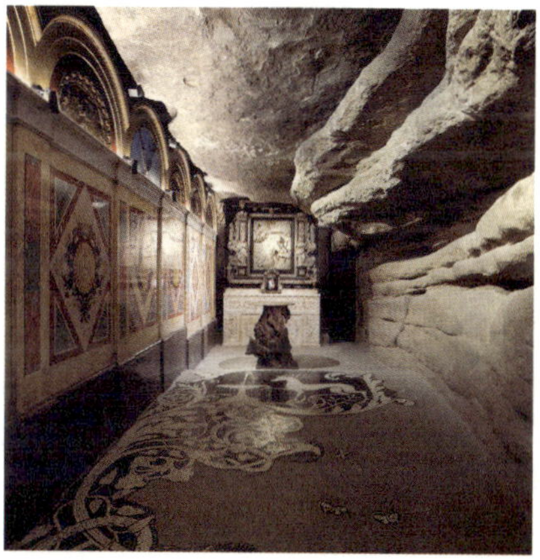

B Image from the early 20th century with the Baroque style that decorated the Holy Cave until the reform in 2019.

C Entrance to the Holy Cave at the beginning of the 20th century.

D The Holy Cave of Ignatius of Loyola, 20th century.

which if not as grandiose and sublime as that of Montserrat is indeed more agreeable, more pleasant. So much so, that it justifies the name Valley of Paradise, being the one it has been christened with since ancient times.' The description continues: 'Surrounding the valley are various hills of different elevations, with their sharp, scaled crags comprised of overlaying layers, with varied density and hardness, and with surface perforations to which the term Caves is given (in Catalan it would be *balmes*). Their formation is attributed by geologists to erosion from waters, when in distant times the Cardener River had reached such a high level. When Ignatius saw this for the first time, the river had already been winding along the valley bottom for centuries, as its banks were lined green. The hills that surround the valley itself feature various flat surfaces lying low, and there we find just as many small vegetable gardens, fertilised by the waters of the ancient irrigation channel.'[6]

This paradisical vision of the valley is not far from the current panorama, despite the industries which set up alongside the river in the last century and which were recently demolished, or the pass of the railway and the highway which run parallel to the water course. This harmonious image of the valley is what Joseph Beuys was still able to see when he went to Manresa in the summer of 1966, a few months before carrying out the MANRESA action at Galerie Schmela in Düsseldorf, on 15 December of that same year.

Although it was confirmed by Eva Beuys to Friedhelm Mennekes,[7] this visit was never documented, despite having gone through all the signatures of visitors to the Holy Cave during the 1960s; the visit was, we believe, the key component to the action. Henning Christiansen prefers to believe that Beuys might have even been in Manresa more than once, given that before 1966 he had already travelled alone to Barcelona and had visited the city on other occasions with Wolf Vostell. The word BARCELONA was written on the windows of Galerie Schmela when Beuys did the action. The distance of 60 km between Barcelona and Manresa would have made it feasible to do a quick visit to the city that would not have to last more than half a day.

Both the landscape of the Cardener River and the medallion from the Christ of Tort influenced the action MANRESA directly, and not just the thought of Saint Ignatius of Loyola. Joseph Beuys clairvoyantly captures the landscape of *The Valley of Paradise*, leaving evidence of it in the preparatory drawing of the action entitled *Where is Element 3?* where the artist's hand jots down the following phrases: 'Good day, where are you going? To the beautiful valley of Manresa' (*Im schönen Tal von Manresa*).

Nor would Beuys have ever used the plate and the crucifix that he had kept since 1957 — a year when the artist was still in the midst of a spiritual crisis — if he had not seen the medallion of the Christ of Tort, before which Saint Ignatius had experienced his vision of the Holy Trinity. The extreme similitude between the Christ on the medallion and Beuys's *Plate Crucifix* is so great that the artist would have been hard pressed to conceive the action in the way he carried it out if he had not known the landscape and instruments of the Ignatian vision. Henning Christiansen, upon visiting the Cave and seeing the Tort medallion, states with a shining face: 'I am totally sure that Beuys was at Manresa. That Christ is, quite strangely, alive.'[8] It should be pointed out that a part of the objects that were left over from the MANRESA action were presented at the documenta in Kassel in 1968, and later conserved in the Block-Beuys at the Hessisches Landesmuseum in Darmstadt, where they can currently be seen.

We also know that he included some rosemary in the action. It has not been demonstrated if this was from Manresa or part of the MANRESA action. In any case, rosemary is easy to find in the Mediterranean region and is abundant in the area around Manresa and the Cardener River. Joseph Beuys planted this rosemary bush in his garden in Düsseldorf until it froze one winter, and then became part of the sculpture *Boothia Felix* as a relic, included in the piece *Lightning with Stag in its Glare*. For Joseph Beuys that rosemary also signified Manresa. Curiously, every 31 July, the day of Saint Ignatius, a group of residents of Manresa line Sobrerroca Street with rosemary as a kind of popular offering, the street being where a good part of Ignatius' life took place during his time in Manresa.

Further to this, Joseph Beuys used the name of the site and not that of the saint for various reasons. On the one hand, the word 'Manresa', both in Scandinavian languages and in Germany, can be

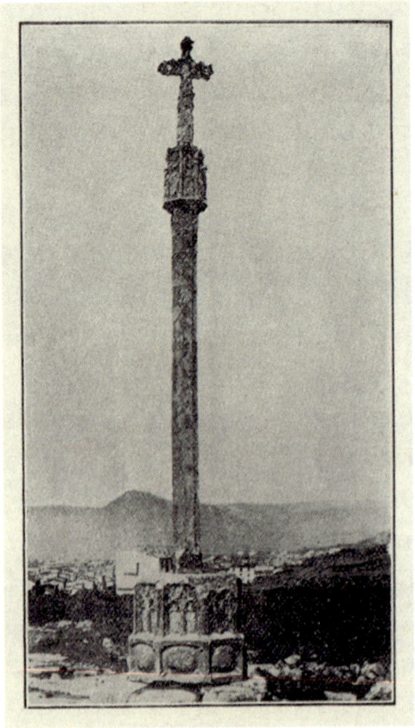 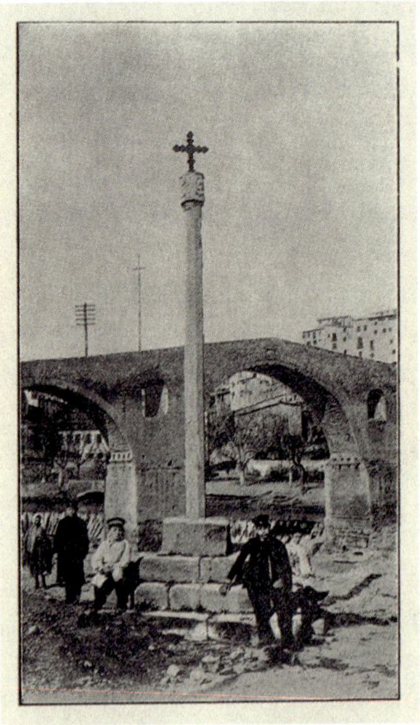

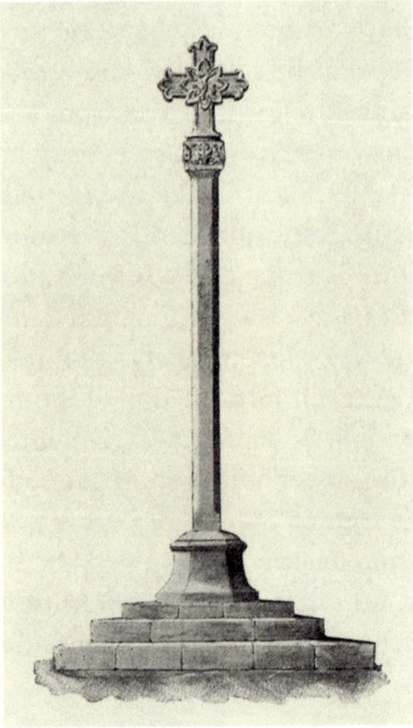

E Culla wayside cross, on the road to Santa Clara.

F Guia wayside cross, near the Old Bridge and the Cardener caves.

G Tort wayside cross, as it would have been in the 16th Century.
In the middle of the cross, the medallion with a crucifix currently held in the Holy Cave in Manresa can be seen. In front of the cross Saint Ignatius had his vision of the Holy Trinity. It is said that during the vigil of Saint Ignatius in 1627, the Christ on this cross started bleeding.

broken down into two concepts: 'man' and 'resa'. In the Nordic languages it would be 'man' and 'reest'; in German, 'man' and 'reise'. In both cases this means 'man who travels'.[9] One more meaning to add the conceptual play of words that the artist almost always employed. We could say that his visual art is one more extension of his language, if we were to honour the principle of logos as the starting point of creation.

The word 'Manresa', then, picks up on various meanings, starting with the intuitive classicism that comes from the ancient *Minorisa* — let us not forget that Manresa and Rome are in this Beuys action the most southern points of Europe where classicism might be found. It then projects itself to the maximum northwards, to the Danish capital, the site of the museum of the sculptor Thorvaldsen, so that the Thorvaldsen Museum is the furthest north this intuition gets. It also includes the idea of nomadism and of permanent travel. Behind MANRESA is concealed the interpretation of the 'traveling man', which fits in perfectly with Saint Ignatius of Loyola and with Joseph Beuys. For the artist, Saint Ignatius is the 'traveller' and the 'wounded man'. These words are the headings in German for the scores by Henning Christiansen: *Der Reisende, Der Verwundete*. Further, in this action Beuys invites man, in general, to take a spiritual journey to heal his wounds, whether physical or of the soul. It is here where the lives of Ignatius of Loyola and Joseph Beuys coincide. Both of them live through war wounds that almost lead to death, and from death they return to life, with their souls revived.

'O Crux, ave, spes unica'

The city limits of Manresa feature wayside crosses that began to be raised well into the Middle Ages; up to the 19th century they were the object of popular devotion. Some of these wayside crosses, found at entrance or exit points to the city, are part of the route of Saint Ignatius, such as the Guia Cross, the Tort Cross, the Culla Cross and the Cal Gravat Cross. Most of the original medieval crosses have not been preserved, although nowadays the corresponding sites have some sort of wayside marker giving testimony to the original.

Of all the crosses that were witness to the prayers and vision of Saint Ignatius, the only one remaining is the Culla Cross, which can be seen at the Museu Comarcal de Manresa (Manresa Regional Museum); the historical crucifix of the Tort Cross, in the shape of a medallion, is found in the Cave. In times of Saint Ignatius this cross was found on a small path that led from the Cave to the path known as the Camí de Santa Clara, quite near the convent of the same name. This site receives direct light from Montserrat and is close to a small creek whose stream turns into a series of waterfalls on its way down to the Cardener. The little valley has its ravine, and is lush and wild, except for the order imposed by four small garden plots. The site is an open viewpoint to Montserrat and the Cardener, along the newer high road from Manresa to Barcelona that was opened up starting in the 14th century, passing through Pont de Vilomara.

The current view still coincides to a great degree with engravings from the 17th century that show the image of the spiritual pilgrim discovering another world. Quite probably this generic iconography of the pilgrim has some relation to Saint Ignatius, the most famous reluctant pilgrim of the 17th Century, as the process to canonise him was carried out with the Company of Jesus expanding in full force.

At that time, the cross was made of stone and raised on a thin yet elegant pedestal, topped by a cross with the centre featuring a small sculpted Christ figure surrounded by a mystical medallion.

Saint Ignatius had various supernational visions in front of this cross, from the one with the diabolical serpent, to another of the unity of the three divine persons; yet clearly that what interests us here is the vision of the Holy Trinity. This is precisely what Joseph Beuys invokes with the action MANRESA, with his insistent question: *Where is Element 3?*

The Tort Cross was greeted in popular parlance with the words *O Crux, ave, spes unica* (Hail O Cross, our sole hope), and Manresans used to say the following prayer, which is not far from the Beuysian idea of Christ: 'Let whoever has died in you be in me. Now and in the hour of my death. Amen.' For Joseph Beuys as well, the descent of God to earth, incarnated in the figure of Christ and the mystery of Golgotha, the death and resurrection of Jesus, has meant that Christ lives in each

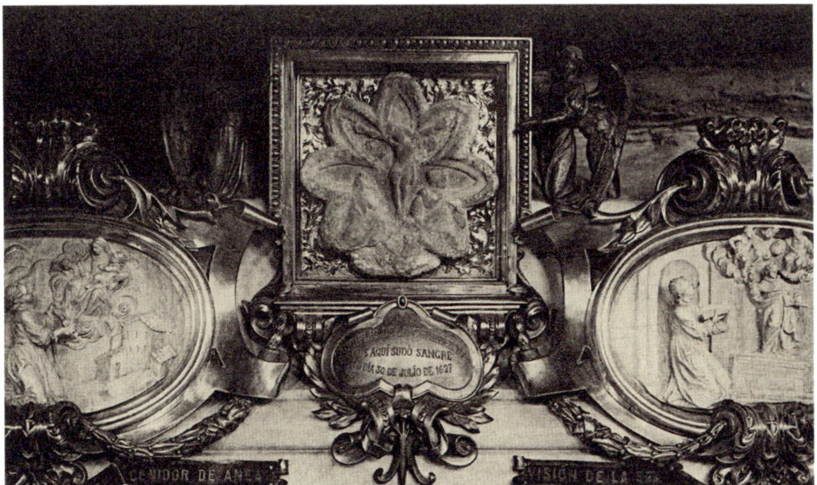

18. MANRESA – Crucifijo de la antigua Cruz del Tort, el cual manó sangre el 30 de Julio de 1627, víspera de San Ignacio

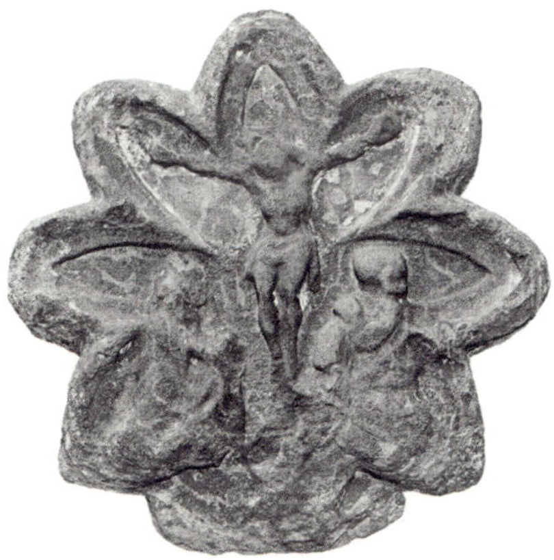

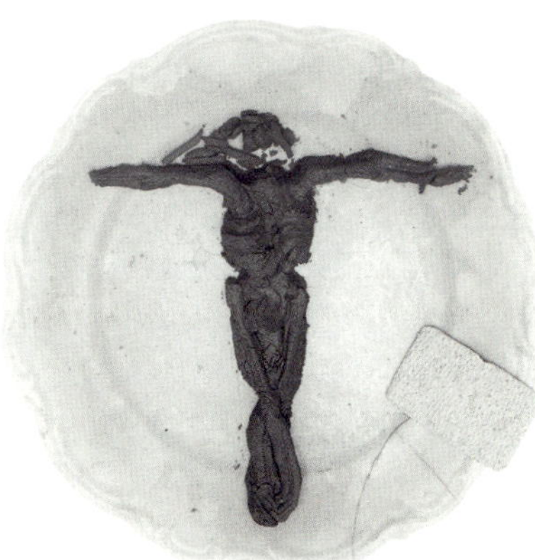

H The historical medallion with the crucifix from the Tort Cross as seen in the Holy Cave, at the beginning of the 20th century.
I Historical medallion with crucifix, from the Tort Cross.
J Plate with crucifix used by Joseph Beuys in the action MANRESA.

and every man and makes up part of human existence. 'Christ lives in each human being', said Joseph Beuys. 'Whether I wish it to be so or not, the essence of Christ exists within me as in every other person.'[10]

The historical chronicles indicate that sometime between 1592 and 1602, a heavy rainstorm with hail and strong wind devasted the smaller Tort Valley and the Cardener Valley: 'So strong was that lightning storm with its terrible thunder, so furious the wind and hail, that it cut through this beautiful district, leaving this "Paradise Valley" a wasteland.'[11] This caused the historical Tort Cross and its pedestal to fall; the remains were gathered up and later set at the foot of the new cross, now topped off in iron. On it, the then Canon of La Seu, Tomàs Fadre, had the following Latin inscription inscribed on the piece that corresponded to the capitol, set out along two lines. Above it read: 'HIC HA-BUIT S. IGNATIUS-TRINITA'; below were the words: 'TIS VISIONEM-1522' (Here Saint Ignatius had his vision of the Holy Trinity).

As for the Christ of Tort, we still need to mention a historical anecdote of a miracle that took place on 30 July 1627, the eve of the festivity of Saint Ignatius, and five years after the saint was canonised. Witnesses from the time saw how the Christ of Tort perspired blood: 'there had been a humour or bloody liquor, that had left on it the remains and sign that blood or similar humours have the custom of leaving when they have passed through some place where they could leave a vestige or sign.'[12]

Movement and action, 'ad amorem'

'Love ought to be put more in deeds than in words.'[13] This is an Ignatian warning. Joseph Beuys is also a man of action, who would find in the spirit of Fluxus an initial path for broadening the concept of art. Drawing, thought and action would be extensions of the word, of language.

After a major spiritual crisis in the years 1957–58, during which Beuys found refuge at the home of his friends the Van der Grintens, in Kranenburg, he set out on a path of personal transformation that would play out with his first Fluxus actions, some of which had clearly Christological references. From amongst these we could mention *The Chief* (1964), *How to Explain Pictures to a Dead Hare* (1965),

MANRESA (1966) and later on, *Celtic* (1971), *Coyote* (1974) and *Show Your Wounds* (1976). Of all these, the action MANRESA is the one that reveals the most direct relationship with the Christ figure, just as it is seen and dealt with in the entire work and thought of Beuys.

It seems to me absolutely essential to gauge the influence of Saint Ignatius of Loyola's *Spiritual Exercises* on the action MANRESA and on Joseph Beuys's first Fluxus actions. The *Exercises* are a practice to attain the freedom and self-determination of the soul, constituting a manual of militancy and discipline to prepare the soul for the consequences of full transformation, choice or renewal of a state of life. With the exercises, 'what is sought, however, is not the will of God in a general sense, but the strength to be able to respond with full disposition to his specific historical call.'[14] What Joseph Beuys admired most in Saint Ignatius was 'the disciplined inner consciousness, the capacity to put everything on the line and make the decision to change life and the very existential direction of being.'[15] We could say that Beuys appreciated the saint for his militancy and discipline in waging an 'internal war', a struggle for the conquest of 'self-awareness', the conquest of the soul and of the principle of freedom and movement.

The application of Christological references, and the putting into practice of Ignatian principles, not only would distance him from other Fluxus actions, more related to musical renewal;[16] it would also endow him with energy and with a mission, bolstering his therapeutic, shamanistic vision of art, meant to lead to a healing of Western man's soul through art conceived as social therapy. On the basis of Ignatian principles and the action MANRESA, Joseph Beuys envisions the expanded concept of the work of art and the famous yet controversial notion that 'every man is an artist'.

When it comes to Fluxus, Beuys kept himself apart from the neo-dada spirit of the movement, as he himself would confirm: '...I only joined externally, on an organisational level but not conceptually, to the neo-dadaists, the people of Fluxus, most of whom worked in the terms of dada, while at the same time I was developing my own concept of Fluxus, independent from dadaism and neo-dadaism.'[17] In his first Fluxus action, *Siberian Symphony, First Movement*, carried out in 1963 as part of the Festum Fluxorum Fluxus in Düsseldorf, this was already clear, as the piece was impregnated with a heightened degree of spirituality, with its allusions to the mystical phenomena of reincarnation. On the other hand, Beuys liked to speak of his Fluxus actions as 'demonstrations', and this was the word he would define them with from that point on. His final connection to Fluxus was the *Piano Duet* ('In Memoriam George Maciunas'), played with Nam June Paik in 1978; it was a requiem for the death of the founder of the movement, and the performance is considered by historians to be the swan song of Fluxus. The declarations of Joseph Beuys, as gathered by his biographers, Adriani/Konnertz/Thomas, are rather explicit in this regard: '...when it comes to the authentically demonstrative actions, the concerts, the interdisciplinary activity, Fluxus has died.'[18]

The other difference Beuys had with Fluxus neo-dadaism is that despite including the prefix 'anti' before certain concepts in his actions, such as *anti-physics*, *anti-chemistry*, *anti-mathematical*, *anti-nature*, and so on, he did not grant these terms the meaning of a simple protest or negation. Rather, their meaning was one of expansion, stretching the immaterial or invisible aspects of such concepts to be able to have their totality at hand. We could almost state that Fluxus since Beuys was not neo-dada but rather anti-dada: 'All the Actions were important in broadening the concept of art. To expand and enlarge the concept as much as possible, so that it could include any sort of human activity.'[19]

Behind Beuys's Fluxus demonstrations, and especially MANRESA, there are Ignatian words and concepts, with a predominance of verbs, the spirit of action, such as: 'feel', the personal experience that implicates the 'entire being' (thought, memory, will, fantasy, body, material environment, and so on). In this way, as Saint Ignatius would say, "everything works together to impregnate those exercising to the bottom of their hearts, from the word of God and the sentiment of Christ."[20] The other important verb is 'repeat', which means to continually return to that which is most heartfelt. This is the spirit and the language of Fluxus in Beuys.

The action and demonstration MANRESA is a practical lesson in love, as the *Exercises* are in turn a 'superior school in love of God.'[21] With the strength of the heart and of love we might come to ourselves and to God. In MANRESA, therefore, Joseph Beuys follows the footsteps of the Ignatian 'mastery of love' and his 'theology of the heart', so that the action MANRESA might be seen as a demonstration of love restoring the unity of the individual and the spirit as received from God. Joseph Beuys begins with the idea that Christ is within each human existence, that he is 'in itself a force, a human force, a divine and human force while, suddenly and for a certain time, he has merged into a historical context.'[22] In this regard, he also follows Rudolf Steiner in believing in the Christ figure as a meeting point between God and Humanity.

His starting point is thus how to restore the unity of man with the cosmos from an anthropological point of view. We should consider that 'every being is a Christophany and only a Christophany. We only exist to the degree that we participate in the Logos.'[23] Here is where the references to Steiner are useful again, as for him the culmination of Christ's sacrifice constitutes the moment when earthly spiritual life absorbs what formerly came to us from without, that is, the power of the logos.

The play that arises between Element 1, Element 2 and Element 3 in MANRESA is a shift of powers, of energies in movement that move in the dynamic internal circularity of the Trinity. Raimon Panikkar seeks to bring us closer to the religious experience of the Trinity, from a perspective that closely approximates the way Joseph Beuys does it.

Grounded in an Augustinian notion, Panikkar draws us nearer to divine mystery through Man himself, 'the image of the Trinity in what is most intimate and most truthful in its being. However, regardless of its validity, its anthropomorphism is obvious: the Father, Being; the Son, Intellect; the Spirit, Love, *mens*, *notitia*, *amor* (or just as well *memoria*, *intelligentia*, *voluntas*).'[24] From here, Panikkar proposes the following formula: 'The Father, Source, the *I*; the Son, Being, the *Thou*; the Spirit, return to Being (Ocean of the being), the *Us*.'[25] For this specialist in religions, Paul's Trinitarian formula of God, 'over all and through all and in all' (Ephesians 4:6) provides us with the key:

1. *Epi panton*—over all, *super omnes*, the Source of Being, which is not Being, since, if so, it would be Being and not its source: the ultimate I.

2. *Dia panton*—through all, *per omnia*, the Son, Being and the Christ, he through whom and for whom everything was made, beings being participants in Being: the *Thou*: still scattered in the many *thous* of the universe.
3. *En pāsin*—within all, *in omnibus*, the Spirit, divine immanence and, in the dynamism of pure act, the end (the return) of Being. Thus Being—and beings—only exists insofar as it proceeds from its Source and continues to flow in the spirit: the *we*, in as much as it gathers all of us into the integrated communion of that perfect reality.[26]

Here we are reminded to refer to the interview Mennekes did with Beuys: 'Where is he now?' asked Beuys himself, referring to Christ. Beuys follows: 'Whoever tries to see with the inner eye sees that he has been there. No longer is he here in a physical form, but he is found in the moving form of substance that is not visible with the outer eye.'[27]

In the Fluxus demonstration MANRESA there are two important moments. The first is when Beuys activates the spirit with the copper rod, in a movement from up to down between Element 1 and Element 2. The other is when he takes the illuminated Geissler tube and draws it near to the plate with the crucifix, then rubbing the other end of the tube against his heart, thus receiving the impulse of Christ, filling it with his experience and with feeling, to then projecting towards the felt cross, or Element 1, in a return to the spirit of Being, as it returns to being Source. To the question, therefore, of 'Where is Element 3?' what is insistently asked during the action finds the following answer: *in omnibus*, in ourselves, as we are the spirit, we are love. MANRESA is thus a demonstration of 'love' that appeals to a transformation of ourselves that begins with the heart, so as to come to personal self-knowledge as a free being. From the power of love we can come to ourselves and to God: '...in everything, love and serve your divine majesty', say the *Spiritual Exercises*, no. 233. This is further driven home in the document of Saint Ignatius' *Constitutions*, written after the *Exercises*, as 'a work to help us to better proceed in divine service.'[28], although always giving priority to 'the interior law of charity and love that the Holy Spirit inscribes and prints in our hearts.'[29]

The birth of a new 'Gestalt' and social sculpture

The action MANRESA has a healing or therapeutic aim, centred on expanding knowledge of man while restoring the totality of his fragmented conscience, split as it is into two halves. Man is ailing because he lives immersed in a daily chronicle of 'heartbreak', where love is lacking. For this reason, the cross in MANRESA is split in two. The right side is material and visible; the left, immaterial and invisible, the outline barely defined by a chalk tracing.

On the right side of the cross, man lives immersed in what is material: physics, mathematics, chemistry, nature, and so on. Meanwhile, on the left side we find the broadening of this knowledge, in anti-physics, anti-chemistry, anti-mathematics, anti-nature, and so on. This 'anti' is not understood as a negation but as an extension of the concepts it accompanies. Restoring the unity of the cross means broadening knowledge, just as Ignatius of Loyola did in Manresa. It also means expanding the concept of art, so that it might encompass both 'art' and 'anti-art', reason and intuition, what is visible and what is invisible, with the definitive confluence of Eastern and Western man. Restoring the totality means overcoming rationalism. In the course of the action, the phonetic repetitions in Danish, like *ikke kann...ikke kann* (I – can – not...I – can – not), play with the phonetic error of 'no to Kant, no to Kant', the sort of play that was in line with Duchamp's *Rose Sélavy* (*eros c'est la vie*), to give an example. Only by way of intuition can we come to higher knowledge and overcome this fragmentation. From this was born the idea of a New Cross that he expresses in his drawings, a new Gestalt.

The action MANRESA is also identified in Joseph Beuys's notebooks as a *Europaïsche happening*, a European happening, behind which one perceives the idea of Western man fused with the map of Europe, just as is seen in the drawing from the Van der Grinten Collection, entitled *Nord/Süd/Ost/West*. This drawing traces a European cross between these cardinal points, going from Manresa and Rome to Copenhagen; from Ostend (the end of the East) to Asia (the land of Samarkand and Genghis Kahn). From Rome to Manresa, classicism, intuition and the light of the south are projected towards the north, towards the capital of Denmark, where the sculptor Thorvaldsen celebrates southern classicism in his own museum. We would be surprised to analyse the similitudes between academic sculpture in Catalonia in the 19th century, represented by Antoni Solà and Damià Campeny, and the sculptures at the Thorvaldsen Museum itself.

As for the horizontal part of the cross, the idea was that it brought East and West together. In relation to having Ostend as an end of the cross and the city furthest to the west for Western man, Henning Christiansen has spoken of a trip by Beuys to Ostend that was perhaps revelatory: 'We had spent a few pleasant days in the home of Anny de Decker and Bernd Lohaus. Later, Eva, Jessyka, Wenzel, Joseph, Ursula and I went to Ostend to visit the tomb of James Ensor. It is covered by a large stone slab where only the word ENSOR has been chiselled in. Beuys confided, apart from this, that he felt a strong affinity with Ensor. He also spoke to me of his *Project for Western Man*, which he sought to build on the sea, just off Ostend. The idea was to construct a large cubic space on the surface of the water, where it would be possible to see *The Samurai's Sword is a Sausage*, while the cement block would be placed on top of an emitter that would broadcast the *ÖÖ PROGRAMM*. When we found ourselves looking at the Atlantic Ocean, Beuys said to his son Wenzel: here you have the end of the Earth.'[30]

For Joseph Beuys visual art is an extension of language, because in the beginning was the Word (logos). And the Word is a Gestalt. For the mystery of Golgotha, seen as the union of the blood of Christ with the earth, man acquires the capacity to take the will of Christ, his movement, with him. 'For Beuys, Christ is essentially a human power, a divine power working in the world through us, a spiritual substance.'[31]

Within this substantial conception of things, the reddish-brown tone enters into the field of play, with its associations to the earth and with flowing blood. MANRESA is mentioned in the action as a 'brown space', as a 'counterspace'. Brown, in the visual language of Beuys, resends 'all forms of substantiality'.[32] For Joseph Beuys, explains Max Reithman, 'brown, as a neutralised colour, could arouse like the grey of felt certain counter images in man; ... a counter image, you could almost say: engender the rainbow in man.'[33] Yet man cannot produce these counter images that are substance only in to the degree that he is the principle of movement. Manresa is thus a site for substance.

In the visual language of Joseph Beuys, art is no longer retinal, and thus cannot be analysed from traditional categories of oil painting, drawing, watercolour, collage and so on. Beuys does not paint with colours, he paints with substances, or better said, with materials that have the value of substance, such as fat, iodine, the blood of a hare, silver bromide, sulphur.... The artist himself clarifies this: 'I do not begin from the problem of colour. I begin with the problem of substance.... In itself it is not the problem of colour, in the sense that I understand it, "but rather a form for substance".'[34]

Joseph Beuys's visual language encompasses, in a single concept, word and thought, feeling and will. The person is, in effect, something visual. Man as a visible/invisible sculpture. The human soul will thus be substance and visual material; it will be mouldable, sculptural.

In the many readings that can be made of Joseph Beuys's work, there is the possibility for an alchemical interpretation of the action MANRESA and its structure as a triadic mandala.[35] When all is said and done, the work of Beuys is grounded in religion, art and science, the tripod of alchemy. In the alchemical philosophical tradition, the number 4, as the natural division of the circle, is a symbol of totality, coinciding with the central Christian symbol that equally represents a quadriplicity, while an oblong cross has the structure of 3+1. Furthermore, in the Christian world the Trinity maintains the proportion 3+1. For C.G. Jung, the four parts together make up a symbol of unfolded wholeness, that is, the *Selbst* (or the Soul), in its empirical manifestation. 'Like God', Jung explains, 'Christ is the unity of the Trinity, and as the historical Son of God and Anthropos is the exemplum and model of the inner, individual man, while at the same time being the point, goal and totality of empirical man.'[36]

The triadic mandala has something unique about it, namely a 4−1 proportional structure, if it is considered from the point of view of wholeness. C.G. Jung says that 'in the triadic mandala, the fourth function is the undifferentiated or inferior one (opposed to the first, or fundamental function), that characterises that part of the personality that is in the shadows. When this aspect is missing in the symbol of

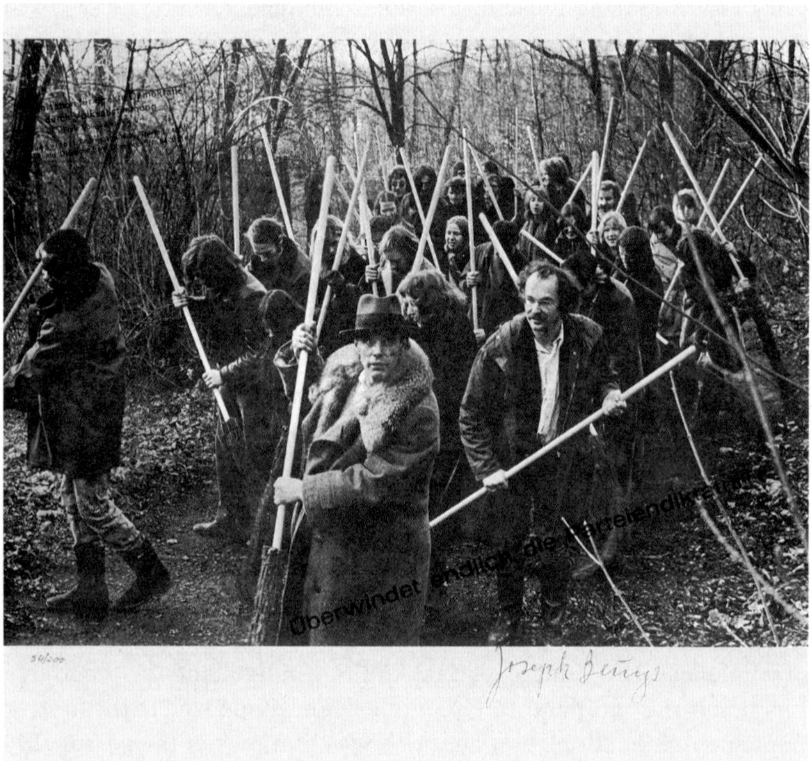

K *Save the Woods*, community action to save the Grafenberger Forest from logging, Düsseldorf, 1972.

totality, there arises a preponderance in the sector of the conscience.'[37] This description is fully in line with the partially-broken cross as a motif Joseph Beuys develops in MANRESA, which leaves the left side of the cross in the shadows, as well as with research into the unknown or Element 3, a basic factor in the reconstruction of wholeness, of the *Selbst*, the human Soul.

Returning to the relations between Ignatius of Loyola and Joseph Beuys, some commentaries point out that what happened during Ignatius' stay in Manresa was the 'substance' of the exercises. There is more. Diego Laínez states that 'Iñigo, in Manresa, came to the substance of these meditations we call exercises.'[38] Thus, for Ignatius, Manresa worked as a 'counterspace' that led him to a broadening of his knowledge and the transformation of his soul, converting him into a new man, into a new Gestalt who with his mission to assist, care for and save souls could be extended to everyone. From this arises the shamanistic coincidence between Beuys and Loyola as 'healers of souls', with Ignatius taking the path of religion and Beuys the path of art and imagination. Each in their own way believed that only individual freedom and the creation of each individual could lead to social utopia and the transformation of society.

We might almost say that Ignatius of Loyola was a pioneer of the new social sculpting advocated centuries later by Joseph Beuys, the first person to join art and religion, or to make religion a 'counterspace' to art — just as would be done by science and by other disciplines — simultaneously inserting it in art, as a totality.

Joseph Beuys's famous phrase that 'all men are artists' is a synthesis of his finest contribution to art and form from a social perspective. It is a call for the self-determination of the soul and creativity in work: 'the Christ substance is realised in matter and in work. The worker is the transcendental essence of man.'[39]

Beuys continually rebels against traditional art, against the idea of art as form of specialised labour. He requires so much more, though not from the artist but from man in general: '...the path that goes through what we call ART is not what contributes most to ART. The concept of the reach of art: every man is an artist, it is not easy, but it is clearly more necessary to ART.'[40]

Here, once again, we find Ignatian coincidences: 'What is important is to *elevate anew* the human soul. I speak here of the soul in a global sense. I am not thinking just of the terrain of emotion, but also of the forces of knowledge, of the capacity to think, of intuition, inspiration, of self-awareness, of willpower. All things are *abysmal* (or collapsed) in our epoch. They have to be saved. It is absurd to think about producing better potatoes without keeping this in mind.'[41] For Joseph Beuys, all men are carriers of this transforming creativity: 'Every man is an artist, in potential. The question here is potentiality.'[42]

Manresa, therefore, is substance and cosmos, and the action MANRESA is an exercise, a paradigmatic demonstration that complete transformation is an inner path we must take, an invitation to inner movement, like the 'spirits' that are often referred to in the *Spiritual Exercises* and which refer to 'inner movements', to 'motions' experienced by those exercising.

Joseph Beuys grounds his entire work in 'heat' or 'warmth' as a main form of energy that is only found between life and death, but not just in the physical sense; we are speaking of human warmth, of love. Warmth refers to the veritable substance of love and the figure of Christ incarnates this domain of love, until death and resurrection. 'It is in the free self that we find Christ', said Beuys; 'I will make you free', say the Evangels.

For Joseph Beuys, the Christ figure is a cosmic event which in fact had transformed substance, in itself and for itself: 'Jesus is for me the man and Christ is the person, the double figure, that man has transformed into. It is, therefore, a complete transformation.'[43]

Joseph Beuys incarnates the image of the solitary traveller, the nomad, the pilgrim in search of experiences that lead him to a superior world. The hat, the Eurasian staff used in the action *Eurasian Staff* or the figure of the shepherd in the action *Coyote*, personify for us the image of the traveller. As early as 1969, Joseph Beuys had written a phrase that still has inevitable relevance for our time: 'We find ourselves in a nomadic culture; the spirit has to be seen without a solid vision of the world.'[44]

Beuys identifies with the nomads of German Romanticism, and especially with those of Friedrich Nietzsche, or with the wanderer on the sea, as painted by Caspar David Friedrich. As Antje von Graevenitz has observed, Beuys gave prominence to the importance of the person in the work and in this way, in a debate with other artists, once remarked: 'Inside of us is the most important question we now confront... the person, the person, central, central, central.'[45]

Mysteries take place at the central station, and not at the "Goetheanum", stated Joseph Beuys in an interview.[46] The action MANRESA has the nomadic, travelling spirit of Beuys, who made his studio into a mental image that could be found anywhere. The demonstration MANRESA constitutes an act of love towards Manresa as the central station of Christ and man in the world.

If the shape of a bird in the work of Joseph Beuys, like in Ancient Egypt, symbolises the mobility of the soul,[47] man as artist might spread his wings over the Cardener Bridge and cry out with Beuys: 'Auch zu Dir fliege ich, MANRESA' (I am flying to you too, Manresa).[48]

1
Alois Martin Müller, 'Chamanes', in *Beuysnobiscum*. In *Joseph Beuys*, Madrid: Museo Nacional Centro de Arte Reina Sofía, 1994, p. 225 [Exh. cat.]. Translation by translator.

2
Idem.

3
El relato del pelegrino: Autobiografía de San Ignacio de Loyola, Bilbao: Ed. Mensajero, 1990, p. 30 and ff. Translation by translator.

4
Ibid. p. 30.

5
See the text 'Joseph Beuys and his energy plan', by Henning Christiansen, in this publication (p. 164).

6
Jaume Nonell, S.J., 'La vista de Manresa', in *Manresa Ignaciana, Nuevo Álbum Histórico*, Manresa, 1915, p. 11. Translation by translator.

7
Friedhelm Mennekes, *Joseph Beuys. MANRESA: Eine Aktion als geistliche Übung nach Ignatius von Loyola*, Frankfurt am Main and Leipzig: Insel Verlag, 1992. p. 113. Translation by translator.

8
Oral declaration by Henning Christiansen during his visit to the Holy Cave in Manresa, before the Christ of Tort, on 29 August 1994.

9
Friedhelm Mennekes, *Beuys on Christ: A Position in Dialogue*. [bilingual edition] Lesa Mason and Jon Boles [trans.], Stuttgart: Verlag Katholisches Bibelwerk, 1989. p. 95. In a stay at Møn with Christiansen, this latter explained that the sound 'reest' in Swedish is similar in the entire Indo-European linguistic area.

10
Dialogue between Joseph Beuys and Elisabeth Pfister (German/English), in Friedhelm Mennekes, "Homily on Beuys", in *Beuys zu Christus/ Beuys on Christ*, Stuttgart: Verlach Katholisches Bibelwerk, 1992, p. 130.

11
San Ignacio en Manresa (1491–1891). Dedicated album *Al Santo Fundador de la Compañía de Jesús en el cuarto centenario de su glorioso nacimiento*, Manresa, 1891, chapter 28: 'La Creu del Tort'.

12
Joaquim Sarret i Arbós, 'Les creus de pedra del terme de Manresa', *Butlletí del Centre Excursionista de la Comarca de Bages*, Year XI, nos. 60, 61, 62, Manresa, March–August 1913, p. 327. Translation by translator. This quotation is from the testimony of doctor Bernat Mas, during the process of the complete solemnities, in the Church of the Holy Cave, on the date indicated for the event.

13
Ignatius of Loyola, *Spiritual Exercises*, Christian Classics Ethereal Library, www.ccel.org/ccel/ignatius/exercises.xvi.html [access: 15 March, 2020].

14
Josep M. Rambla, 'Introduction', Ignatius of Loyola, *Exercicis espirituals*, Barcelona: Fragmenta, p. 24. Translation by translator.

15
Mennekes, *Beuys zu Christus*, p. 92.

16
We refer to the first Fluxus concerts begun in Darmstadt in the summer of 1962, which were followed afterwards with the name of International Music Festivals, at the Museum Wiesbaden.

17
Juri Steiner, 'Fluxus', in *Beuysnobiscum*. In *Joseph Beuys*, Madrid: Museo Nacional Centro de Arte Reina Sofía, 1994, p. 266 [Exh. cat.].

18
Ibid., p. 267.

19
Quote from Uwe M. Schneede, in 'Acción', *Beuysnobiscum*. In *Joseph Beuys*, Madrid: Museo Nacional Centro de Arte Reina Sofía, 1994, p. 241 [Exh. cat.]. Quote from 'Beuys's, in *Robert Filliou, Lehren und Lernen als Aufführungskünste*, Cologne-New York: ed. Kaspar Köenig, 1970, p. 161.

20
Rambla, op. cit., p. 25, note 56: Cardenal Gaspar Contarini, after completing a month of exercises under the guidance of Saint Ignatius, expressed his impression with these words: 'I have found a master of love' (quoted in W. Sierp, *Hochschule der Gottesliebe, I-II*, Warendorf i. W. 1935–1937; v. I, p. 22). In effect, Ignatius is not a master of speculative theology, but of the 'theology of the heart'. See A. Haas, 'Gedanken su einer "Theologia cordis"', in *Ignatius von Loyola, Geistliche Übungen*, Freiburg, 1985, pp. 140–150.

21
Ibid., p. 25, note 59: 'Superior School of the Love of God' is the title of a classic commentary on the *Exercises* (W. Sierp, cited in note 19).

22
Friedhelm Mennekes, interview with Joseph Beuys in Max Reithmann, *Joseph Beuys: La mort me tient en éveil*, Toulouse: ARPAP, 1994, p. 63. Translation by translator.

23
Raimon Panikkar, *La Trinidad y la experiencia religiosa*, Barcelona: Ediciones Obelisco, 1989, p. 102.

24
Ibid., p. 103.

25
Idem.

26
Idem.

27
Reithmann, *Joseph Beuys. La mort me tient en éveil*, p. 86.

28
Rambla, op. cit., p. 45.

29
Idem.

30
Henning Christiansen, in Joseph Beuys *Eurasienstab*, Antwerp: Galerie Anny de Decker, 1987 [Exh. cat.]. The display case piece *The Samurai-Sword is a Blutwurst* is currently in the collection of the Museum of Modern Art in New York.

31
Dialogue between Joseph Beuys and Elisabeth Pfister (German/English), in Friedhelm Mennekes, "Homily on Beuys", in *Beuys zu Christus/ Beuys on Christ*, Stuttgart: Verlach Katholisches Bibelwerk, 1992, p. 139.

32
Mennekes in Reithmann, *Joseph Beuys. La mort me tient en éveil*, p. 225.

33
Ibid., p. 226.

34
Ibid., p. 219.

35
C. G. Jung, *Sobre cosas que se ven en el cielo*, Buenos Aires: Ed. Sur, 1961, p. 168. The author here observes that on the basis of ethno-comparative observation studies, he came to the conclusion that the majority of triadic 'mandalas' came from his German patients.

36
Ibid., p. 146.

37
Ibid., p. 169.

38
Diego Laínez, Letter n.12; FN, I, 82.

39
Reithmann, *Joseph Beuys. La mort me tient en éveil*, p. 436.

40
Mennekes in Reithmann, *Joseph Beuys. La mort me tient en éveil*, p. 77.

41
Ibid., p. 76.

42
Ibid., p. 77.

43
Reithmann, *Joseph Beuys. La mort me tient en éveil*, p. 447.

44
Antje von Graevenitz, 'Nomadas', in *Beuysnobiscum*. In *Joseph Beuys*, Madrid: Museo Nacional Centro de Arte Reina Sofía, 1994, p. 279 [Exh. cat.]. Quote from Ernest Günter Engelhard, *Joseph Beuys*: 'Ein grausames Wintermärchen', in *Christ und die Welt*, Year XXI, no. 1, 3 January 1969. Reproduced in: *Joseph Beuys*, Kunstmuseum Basel, 1969/70, p. 34 [Exh. cat.].

45
Antje Graevenitz, quote from *Ein Gespräch – una discussione. Joseph Beuys, Janis Kounellis, Anselm Kiefer, Enzo Cucchi*, Zürich: Jacqueline Burckhardt, 1986, p. 110. Translation by translator.

46
Peter Brugge, 'Die Mysterien finden in Hauotbahnhof statt', *Der Spiegel*, no. 23, 1984, p. 179.

47
Reithmann, *Joseph Beuys. La mort me tient en éveil*, p. 427.

48
This is a Joseph Beuys annotation in the preparatory drawings for the action *Partitur zu Manresa, 1966*.

HENNING CHRISTIANSEN

JOSEPH BEUYS AND HIS 'ENERGY PLAN'

'Our life between birth and death calls for the exploration of *Gegenraum-Wärme-Zeit* (anti-space-warmth-time) — humanity's immortal essence and life after death. In this context (anti-art) it depends on our insight whether we can obtain reliable possibilities for controls and measures concerning what we do in space and time.'

Opus 16: Look for the reason!

THE ABOVE QUOTE and *Opus 16*[1] are central to understanding Beuys's activities. He tries to avoid philosophical terminology. It is not the How, but the What that matters. He believes that only the 'anti-stance' or the 'anti-thought' are significant. For him, humans are 'anti-nature'. And this is precisely why humans can move beyond sensory perception, to break through to what Beuys refers to as *Gegenraum* (counter space) — the state in which we intuit something without understanding it. 'Energy', according to Beuys, is the most precious element of all and therefore the new principle with which to infiltrate everything. Physics → anti-physics, chemistry → anti-chemistry, music → anti-music, mathematics → anti-mathematics, etc. helps us rise above the 'space' of reason.

Beuys constantly chases after the place in or near the human body where this 'super generator' of time-overtime (*Zeit-Überzeit*) and space-counter space (*Raum-Gegenraum*) is produced.

Surely it must be somewhere...?

1 Translator's note: Christiansen sent a tape to Beuys with a recording of a radio programme in which he had participated. Among the pieces that were recorded on the tape was *Opus 16* that Beuys played during his second performance of the piece *Der Chef* [The Chief] in Galerie Block in Berlin on 1 December, 1964. This fact marked the beginning of the collaboration between the two artists.

This might seem like a triumph of the absurd, but Beuys takes it further by making fun of physicists:

> For the physicist, only what is real can be measured! Loud shouts are heard from the leader of stags (*Hirschführer*)[2] on the right: How much longer will you stay at step one?'

And as a sculptor, he creates a reality that humans can intuit through their 'anti-nature'.

During the May Exhibition in 1964 in Charlottenborg (Copenhagen), Beuys showed how a walking stick could be turned into an experience by transforming it into counter space (*Gegenraum*). With a slab of margarine, he lengthened its handle by about 30 cm. Beuys also completely transformed one room in Charlottenborg by filling a corner with yellow margarine. The event literally burst open the space. Later he performed an 'anti-procedure' by covering a protrusion with thick grey felt, thus 'stopping up' a corner. In this context he speaks of a 'positive' and 'negative' process.

Beuys always wears a fisherman's waistcoat and a felt hat. This is not for exhibitionist reasons, but so that wherever he goes and stands, he is an object for *Antinatur*, the *Supergenerator* and *Gegenraum* (anti-nature, the super generator and counter space).

When asked how he felt about the term *Verfremdung* (alienation), he replied that he was not interested in it at all as it was too clumsy and based on a misunderstanding of life.

Some believe that Beuys is a mystic, an artist who works in metaphysical space, but ultimately his work centres on creating clarity around the phenomena of 'anti-nature': *Energie-Gegenraum-Wärme-Zeit* (energy-counter space-warmth-time). He is not interested in illusions. His philosophy may well be pseudo-philosophy. But it is qualified.

Beuys's relationship to time is expressed in his actions, many of which take place over a long time. During the May Exhibition in 1964 in Copenhagen, he lay in the exhibition room for six hours, carefully rolled up in a grey felt blanket. Just as carefully, he had placed two dead hares at the extensions of his body — one at his head and one at

2
Translator's note: *Hirschführer* was one of Beuys's favourite names for himself. It literally translates as 'leader of stags'.

his feet. Next to him inside the felt blanket was a microphone. And over a loudspeaker the audience could hear regular guttural sounds coming from his throat. On the wall hung a small picture with something that looked like wool inside. This entire sculpture in grey (Beuys has a preference for grey, minium and yellow) was an expression of Beuys's concept of life and death. What separates them is warmth — or body heat — that only he transmits.

Beuys very often uses his body as a sculpture during his 'demonstrations'.[3] He performs with fantastic concentration and extreme body control. Based on the description in the book *24 Stunden* (24 Hours) by Hansen & Hansen, Itzehoe, published in 1964, with a little imagination we can picture the precision with which Beuys performed on two blocks of margarine using his feet. Every ten seconds, he changed the position of his legs in relation to the blocks — without touching them. This concept requires great mastery and concentration to reproduce as an experience.

Currently there is a fierce dispute raging over Professor Beuys's chair at the Kunstakademie Düsseldorf. Influential forces surrounding the academy and in the political world are trying to remove him from his post. This is due to his statement to the press in relation to the large-scale simultaneous happening organised by the Technische Hochschule in Aachen on 20 July 1964, the 20th anniversary of (Stauffenberg's) attempt to assassinate Hitler. Beuys mentioned in passing that the Berlin Wall should be made 5 cm higher: that way, it would be better proportioned. With this remark, he hurt the feelings of the German public and sparked enthusiasm among German youth.

Düsseldorf, 15 December 1966

This article appeared in *Hvedekorn* magazine, vol. 40, no. 5, 1966, pp. 175–176.

3 Translator's note: Beuys called his Fluxus actions 'demonstrations'.

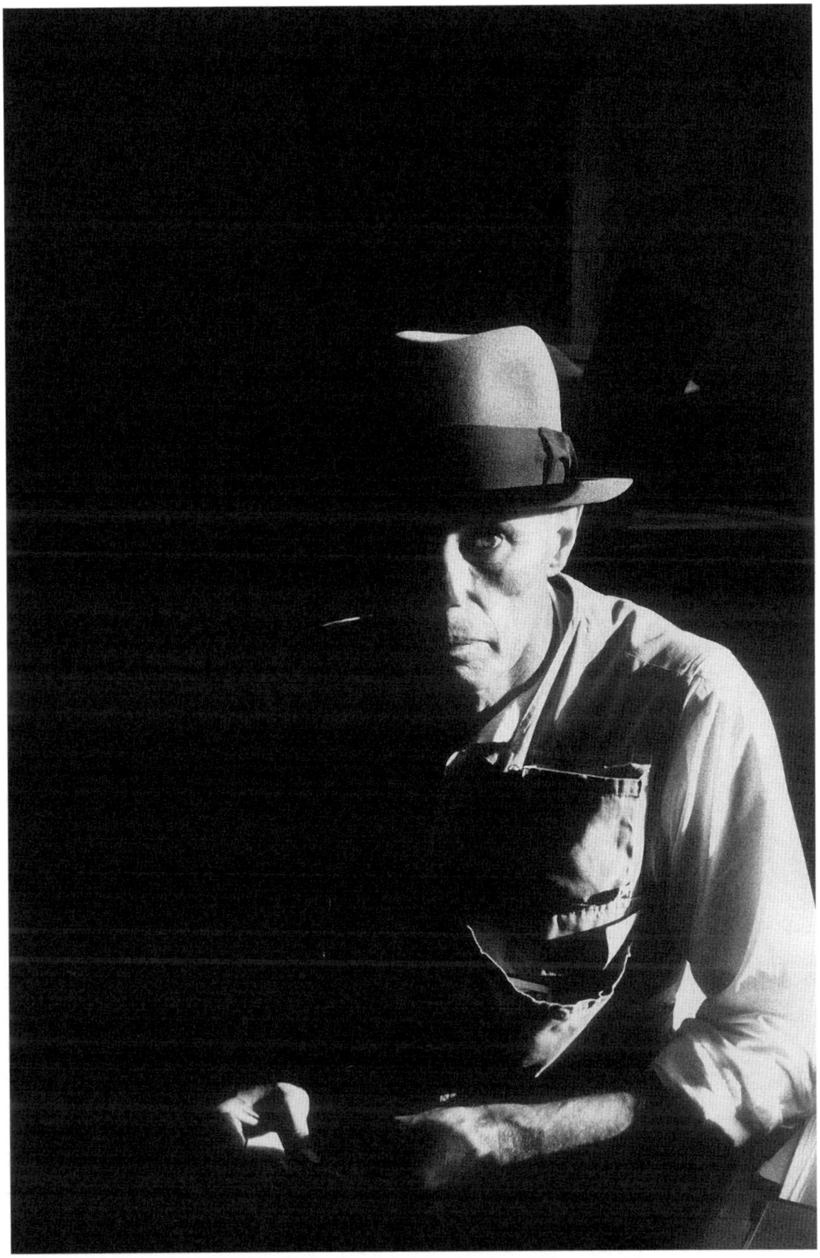

A *Joseph Beuys as a halved cross*, Møn, Denmark, 26 July, 1982.

BJØRN NØRGAARD

THE PRESENT IS WHERE THE PAST MEETS THE FUTURE

AT THE AGE OF SEVENTY-THREE it is difficult — extremely difficult — to write a text on an event that took place fifty-four years ago. That was when Joseph Beuys asked me, then a young man of nineteen, to participate in an action he called MANRESA at Galerie Schmela in Düsseldorf, to be held on 15 December 1966.

That same year, on the 14th and 15th of October, Beuys had participated in a series of actions, entitled *Tilstande* [Situations], organised by Den Eksperimenterende Kunstskole [The Experimenting Art School] in Copenhagen, with the presence of eleven Danish artists.

Over the two days Beuys performed *Siberian Symphony, Thirty-Fourth Movement*, and carried out a series of minor actions. My contribution was to work on various materials and objects with my feet, on a scale from soft to hard. Meanwhile, a tape player reproduced a blurry, scratched message, which sounded like something that could be interpreted as *rederecherche*.[1] Beuys asked me to accompany him for the repetition of this action for MANRESA, in Düsseldorf.

In order to keep moving forward today, we must take a look back and try to remember; now, fifty-four years later, when we set out to describe ideas and movements over time, it makes sense to speak of 'Spaces'. Not of geometric or physical spaces, but of spaces of time, conceiving their nature and the way that the *Zeitgeist*, the spirit of the time, has an influence on actions and ideas, on dreams, and in this case on art.

The first MANRESA, in Düsseldorf, took place in a space we could call the 1960s, which in reality took place from 1959 to 1974. *Manresa Hbf*, which we presented in the city of Manresa, is from a space of time that could rightly be understood to span the period from

1
Editor's note: Joseph Beuys wrote a letter to Henning Christiansen on 20 November 1966 (pp. 23, 24), requesting him to revive the recording used for that action, where the word *rederecherche* was repeated rhythmically, mixed in with other sounds. Joseph Beuys had already done the drawing *Cerche* (1966), with this word appearing various times on the back of the drawing, linked together along two lines (p. 12).

1979 to 1994. Now we find ourselves in the space of time that has been taking place since 1995, carrying us up to the present; it is from this space that we describe those other two spaces of time. If this seems unattainable, then quite possibly that is the case.

Why do we speak of 'Time', of 'Space',
as the dominant metaphor?

Braunräume, cold-warm, reason-intuition, science-spirituality, east-west... There was Beuys's visions in various spaces of time, and the tension arising in the interval. There was Element 3, which brings together different spaces and energies, while also revealing their differences. His felt hat is an insulator, so that the brain and the processes taking place under the hat have an ongoing cold-warm energy.

The various 'Spaces of Time' from 1960 to 2020 mean that, in spite of the felt hat, warmth and the energies in our heads alternate between the 'Space of Time' and the 'Spirit of the Time'. I will try to describe this, although beforehand I should apologise for my lack of skill in the art of writing: I am a sculptor.

1964, Copenhagen. At the age of seventeen I joined Den Eksperimenterende Kunstskole, the EKS. Previously, in 1961, the first Fluxus events in Copenhagen had taken place at the St Nicholas Church. In 1963, Beuys, Henning Christiansen and others participated in a Fluxus action in the auditorium of the Academy of Fine Arts in Copenhagen. In 1965 I participated in the first actions with the EKS school and Henning Christiansen.

In the space of time of the 1960s, the spirit of the time found itself in student revolt and the art that rejected the great utopias of the 19th C, socialism/liberalism, as valid for the creation of a new political mentality. There was a will to reach an open, diverse world where rational science and economy might join with spiritual forces and decentralised, autonomous social structures. Democracy needed to take a step forward. In this spirit of the time, with Fluxus' break with art as an institution, Beuys developed his ideas in the search of the way to give 'shape' to them. Beuys developed the 'expanded concept of art', the idea that 'any person can be an artist', and the idea of 'Soziale Plastik' [social sculpture], so that on the basis of these formal ideas new political organisational principles might be developed.

The spirit of the time sought to eliminate the dividing line between private and public, between life and art. Love was held up as essential in our relationships, freeing ourselves from 'old' ideologies and organisational principles, which would have to be dissolved. It was here where Beuys, with what he brought with him from his German identity and participation in the war, caused a great impression on the generation of the post-war, including myself.

The actions *Siberian Symphony, Thirty-Fourth Movement*, from 1966, MANRESA, also from 1966, and *Eurasian Staff*, from 1967 and 1968, demonstrate through structure and materiality the physical and mental energies through which the artistic method might convert itself into a political force.

Shortly before his death, upon receiving the Lehmbruck Prize, Joseph Beuys explained that the idea of 'Soziale Plastik' was inspired quite precisely by the work of Wilhelm Lehmbruck. Lehmbruck held that sculptural form arose from the pressure placed by society / the State on art. This pressure became so overwhelming that, after the war, Lehmbruck would commit suicide. Beuys, who in his earliest sculptures was clearly influenced by Lehmbruck, and especially by his idea of the pressure all of society places on the creation of forms in art, decided to invest his energy in such a way that art might put pressure on society. This is why the German concept of 'Plastik', and not sculpture, was so determinant. 'Plasticity' is the formal ground in process; in formal creation using clay, wax or plaster, it is when the final form is persistently being pursued. Beuys conceived this way of working / the malleable artistic principle, as a possibility to send out into society as a thought, in an active political process. Starting with his idea that 'every person is an artist', we are all called to shape social structures through this 'expanded' artistic concept.

In 1966, on the train on the way to Düsseldorf, Henning and I tried to decipher the concept MANRESA, but for two artists raised in a Protestant context in Northern Europe the Company of Jesus and Ignatius of Loyola were just a chapter in history; when we asked Beuys about it, he was evasive. That was not what it was about, as it would have to be interpreted by every individual in his or her own way. It was not until many years later in Spain, in Zaragoza, for an exhibition, that

I found out that Manresa was a city, and was able to situate the story of Ignatius of Loyola and the Company of Jesus, along with Beuys's identification with Ignatius and his spiritual visions. The action (and actions were exercises) and artistic/spiritual ideas, were revelations the actions could give rise to. They could be transformed into formal social actions and creations where the material and the spiritual were fused.

At the same time, the idea that every human being is an artist became the starting point for everyone to be able to train to work politically from the foundation of formal artistic creation. In this way, therefore, politics was defined as a common organic power where each human's capacity and will to create forms was what created everything, and with all things, society.

A society that has been decentralised by direct democracy, formulated by Beuys through artistic form, yet within a spirit of the time that wanted it and conceived in terms of both possible and impossible principles. Or as Beuys would also come to express it: in this chaos, by means of formal spiritual creation, new social structures are born.

In 1994, Henning and I finally travelled to the starting point of the 1966 action MANRESA, a city by the name of Manresa. The name of the action we did there, *Manresa Hbf*, no doubt arose when in his day Beuys got off the train in another time and space.

While in the 1960s, when Beuys developed his ideas, there were many of us at the same time who were seeking new answers and rejecting older ideas, the 1970s explored how various challenges made it more difficult for 'Soziale Plastik' and 'every human is an artist' to modify political reality in a significant way.

In contrast, other, equally progressive forces were revived to take on materialist ideologies. European states continued to depend on cheaper primary resources from their former colonies. Beuys went ahead with the Deutsche Studentenpartei [German Student Party], Die Grünen [The Greens] and his own 'exercises'. Henning and I did a series of actions together, such as *World Peace Economy*, *The New Europe*, *Pre-National*, *Unity Through Diversity*, and so on. However, in the 1980s neo-liberalism came to dominate the spiritual space.

The fall of the Wall in the 1990s gave us the fleeting hope that we would be able to redefine the relationship between East and West, just as Beuys had expressed in his actions, as seen both in *Siberian Symphony, Thirty-Fourth Movement*, and *Eurasian Staff*.

It is in this space, in this spirit of the time of the 1990s after the fall of the Wall, that Henning and I set out to carry out the action we had been invited to do in Manresa. Our action was conceived as a long 'epic' route where the definitive image might be attained through 'exercising' exercises, developing the ideas of Ignatius and Beuys over the course of the sequence, as two identifications where a revelation/artistic/spiritual construction could be thought of in terms of action in a material space. We followed the route that Ignatius most probably had taken: from the Shrine of Our Lady of Guidance to the Cardener River, then crossing over the Old Bridge as far as the Holy Cave. Later, inside an ecclesiastic space, the previous actions/exercises and features of the 1966 MANRESA, and through a sermon featuring Christian rhetoric included in the action, all the various components were put in play, until they came to be transformed into a figure. This was a synthesis of Ignatius and Beuys, of Christian liturgy and the effort to forge a new path able to mould what is material and spiritual through artistic form. In the end this all came together. We are all artists, and then there is the Christian image of the loaves of bread and fish, where the spirit might continue to develop through thought and conversation.

When today, with this text, I look backwards towards the temporary space that MANRESA was performed in, it is with great hope that the idea of converting spirit into action might be present amongst young people the world over, just as Ignatius imagined it in his day, just as Beuys dedicated precise reasoning and various physical spaces to in the 1960s and 1970s. Yet at the same time I am concerned when avarice, short-term benefits and inhuman thought threaten Creation, our planet, with petrified materialism.

The mission of MANRESA remains intact.

We must understand *Beuys Cross*, so beautifully installed between the Cardener River and the Old Bridge, as a 'musical score', as a 'manuscript' for the action *Manresa Hbf*. Not literally, but on a visually syntactic level: a horizontal action rises vertically to become a spiritual image, like the Cross, and like *Eurasian Staff*.

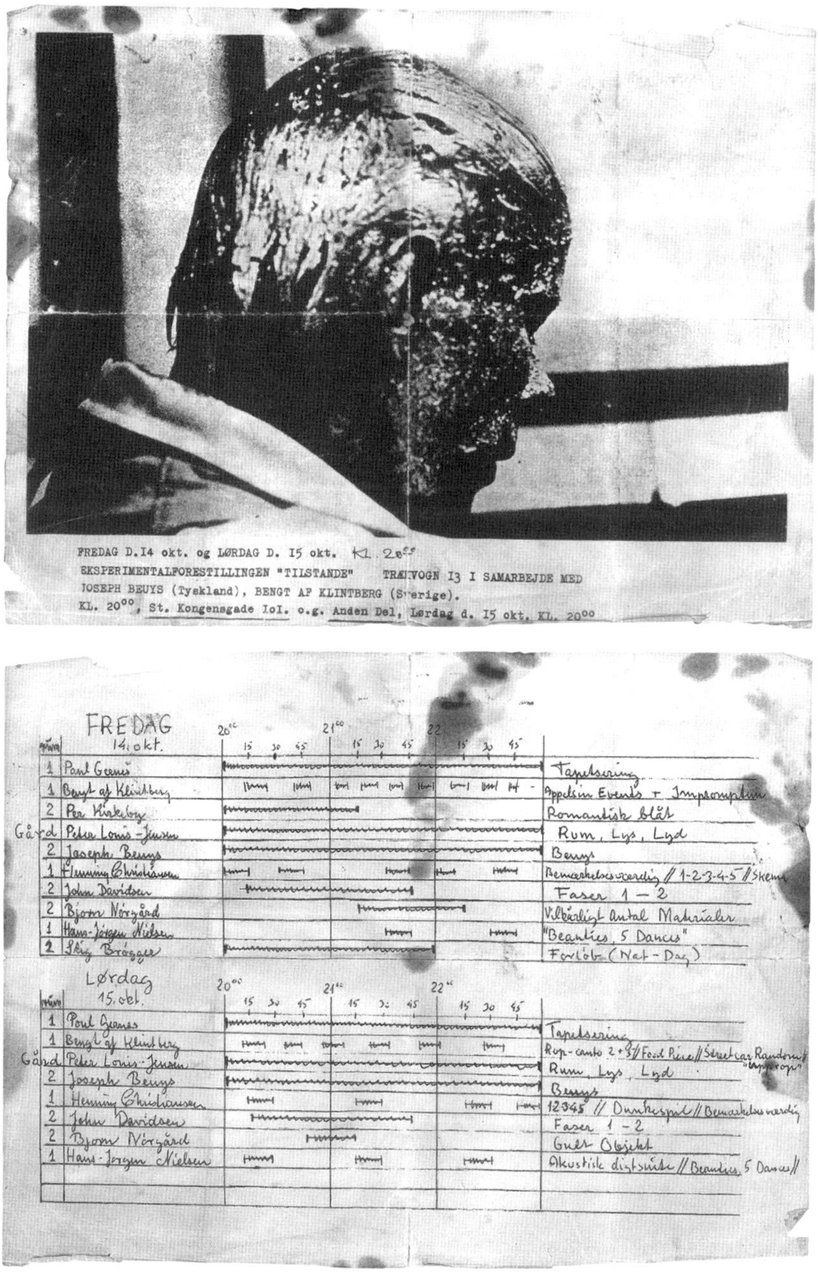

A Programme of the festival *Tilstande* [Situations], which took place on 14–15 October 1966 in Copenhagen.

Edition
Pilar Parcerisas
Editorial Tenov

Translation
Lucy Jones - Transfiction
Jacob Daniel Schneider
Jeffrey Swartz

Correction
Gallina Green - Trend translations
Jeffrey Swartz

Graphic design and layout
Bendita Gloria

Preprinting
Xavier Tulleuda

Printing and binding
Agpograf

Arxiu Festiu Catalunya, Jordi Pablo, Barcelona: p. 141 (B, C), 144, 147 (H). ▸ Henning Christiansen: p. 167. ▸ Institute for Foreign Cultural Relations, Stuttgart: p. 19, 23, 24. ▸ Kunstpalast – ARTOTHEK: p. 28 (A), 29 (B), 31 (C), 33 (E), 36 (H), 40 (N), 45 (T), 46 (U). ▸ © Kunstpalast – Horst Kolberg – ARTOTHEK: p. 9, 12, 13. ▸ © Kunstpalast – LVR-ZMB – Stefan Arendt ARTOTHEK. © Stiftung Museum Schloss Moyland / Ute Klophaus: p. 49 (Y), 130 (D). ▸ © Marc Leve, Estate of Manfred Leve: p. 49 (Z), 50 (‡). ▸ © mumok – Museum moderner Kunst Stiftung Ludwig Wien, On loan from the Austrian Ludwig Foundation: p. 22. ▸ Private collection: p. 14, 20, 130 (E). ▸ © The Estate of Per Kirkeby. Courtesy of Museum Jorn, Silkeborg: p. 108 (G). ▸ Tenov Archive: p. 25–27, 103 (A), 115 (K). ▸ Parcerisas Archive: p. 139. ▸ © Wim Cox: p. 6, 79–81.

Front cover image: Galerie Schmela after Beuys's MANRESA action. ▸ AGNSW: Art Gallery of New South Wales. © Stiftung Museum Schloss Moyland / Ute Klophaus.

ISBN: 978-84-944234-6-8
DL: B 12645-2021

The paper used in this publication is FSC® (Forest Stewardship Council®) certified, indicating that it comes from sustainable forests and that all the supply chain is managed responsibly.

Acknowledgments

The editors wish to express their gratitude to the institutions and people who have contributed to the conception and realisation of this book. We thank Friedhelm Mennekes for his advice, the Town Hall of Manresa for its interest in our project and the Embassy of Denmark for its support.

This book has been published with the support of:

Ajuntament de Manresa

Manresa 2022 Transforma

EMBASSY OF DENMARK
Madrid